Yale Series in Economic History

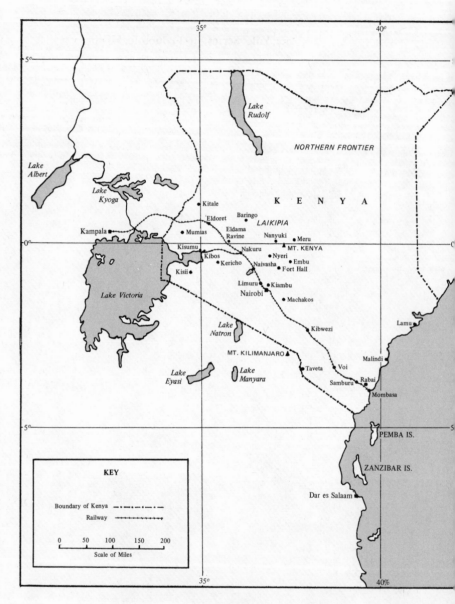

Colony and Protectorate of Kenya in the 1920s

THE ECONOMICS OF COLONIALISM

BRITAIN AND KENYA, 1870-1930

Richard D. Wolff

New Haven and London: Yale University Press

1974

Designed by John O. C. McCrillis
and set in Baskerville type.
Printed in the United States of America by
The Murray Printing Co., Forge Village, Massachusetts.

Published in Great Britain, Europe, and Africa by Yale University Press,
Ltd., London. Distributed in Latin America by Kaiman & Polon, Inc.,
New York City; in Australasia and Southeast Asia by John Wiley & Sons
Australasia Pty. Ltd., Sydney; in India by UBS Publishers' Distributors
Pvt., Ltd., Delhi; in Japan by John Weatherhill, Inc., Tokyo.

With love, respect, gratitude, and a touch of
angry sadness, I dedicate this book to
Max Wolff, 1905–1973.
I have been extremely fortunate:
my father was a wise and beautiful man.

Contents

Maps

Tables

Acknowledgments

Four people who greatly influenced the reading and reflection that led ultimately to this book were forced out of their native Europe because of profound social upheavals there. My mother and father fought fascism and fled for their lives. So did Fritz Pappenheim, who, although holding no academic position, generously and encouragingly guided me through the classics of European social science during my four undergraduate years. And so did Paul A. Baran, whose animated discussions as my teacher and friend sharpened my interest in economics and focused my mind on the area of economic history.

The realities of social change transformed their lives, deeply impressed their thinking, and hence left their mark indirectly, but not slightly, on me. Their thinking arose from their passion to understand what had caused the upheavals of their time. To act against fascism and war, they—each in a particular manner—worked to understand the processes of social change, the "laws of motion of modern capitalism" as one of them loved to quote.

The education and inspiration I drew from these four were supplemented by two similarly motivated American scholars and activists. Harry Magdoff has spent much time as an encouraging teacher and as a critic of my thinking in general and of aspects of this book in particular. Paul M. Sweezy has played a similar role.

It should be needless to add that, in acknowledging the influence of these individuals and the understanding which they transmitted, I am also indicating my debt to the Marxian tradition of social science. They found it indispensable, and so have I.

This book grew out of a doctoral dissertation prepared for the Economics Department of Yale University. The support and constructive criticism of William N. Parker accompanied this study from its early forms through major revisions and additions to its present state. My conversations with Stephen Hymer provoked helpful thought and research. Research

among various African archives in London was facilitated by
a grant from the Yale Concilium on International and Area
Studies. Anne J. Granger contributed valuable ideas in addition to her superb typing skills. The manuscript benefited
significantly from the attention of three Yale University Press
experts: Marian Ash, Ellen Graham, and June Darge.

A final word on the origins of my interest in Africa. The
overabundant privileges accorded undergraduates at Harvard included, in my case, a trip to East Africa and a pre-
paratory course in the Swahili language, which permitted at
least some rudimentary conversations. In East Africa, I confronted the stark realities of colonialism and conceived then
the intention to understand how and why such a situation
had come into being. This book summarizes a good part of
what I have learned.

R.D.W.

Introduction

According to J. B. Carson, former District Officer of Kitui District, Ukamba, Kenya, "Sixty years is a very short span of history, yet it is doubtful if a greater transformation has taken place in the general pattern of life of the people of any country than has happened in East Africa since the turn of the century."[1] While obviously agreeing with this summation, an African leader who was active over much of the period adds, "There have been consistent threads running through our struggle from the early years until the present."[2]

Kenya's economic history as a British colony exhibits both the radical transformation of African society and the consistent application of British colonial development strategy. I will seek to demonstrate that such a strategy made economic sense, did operate, and did cause the transformation of Kenya. After a brief analysis of the economic purposes and patterns of Britain's colonial empire after 1870, this study will focus on the total reorganization of the Kenya economy that British policy makers carried out.

A study of this type belongs to the large and growing body of literature on the economics of colonialism and imperialism. That literature and the outline of this study have been significantly influenced by the theoretical contributions of Marx and several later Marxists.[3]

Of particular relevance here is a central theme in the Marxist approach: that the development of capitalism in Europe, especially in Britain, involved the revolutionary conversion of "one part of the globe into a chiefly agricultural field of production, for supplying the other part which remains a chiefly industrial field. This revolution hangs together with radical changes in agriculture. . . ."[4] The conversion is held to be a continuing process which itself undergoes changes as the features of the metropolitan center evolve over time. The colonial or "periphery" economy is seen to develop within the context and subject to the constraints of the general economic development of the industrialized metropolis. Capitalism brings into being a world-

wide economic system but develops different regions un-
evenly, assigning different roles to each region in a global
division of labor. Corresponding to these roles are different
levels of income, different rates and types of economic growth,
and different "gains from trade."

The linkages between economic development in the colony
and in the metropolis have not been extensively analyzed on
a case-study basis; this perspective has certainly not been applied to Kenya's formative years as an appendage of the British
Empire. In this study the economics of British colonialism in
Kenya are presented as an episode in the development of a
world economy.

To analyze the first thirty-five years of the colonial Kenyan
economy, 1895–1930, I present first a brief and indicative,
rather than exhaustive, sketch of some basic features of the
evolving imperial economy from 1870 to 1914 (chapter 1).
The latter is the relevant time period because during these
years Britain's economy absorbed a number of new colonial
territories and developed a set of beneficial economic relationships with them. The establishment of some or all of such
relationships became the typical objective of colonial policy
in each new territory by the turn of the century—the precise
time when the modern outlines of Kenya's economy were
first formulated and established by colonial officials.

In Kenya from 1895 to 1930, British colonial officials totally transformed the preexisting patterns of economic behavior, erecting in their place a very different basic economic
structure whose essential features have confronted policy makers in Kenya to this day. Why, how, and with what economic
results did the colonial officials create the modern Kenyan
economy? What does it mean for an economy to experience
colonial status? Chapters 2–7 present answers to this question.

These chapters have two characteristics that deserve explicit explanation. First, the limitations of the data available
to me prevented my drawing many fine distinctions among
subgroups, usually tribes, of the African population. Thus, in
general statements about the conditions of the African population, some distortion of a complex reality was unavoidable. However, where such distinctions could be made and
were relevant, I have indicated them.

Second, within the European population the distinction
most germane to this study, between settlers and officials, has
been consistently deemphasized. The underlying explanation
for this is my judgment that differences of economic interest
between them were of fundamentally less significance—within
the framework of this study—than their common goals. There
were, of course, frequent and often bitter disputes between
settlers and officials. Yet these disputes were political rather
than economic. They hinged mainly on the settlers' demands
for ultimate control over governmental policy in Kenya. In
the period under review, the settlers sought full control in
order to ensure the continuation of basic economic policy in
Kenya, not to change it. They clearly felt that its continuation was more secure under their direct authority than if it
were subject to the broader considerations of officials looking
finally to London for direction. The officials were not eager,
however, to relinquish their powers. This was the root of
significant disputes between them. On basic economic policy
after 1908—that is, after the initial period of trial and error
with European settlement was resolved in favor of such settlement—settlers and officials were essentially in accord.[5] In any
case, where conflicts between the two groups were relevant
to this study, they have been discussed.

The third basic ethnic subgroup in Kenya, the Asian population, has received minimal attention in this study because
of its tangential relation to the focus of our investigation.

It is not my purpose to affix blame on any participant in
the development of the Kenyan colonial economy. Rather
the objective is to ascertain why, how, and with what concrete economic consequences the colonial administration pursued specific economic goals in Kenya derived from British
perceptions of the specific economic needs of the empire.

1 Britain and the New Empire, 1870–1914

In the generation before 1914, "an Empire whose nucleus is only 120,000 square miles, with 40,000,000 population [added] an area of 4,754,000 square miles with an estimated population of 88,000,000." This, concluded J. A. Hobson, "was a historical fact of great significance."[1]

As Great Britain added this "new" (i.e. post-1870) empire to the "old" (i.e. Canada, Newfoundland, Australia, New Zealand, and South Africa),* there developed at home simultaneously a momentous debate that became a major factor in British politics throughout the period 1870 to 1914.[2] The "imperialists" included men of widely divergent basic interests and motivations. Some favored an expanding British Empire because it offered a wider field for Englishmen to fulfill a "civilising mission." Some favored imperialism for security or military reasons. Others justified their position in terms of the economic benefits which, they argued, a greater British Empire would convey to Britain. While there were different kinds of arguments for the new imperialism, we will focus here on aspects of the economic argument.

Needless to say, British politics also contained a strong school of anti-imperialists, encompassing proponents with differing reasons for their anti-imperialism. Some were isolationists or cultural relativists convinced that Great Britain had little to offer the world. Some associated imperialism with military operations and the consequent taxes, and therefore they opposed it. There was also a school of thought which directly denied that Great Britain would or could derive any significant economic benefits from holding colonial possessions. This school, generally advocates of "free trade," argued that the gains from imperialism for Britain were small and

*India was an old colony, but as a tropical possession it shared many important characteristics with the new empire. Hence it will generally be treated here in a special category by itself. Also, statistical difficulties have required that the British West Indies be included as part of the "new empire" in several tables. However, this does not materially affect the argument.

1

therefore insignificant and, furthermore, that they fell short
of its costs.

Political and academic argument about the economic benefits and costs of British imperialism has continued to the
present. Nor is there any lessening of the closely related debate over the importance of economic considerations among
the motivations for imperial expansion. While this chapter
will hardly resolve the controversy, I will attempt to develop
it here beyond its present state in the literature of economic
history.

Stated simply, my general hypothesis is that the basic economic policies of British imperial authorities in Kenya after
1895 constituted a consistent application and extension of the
accumulated British experience with the new imperialism. The
aim of this chapter is to establish at least the presumption
that the late nineteenth-century British economy derived significant economic advantages from its colonies, that it could
reasonably expect these advantages to increase absolutely and
relatively, and, finally, that these advantages would most probably not have been available in the absence of a colonial tie.
A convincing case for this presumption will then permit the
further argument that Britain's economic activities in East
Africa were, within limits, rational responses to her current
economic problems and opportunities.*

My method is to analyze selectively the basic statistics of
Britain's international economic position from approximately
1870 to 1914: exports, imports and re-exports of commodities,
and capital flows. An underlying theme emerges from a glance
beneath the aggregated data: in short, Britain's acquisition
and development of her post-1870 empire was an economically significant—and frequently successful—response to the
real problems of Britain's economic situation at the time.
Kenya's economic history provides then a detailed case study
of this response.

*The word "presumption" is meant to indicate that I am not attempt-
ing anything approaching a formal proof, which is, in any case, probably
impossible for reasons discussed below. The word "rational" is meant in
its looser sense of logical and intelligent allocation of resources—not in
terms of the more formal criteria of global efficiency.

THE TRADE ACCOUNT

My case for the economic importance of the new empire in Britain's commodity trade begins with a critique of a prevailing set of assertions. At the turn of the century, J. A. Hobson argued that the new imperialism involved a wasteful expenditure of resources with no significant advantage for the British economy. He reasoned that, since trade with the tropical colonies was "small, precarious and unprogressive . . . no serious attempt to regard them as satisfactory business assets is possible."[3]

More recently, this line of reasoning has been frequently reiterated by D. K. Fieldhouse as well as by W. W. Rostow, R. E. Robinson and J. Gallagher, and M. B. Brown, to name but a few.[4] These and other writers emphasize the point that trade between Great Britain and the new empire between 1870 and 1914 was a very small share of total British trade. Since it was small, they argue, it was insignificant. Hence, any claim that economic advantage in general commodity trade motivated imperialist policy is an incorrect analysis, probably derived from mistaking the rhetoric of the time for the reality. Fieldhouse develops this argument into an alternative theory that the new imperialism was a political, rather than an economic, phenomenon.

There are several problems with these general assessments of the economic aspects of Britain's new imperialism. First, the fact that the trade would be small was presumably neither known nor expected when imperialistic decisions were made. It is certainly possible, and quite likely, that economic calculations and expectations—more or less justified—played a significant role in determining British colonial activities. Perhaps the very pace and size of colonial acquisitions exercised a stimulating effect on the British economy that was expected and welcomed after 1870.

Second, and more importantly, the argument that Britain's trade relations with her new empire were small neglects the historical reality that the increasing protectionism of Britain's European and American competitors confronted her with the risk of losing access to territories outside her colonial control and therefore within theirs. A focus on the size of aggregated trade statistics alone tends to ignore the likelihood that Britain faced the need to undertake an economically advantageous "preemptive imperial expansion."[5]

These criticisms of what may be termed the Fieldhouse position are germane here insofar as they suggest possible and plausible interpretations of the new imperialism that make it in part a consequence of rational economic calculation by British policy makers. However, a more fundamental criticism of the Fieldhouse position is possible, one which will establish the basis for our argument that Great Britain did in fact derive significant economic benefits from her new empire.

Common to most versions of the Fieldhouse position is an unjustified—in terms of strict economic theory—leap from a judgment that trade relations between Britain and the new empire were "small" to a judgment that they were therefore "insignificant" or "valueless." In this context, the word "small" has no meaning without a specification of the underlying economic structure. For example, with a plausible combination of supply and demand curves in the post-1870 British economy, a 3 to 5 percent increase in exports to newly acquired colonies might make the difference between the continuance or demise of one or more industries in Britain.[6] Abstractly, 3 to 5 percent may be small, but it need not therefore be insignificant. The proponents of the Fieldhouse position have not specified any underlying economic structure to justify their repeated equation of small with insignificant. Hence their argument is not convincing.

While I have shown why the conventional assessment of the economic aspects and significance of the new empire is without sufficient foundation to be persuasive, it is beyond the scope and purpose of this study to try to estimate the parameters required for a formal proof. Rather, conscious of the pitfalls of such analysis, I will try to demonstrate, from what evidence there is, the significance of the trade relations between Great Britain and the new empire between 1870 and 1914. As we proceed, I will specify such aspects of the underlying economic structure and history as can reasonably be surmised. This will unavoidably be an incomplete argument, but it should represent as much as is possible, given the material readily available.

Imports

We begin with a discussion of Britain's imports. We focus attention on imports according to commodity group first, in order to suggest the role of imports in the domestic British economy. Within Great Britain's manufacturing sector, the labor force was allocated as shown in table 1.1. Three industries—textiles, clothing, and metals and machinery—ac-

TABLE 1.1: British Labor Force in Manufacturing Industries
(In percentages)

Industry	1891	1911
Bricks, pottery, glass	3.2	3.0
Chemicals	1.7	2.6
Metals, machinery, vehicles	24.3	29.0
Textiles	28.2	22.6
Clothing	24.8	20.1
Food, drink, tobacco	4.1	5.6
Wood	4.7	4.8
Paper	4.9	6.4
Other	4.1	5.9
Total	100.0	100.0

SOURCE: P. Deane and W. A. Cole, *British Economic Growth*, p. 146.

counted for 70 percent of employment in manufacturing. Together they accounted directly for 25 percent of Britain's total labor force. We focus our analysis largely on these industries as the dominant core of the British economy because their economic problems and the strategies devised for solving them strongly influenced the nature of national economic development both in Britain and in the empire. "They were the half dozen or so industries which in the hundred years before 1870 had taken the lead in the industrialization of Britain. . . . The technique, the organization and the methods of British industry were largely due to them and to the leadership which they exercised. . . . Their control was to remain unchallenged until the 1920s and their activity, although highly regional, *influenced business expectations, employment and investment throughout the nation.*"[7] (Italics added.)

In British textile production, cotton goods always predominated in value. All raw cotton had to be imported. Woolen raw materials that had to be imported rose from 50 percent in 1870 to over 80 percent by 1913.[8] The smaller silk and jute manufacturers relied, of course, on imported raw materials exclusively.

Within the metals and machinery industry, raw materials imports were likewise large and were increasing over the period. By 1913, the situation appeared as shown in table 1.2.

TABLE 1.2: Ores and Metals, British Production and Imports, 1913
(In thousand tons)

	British Output	Imports
Ores		
Iron	15,991	7,231
Tin	8	35
Copper	......	133
Metals		
Pig iron	......	218
From British ores[a]	5,139	......
From imported ores	5,121	......
Tin	5	46
Copper	0.42	105
Lead	18	204
Zinc	6	145

SOURCES: GB, *Statistical Abstract for the United Kingdom*, no. 70, pp. 228, 238, 308, 312; William Page, *Commerce and Industry*, 2: 200, 202.

[a] British iron ore was of an inferior variety compared to imported iron ore.

While domestic British pig iron production rose some 23 percent from 1885 to 1913, domestic output of copper, tin, lead, and zinc fell in amounts ranging from 50 to 85 percent over the period.[9] For all metals, including pig iron, the share of imports in domestic consumption rose substantially over the period.[10] To conclude this brief survey of raw materials imports: Great Britain had to rely almost completely on imports for mineral and vegetable oils, hides and skins, wood pulp for paper manufacture and crude rubber.

Food imports were as essential for consumption as raw materials imports were for production. The largest single item of food imports was wheat. Its relation to British wheat production is shown in table 1.3. The proportion of food consumption Great Britain obtained from imports by 1910–14 is shown in table 1.4. Finally, sugar, coffee, tea, spices, and tobacco were items whose consumption depended entirely on

TABLE 1.3: British Wheat Consumption
(In million cwts.)

Yearly Averages	Net Home Grown	Net Imports
1880–89	40.0	75.2
1890–99	32.6	93.8
1900–09	27.5	110.2

SOURCE: J. H. Schooling, *The British Trade Book*, p. 51.

NOTE: Grain and flour stated in grain equivalents.

imports. In summary, imports of raw materials (including some semimanufacturers) and food were becoming further integrated into and essential for British manufacturing and consumption between 1870 and 1913.

TABLE 1.4: Percentages of Imports in British Food
Consumption, 1910–14

Wheat	81
Cheese	81
Butter	75
Fruit	64
Meat	42

SOURCE: A. D. Hall, *Agriculture after the War*, p. 12.

We turn next to the share of the whole empire in providing Great Britain's imports, shown in table 1.5. The modest growth of the empire's share of imports of all goods has led some observers to infer no change in the empire's importance across the period.[11] Others admit the empire's growing importance, but argue that only the old empire was relevant in this regard.[12] Yet in fact, imports from the old empire accounted for but half of all empire imports between 1870 and

TABLE 1.5: Empire Share of All British Imports
(In percentages)

Year	Foodstuffs	Raw Materials	All Goods
1870	19.8	35.9	21.4
1880	18.5	39.9	22.5
1890	21.5	37.6	22.9
1900	23.7	28.8	21.0
1913	30.3	34.5	24.9

SOURCE: W. Schlote, *British Overseas Trade from 1700 to the 1930's*, pp. 123, 164–65. The percentages are based on data for 85 percent of all food imports and 75 percent of all raw materials imports.

1913.[13] In any case, to assess the role of the empire—old and new—in British imports, we turn to a more detailed breakdown of the data.

Most important among food imports was wheat. The empire share of wheat imports rose dramatically from 9.8 percent in 1870 to 48.5 percent in 1913.[14] Table 1.6 divides wheat imports according to geographic origin. While empire

TABLE 1.6: British Wheat Imports from the Empire
(In thousands of quarter cwts.)

Year	India	Canada	Australia– New Zealand	Egypt	Total
1870	2	794	22	26	843
1875	311	950	295	493	2,049
1880	754	1,060	1,076	375	3,265
1885	2,841	493	1,272	26	4,632
1890	2,126	566	756	100	3,548
1895	2,054	1,190	837	1	4,082
1900	1	1,866	947	0	2,814
1905	5,336	1,856	2,660	3	9,855
1910	4,184	4,740	3,240	0	12,164
1913	4,379	6,435	2,489	0	13,303

SOURCE: Page, *Commerce and Industry*, 2: 142–43.

wheat imports came chiefly from the old empire and India, after 1870 Britain sought to develop sources in the new empire as well. Officials had seen Britain's wheat sources partially lost, first in Europe and then in the United States, as industrialization in these areas diminished wheat supplies available for export. Such officials could and did fear comparable developments elsewhere, particularly in the old empire. Consequently, they looked increasingly to India and the new empire to produce wheat for export. In Kenya, for example, imperial officials successfully encouraged wheat production (see below, chapter 4).

The empire, and especially the new empire, supplied significant proportions of many other foods, as shown in table 1.7. The only two items in which the role of the empire exhibited a marked decline were coffee and raw sugar. The raw sugar figures reflect British preference for European beet sugar rather than tropical cane. The decline in coffee imports stimulated the search for possibilities of producing cof-

TABLE 1.7: Selected British Food Imports from the Empire, 1870–1913
(In percentages of total imports for the given item)

Food	1870	1880	1890	1900	1913
Fresh fruits, nuts	3.9	6.5	9.4	12.1	14.3
Coffee	73.7	62.2	33.0	22.3	18.7
Tea	11.4	26.7	71.7	91.2	87.3
Cocoa	55.9	52.4	55.9	45.1	50.9
Spices	87.2	79.2	79.0	58.0	72.2
Raw sugar	35.8	28.7	15.8	12.9	8.7
Meat	7.6	3.0	15.4	20.1	24.7
Butter	4.3	4.8	2.2	18.1	19.0
Cheese	5.3	15.1	39.8	58.8	81.7

SOURCE: Schlote, *British Overseas Trade,* pp. 164–65.

fee inside the empire, which will be examined in chapter 4 of this study.

Table 1.8 indicates the prominence of the role of the colonies and dependencies in some of these food imports.

TABLE 1.8: Share of Major Producers in Total Empire Food Production

Product	Year	Major Producers	Percentage of Total Empire Production
Coffee	1900	India, West Indies, Malay States	92
	1913	India, West Indies, Malay States, East and Central Africa	99
Tea	1900 to 1913	India, Ceylon	99
Sugar	1900	India, Mauritius, West Indies	91
	1913	India, Australia, Mauritius, Fiji	92
Cocoa	1900	West Indies, Ceylon	97
	1913	British West Africa, West Indies	96

SOURCE: Page, *Commerce and Industry,* 2: 206–08.

Among raw materials imported, those required for textile production came in significant part from the empire. Table 1.9 details the history of the all-important cotton imports. British officials were extremely concerned about their dependence on the United States for raw cotton. They actively sought to use the new empire to develop alternate cotton sources free from the dangers of American speculators in cot-

TABLE 1.9: British Raw Cotton Imports
(In million lbs.)

Year	Total	U.S.A.	Egypt	India	Total British Empire
1870	1,339	716	144	342	488
1880	1,629	1,224	155	207	361
1890	1,793	1,317	181	239	422
1900	1,760	1,365	312	37	349
1913	2,170	1,580	400	50	480

SOURCE: GB, *Statistical Abstract for the United Kingdom,* no. 32, pp. 68–69; no. 52, pp. 118–19; no. 70, p. 330.

ton (see below, chapter 4, especially tables). The scope and purpose of official British ambitions was indicated in an official report of 1910, which stated that it was intended "eventually to satisfy from Imperial sources Lancashire's main demand for raw material."[15] With the rapid shrinkage of cotton exports from India after 1870, official and private attention turned increasingly to new empire territories. In Uganda, for example, officials successfully developed cotton growing for export. Raw wool, the other major textile raw material, came mainly from the empire. In 1870, 88.5 percent of wool imports came from Australia, New Zealand and British South Africa; the corresponding figure for 1913 was 80.2 percent. Raw jute for jute manufactures came from India, which supplied 99 percent of Britain's jute imports throughout the period 1870–1913.[16]

The empire also provided British imports of ores for industrial production, as set forth in table 1.10. Empire iron ore came chiefly from Newfoundland and Australia, which provided 67 and 29 percent respectively of total empire production in 1903. By 1913, however, Southern Rhodesia and

TABLE 1.10: Empire Share of British Ore Imports
(In percentages)

Ore	1870	1880	1890	1900	1913
Iron	0	0.3	0.5	2.4	8.4
Tin	40.9	0	11.3	2.9	18.3
Copper	19.0	17.4	12.8	15.2	37.4

SOURCE: GB, *Statistical Abstract for the United Kingdom,* no. 52, p. 97; GB, *Statistical Abstract for the Several British Overseas Dominions and Protectorates,* no. 54, pp. 406–11, 422; Schlote, *British Overseas Trade,* pp. 164–65.

India had greatly increased their output, providing 17 and 5 percent respectively of empire production of iron ore. In 1903, over 99 percent of tin ore produced in the empire came from Australia, but by 1914, Nigeria accounted for 41 percent of total empire production, compared to 38 percent for Australia. Throughout the period, Newfoundland and Australia were the chief copper ore producers.[17] In metals the Straits

TABLE 1.11: Empire Share of British Metals Imports
(In percentages)

Metal	1870	1880	1890	1900	1913
Copper	79.4	28.7	27.9	23.3	21.0
Tin	49.1	91.0	94.4	88.3	94.8
Lead	0	0	25.2	29.1	36.7
Zinc	0	0	0.5	0.4	0.9

SOURCE: Schlote, *British Overseas Trade*, pp. 164–65.

Settlements provided 99 percent of United Kingdom tin imports from the empire, for the important British tinplate industry. Canada and Australia provided British copper imports from the empire until the first decade of the twentieth century, when Northern Rhodesia began her steady rise to her future role as the United Kingdom's chief supplier of the basic ingredient of the modern electrical products industry.[18]

Other raw materials and semimanufactured imports further demonstrate the empire's importance to Britain, as illustrated in table 1.12. The imports indicating the greatest role

TABLE 1.12: Empire Share of British Imports Other Than Ores and Metals
(In percentages)

Commodity	1870	1880	1890	1900	1913
Mineral oils	3.4	0	0	0.3	7.6
Timber, joinery	35.2	43.1	26.7	24.9	16.2
Raw hides	44.7	54.7	41.0	50.5	41.8
Oil seeds	37.0	42.8	42.3	34.0	53.3
Raw rubber	21.9	19.5	14.2	12.6	57.2
Jute yarn, goods[a]	—	—	94.2	88.9	82.3
Leather, tanned hides[a]	38.5	24.5	39.1	43.1	35.9
Printing paper[a]	—	—	—	3.2	19.6

SOURCE: Schlote, *British Overseas Trade*, pp. 164–65.

[a] Semimanufactures.
[b] Dash indicates data not available.

for the empire are commodities originating chiefly in the new empire countries. Jute yarn and goods, raw rubber, oil seeds, and hides came largely from the newer Asian and African colonies and dependencies. Britain also derived very appreciable benefits from developing rubber in her new Asian colonies (see chapter 4 below).

This brief survey of commodity imports in Great Britain from 1870 to 1913 concentrates attention on foodstuffs and raw materials, which together accounted for over 80 percent of the value of British imports in current prices throughout this period. The picture emerging from these statistics suggests that for Britain the role of the empire, including the new empire, was significant in providing the imports that became increasingly crucial for domestic production, employment, and consumption.

Exports

We noted above that textiles, clothing, and metals and machinery manufacturing accounted for 70 percent of employment in manufacturing in the United Kingdom. Exports were as important to the profitability and growth of these basic industries as the imported raw materials they required. In addition, exports absorbed large shares of the outputs of other increasingly important industries.

For Britain, prosperity in textiles depended on exports (see table 1.13). In addition to cotton and woolen textiles,

TABLE 1.13: Exports of Textiles as Share of British Production
(In percentages)

Textile	1874–79	1879–84	1884–89	1889–94	1894–99	1899–1908
Cotton	70	74	69	71	79	79
Wool	35	33	32	29	27	29

SOURCE: Deane and Cole, *British Economic Growth*, pp. 187, 196.

NOTE: The dates and figures are approximate, especially in the case of woolen textiles.

the proportion of linen output that was exported rose steadily throughout the nineteenth century from 20 to 50 percent.[19] Prosperity in metals and machinery manufacturing likewise depended upon exports, as illustrated in table 1.14. One important matter excluded in this table, the influential ship-

TABLE 1.14: Exports of Iron and Steel as Share of British Production
(In percentages)

1875–79	1880–84	1885–89	1890–94	1895–99	1900–04	1905–07
32.8	37.2	40.1	38.5	36.2	42.0	50.0

SOURCE: Deane and Cole, *British Economic Growth*, p. 225.

building industry and the export of ships, is indicated in
table 1.15.

Only a complete input-output matrix for British trade and
production would give us the precision desirable in specifying the role of exports in British prosperity. Since it is not

TABLE 1.15: Net Tonnage and Exports of British Steam Vessels

Year	In U.K. Register	Newly Built	New Exports[a]	Old Exports[a]
1890	5,042,500	660,509	131,720	52,361
1900	7,207,610	886,627	188,297	306,180
1913	11,273,387	1,170,107	220,079	450,431

SOURCE: GB, *Statistical Abstract for the United Kingdom*, no. 52, pp. 206–07; no. 64,
pp. 304–05.

NOTE: This table excludes the tonnages constructed for the British and foreign navies.

[a] "New" refers to ships built in the given year, while "old" refers to ships built at
some earlier date.

possible to construct such a matrix, the above tables serve
as evidence of the significant market for manufactures provided by exports.[20] Moreover, as table 1.16 shows, in discussing finished manufactures we have accounted for the lion's
share of all British exports. The composition of finished

TABLE 1.16: British Exports by Type
(In thousand £, at current prices)

Year	Total	Livestock	Foodstuffs	Raw Materials	Manufactures
1870	199,587	325	9,192	14,667	175,403
1880	223,060	425	10,869	24,337	187,429
1890	263,531	862	11,776	37,393	213,500
1900	291,192	902	14,344	58,796	217,150
1913	525,254	2,273	29,748	96,551	396,673

SOURCE: Schlote, *British Overseas Trade*, pp. 125–26; GB, *Statistical Abstract for the
United Kingdom*, no. 70, p. 344.

NOTE: Only exports of domestically produced goods are included here; "Raw Materials" include some semimanufactures.

manufactured exports is suggested by the data for 1913 shown
in table 1.17. Throughout the period 1870 to 1913, the textile and metals manufacturing industries accounted for over

TABLE 1.17: British Exports of Finished Manufactures, 1913

Type of Manufacture	Value (in million £)	Percentage of Total Exports of Manufactures
Iron and steel (excluding machinery, vehicles)	55.4	14
Machinery	33.7	9
Textiles and apparel	192.3	48
Vehicles		6
Rail	6.2	
Road	6.4	
Sea	11.0	
Total above	305.0	77
All manufactured exports	396.7	100

SOURCE: GB, *Statistical Abstract for the United Kingdom*, no. 70, pp. 366–44.

half the labor force in manufacturing, half the industrial capital stock in mining and manufacturing, and over two-thirds
the manufactures exported from the United Kingdom (thus
over one-half of *all* exports).[21] In assessing the role of the
empire in Britain's export markets, our attention will focus
on these two industries. Where the availability of data per-
mits, other exports will enter the discussion.

The role of the empire as a market for major British manufactured exports is presented in table 1.18. In addition to
these commodities, the empire's share in exports of certain
other industries remarkable for their relatively rapid growth
between 1870 and 1913 is indicated in table 1.19.

The most rapidly growing categories of British exports
before World War I were machinery (including electric machinery); motor vehicles (chassis and rubber tires included);
and electrical engineering goods. These three categories together more than tripled in value as a proportion of all
finished manufactured exports between 1870 and 1913; together, they accounted for over 10 percent of such exports.
A second group of finished manufactures exported doubled
in value as a proportion of all finished manufactures over

TABLE 1.18: Empire Share of Major British Exports
(In percentages)

Manufacture	1870	1880	1890	1900	1913
Cotton goods	34.7	44.1	47.4	45.8	51.7
Woolen goods	14.0	25.4	20.8	29.4	33.5
Clothing	55.5	61.7	72.3	80.9	68.6
Total textiles[a]	26.6	36.8	37.2	39.7	43.9
Iron and steel (excluding machinery)	23.0	33.0	37.0	40.0	50.0
Machinery	19.0	18.3	24.6	22.3	32.5
Vehicles					
Rail carriages	6.3	56.9	33.9	55.9	58.4
Locomotives	16.0	67.5	27.8	49.5	58.6
Motor vehicles	......	......	......	38.7	67.4
Steamships	—[b]	—	—	7.0	20.6

SOURCE: Based on Schlote, *British Overseas Trade*, pp. 166–67.

NOTE: Schlote consistently underestimates the role of empire by excluding British exports to Egypt from his calculations. Note also that exports here refer only to goods manufactured in the United Kingdom.

[a] Cotton and woolen yarn exports are not separately listed; they amounted to some 10 percent of all textile exports.
[b] Dash indicates data not available.

the same period. Data on both groups are presented in table 1.20, which shows that the role of the empire was significant in just those industries that achieved most rapid growth within Britain's export mix. Together, the goods in groups I and II rose from 4.8 to 15.7 percent of the value of all manufactured exports between 1870 and 1913. To summarize: tables 1.18, 1.19, and 1.20 support the strong presumption that the empire took an economically significant share of British exports. It is warranted therefore to conclude that

TABLE 1.19: Empire Share of Selected British Exports
(In percentages)

Manufactures	1870	1880	1890	1900	1913
Electrical engineering goods	65.4	43.0	51.8	25.2	61.6
Arms, munitions	13.2	39.8	42.2	49.2	48.4
Paper, paper goods, etc.	71.5	79.0	69.6	63.7	62.0
Drugs, medicines	49.7	59.0	61.8	67.7	59.9
Books	42.0	57.2	59.2	60.6	60.1
Rubber tires	......	......	......	......	36.1

SOURCE: Schlote, *British Overseas Trade*, pp. 166–67.

TABLE 1.20: Growth of Exports of Selected Manufactures
(In percentages)

Commodity	Proportion of All Finished Manufactures Exported			Empire Share of Exports		
	1867–69	1890–92	1911–13	1870	1890	1913
Group I						
Machinery (including electric)	2.4	6.9	8.8	19.0	24.6	32.5
Motor vehicles (including chassis, tires)		0.1	0.8			67.4
Electrical engineering goods	0.3	0.8	1.1	65.4	51.8	61.6
Group II						
Books, pictures, prints	0.6	1.1	1.3	42.0	59.2	60.1
Drugs, perfumes, soap, candles, etc.[a]	0.8	1.3	1.6	—[b]	—[b]	55
Tobacco products	0	0	0.7	39.3	67.7	44.5
Paper, paper goods, office materials	0.7	1.3	1.4	71.5	69.6	62.0

SOURCE: W. Schlote, *British Overseas Trade*, pp. 74, 166–67.

[a] Empire shares for this category of exports are approximate, but they were over 50 percent during the whole period, 1870–1913.
[b] Dash indicates data not available.

the growth of British exports would have been less marked in the absence of empire markets.

Finally, the relative importance of the old empire, India, and the new empire as recipients of British manufactured exports is set forth in tables 1.21 and 1.22. The data in these tables demonstrate the likelihood that, both absolutely and relatively, the exports of Britain's three main manufacturing industries which the new empire absorbed were neither so "small" as to be meaningless nor insignificant. After 1870, as Great Britain agonized over the loss of her export markets because of growing protectionism and effective competition —particularly from the United States and from Germany— she could not but welcome the new empire markets with pleasure and expectation.[22] Well before 1913, the rapid growth of exports to the empire and further growth possibilities in this area had been noted and applauded in Britain. Whatever the long-run effects on overall British industrial efficiency and competitiveness may have been, in the short run between 1870 and 1914 the absorption of British exports in the new empire at the very least significantly lessened the depressive impact of changing world trade conditions on the British economy.[23]

Re-exports

The United Kingdom's re-export trade further illustrates the importance to Britain of the new empire. In the United States and Western Europe, a growing demand for tropical foods and raw materials generally was confronted by the naturally limited supplies of such goods. As the size of firms grew and international competition sharpened, national governments felt an urgent need for secure access to the supplies needed. Concomitantly, many foresaw rich opportunities for fruitful investment in the tropical sources of such supplies. As we shall see, British investors moved successfully to arrange for the production of several tropical commodities, particularly within the new colonies of the empire. They secured for British industry and British consumers the raw materials and food necessary for modern industry and rising standards of consumption.

Beyond securing needed access to tropical resources, the

TABLE 1.21: British Manufactured Exports, by Destination
(Columns 3, 4, 5, 7 in thousand £)

Commodity	Year	Old Empire	India	New Empire		Total Empire	
				Amount	Percentage of Exports to Total Empire	Amount	Percentage of Total Exports
Textiles	1876	12,849	15,961	1,300	4.3	30,000[a]	26.6[b]
	1900	18,214	19,069	2,700	6.8	40,000	39.7
	1913	31,609	40,729	15,729	17.8	88,000	43.9
Machinery	1876	656	724	20	1.4	1,400[a]	19.0[b]
	1900	2,149	1,529	300	7.4	4,052	22.3
	1913	5,360	4,558	2,111	17.5	12,029	32.5
Iron, steel	1876	5,191	1,864	500	6.4	7,555[c]	23.0[b]
	1900	7,368	3,280	2,322	17.8	12,970	40.0
	1913	15,072	9,801	3,670	12.9	28,545	50.0

Vehicles (incl. parts, tires)	1913	1,478	679	1,053	32.8	3,210[d]
Electrical engineering goods	1876	48	145	—[e]	—
	1900	611	76	—	—
	1913	1,513	362	1,443[f]	43.5	3,318

SOURCES: GB, *Statistical Abstract for the United Kingdom*, no. 52, pp. 78–85, no. 62, pp. 134–45; and no. 64, pp. 203–17; also Schlote, *British Overseas Trade*, pp. 166–67, 172–74.

[a] For 1876, we calculated that 30 percent of textile manufactures and 19 percent of machinery exports, respectively, went to the empire.

[b] These figures are for 1870, not 1876.

[c] Calculated by assuming that 30 percent of such exports went to the empire. Included in this category were iron and steel goods, cutlery, hardware, but not telegraphic wire.

[d] Calculated by assuming Schlote's data for motor vehicles apply equally to parts and rubber tires (pp. 166–67).

[e] Dash indicates data not available.

[f] This amount covers chiefly telegraph and telephone cables, switchboards, transformers, meters, etc.

TABLE 1.22: Growth of British Manufactured Exports, by
Destination, 1876–1913
(In percentages based on 1876)

Commodity Group	Old Empire	India	New Empire	Total Empire
Textiles	146	154	1,107	193
Machines	677	557	10,500	757
Iron, steel	190	416	640	275

SOURCES: Same as those for table 1.21 above.

colonies also secured Britain's overall international balance
of payments position by providing her with more commodities which were re-exportable.[24] Moreover, these benefits were
particularly important for Britain's balance of payments with
her advanced industrialized trading partners (see table 1.23).

TABLE 1.23: United Kingdom Foreign Trade
(In million £)

Country	Year	Imports	Exports	Re-exports
Russia	1880	16.0	8.0	3.0
	1900	22.0	11.0	5.4
	1913	40.3	18.1	9.6
United States	1880	107.1	30.9	7.1
	1900	138.8	19.8	17.6
	1913	141.7	29.3	30.2
Germany	1880	24.4	16.9	12.1
	1900	31.4	28.0	10.5
	1913	80.4	40.7	19.8
France	1880	42.0	15.6	12.4
	1900	53.6	20.0	5.9
	1913	46.4	28.9	11.9

SOURCE: R. B. Mitchell and P. Deane, *Abstract of British Historical Statistics,* pp.
314–27.

She was able to offset her decreasing ability to compete in
the economies of the United States and Europe with exports of home produced manufactures by increasing re-exports
of tropical goods to them, as well as by shifting exports of
manufactured goods to the less developed Latin American,
Eastern European, and empire markets.

Throughout the period 1870 to 1913, re-exports never fell
below 20 percent of the current value of exports of home

produced British goods. On occasion the figure reached 30 percent.[25] Table 1.23 indicates the sharp changes which took place in the direction of the re-export trade. Re-exports played an important role in the United Kingdom's balance of payments throughout the period 1880 to 1913. The bulk of re-export products—except to some extent wool and cotton —originated chiefly in the colonies and dependencies of the new empire. Table 1.24 presents a ranking, by importance

TABLE 1.24: Ranking of Re-export Commodities
(In current values)

Commodity	1880	1890	1900	1913
Raw wool	1	1	1	2
Raw cotton	2	2	2	3
Rubber	....	....	6	1
Oils[a]	4	4	5	6
Coffee	3	6	7	8
Tea	5	7	8	7
Hides, skins	7	5	3	4
Nonferrous metals[b]	6	3	4	5

SOURCE: Mitchell and Deane, *Abstract of Statistics*, pp. 307–08.

a Includes oil seeds, gum, resins, tallow, etc.
b Includes semimanufactures using these metals.

to the United Kingdom, of the various items that predominated among the re-export commodities. In the late nineteenth century, changing market considerations began to focus British attention on rubber, which led the way in the growing importance of tropical re-exports, becoming Britain's most important re-export by 1913. A brief economic history of rubber, together with the general statistical picture presented above will complete the basis for our conclusions on the relevance of certain imports and re-exports in an assessment of the economic importance of Britain's new empire.

Growing world demand, stimulated by the versatility of vulcanized products and later by the rubber tire industry, confronted limited and inelastic supplies. Until 1910, Brazil had been the largest single world source of rubber, producing its exports by tapping wild rubber plants.[26] The distance and unreliability of the Brazilian source, however, prompted the India Office under Disraeli to experiment with rubber plants as early as 1873.[27] The research on rubber at the Royal

Botanic Gardens in Kew led to the planting of new strains
of rubber trees in Ceylon, the Malay peninsula, and West
and East Africa.[28] Both the African and the Southeast Asian
plantings resulted in sharp increases in output, but hardly
enough to approach the output of Brazil. This reality led
to a crisis when American speculators cornered the Brazilian
rubber stocks in 1904–05 and again in 1908–10. The enormous price increases the speculators were able to achieve
—from a low in 1901–02 of 49.4 cents per pound to a high
in 1909–10 of $3.06 per pound—gave a strong incentive to
British officials, trading companies, and investors to find and
exploit real and potential alternative sources.[29]

By 1913 Ceyon's exports of rubber were worth £4.5 million,
accounting for over 33 percent of Ceylon's total exports. The
successful plantings of the Malay peninsula boosted rubber
exports from Singapore to £3.1 million in 1913, making
rubber second only to tin among all exports of the Straits
Settlements.[30]

The price mechanism of textbook fame worked rather well
to guide investment into the "re-export colonies." Basic foods
and raw materials experienced upward price movements in
London which resulted in decisions by both private businessmen and officials to push investments in the empire. British
trading companies and investors anticipated that there would
be potential sources of imports and re-exports in every tropical
region. The more tropical regions available, the better. No
one could know in advance how the course of prices might
make first one region, then another, first one primary commodity, then another, present not only opportunities for
lucrative private investment, but also balance of payments
advantages for Great Britain. Access to the tropics was desired for economically sound reasons of actual or potential
gains for the British economy. The value of re-export colonies as objects of private and public economic policy played
an important role in Britain's new imperialism in the late
nineteenth century.

Before I complete the general argument of this chapter,
an assumption implicit in the reasoning so far requires explicit formulation and demonstration, that is, that the eco-

nomic advantages Britain derived from her new empire would not have accrued to her in the absence of direct control of her colonies.

In terms of supplying food and raw materials imports, colonial administration meant for Britain ultimate control and hence a greater measure of security than would have obtained if France or Germany or another power had annexed the territory.[31] Also, whatever the final destination of food and raw materials exports from any colony, British political control almost always meant British predominance in the financing, insurance, and freight for the colony's exports, and hence British balance of payments advantages. Foreign political control could and frequently did deny Britain such predominance, regardless of the relative prices of the services provided by Britain and other countries. Finally, as chapter 4 below will illustrate, colonial control enabled the British authorities to determine to a large extent the choice of foods and raw materials developed and exported from any colonial territory. Thus it is reasonable to conclude that, in the absence of Britain's new empire, her security, her gains from invisible exports, and both the general mix and the quantities of food and raw materials supplied to world markets would have been less favorable for her.

The special advantages to British exports resulting from her colonial control over the empire, and the new empire in particular, are suggested in table 1.25. The table indicates that steel products, one of the United Kingdom's principal exports, enjoyed a favored position in the new empire unlike that which they enjoyed in any other world market, including India and the old empire.[32] Information on the cotton and wool industries, chemicals, shipping, engineering, electrical machinery, and locomotives gives evidence of similarly favored positions for Britain in exports to her colonies.[33] In 1904, the Colonial Office sent instructions to all colonial administrations ordering them to buy British, not only when British prices were more attractive than foreigners', but also when there was any doubt about differences in price or when the benefit from buying non-British was only "marginal."[34] In the new empire, of course, the colonial administrations were major customers who did most of their purchasing, financing,

TABLE 1.25: Trade in Semifinished and Finished Steel Products, 1913
(In thousand metric tons)

| | Exporters | | | |
Importers	United Kingdom	United States	Germany	Belgium
Old Empire	823	1,402[a]	212	101
India, Ceylon	573	22	197	135
New Empire	117	16	8	14
Europe	373	298	2,614	645
Latin America	310	421	466	248
U.S.A.	48	......	32	7
Far East	172	169	270	99

SOURCE: P. L. Payne, "Iron and Steel Manufactures," in D. H. Aldcroft, ed., *The Development of British Industry and Foreign Competition, 1875–1914*, p. 85.

[a] This exception to the pattern of British advantage in empire imports is fully accounted for by the special circumstances of U.S. exports to Canada.

and other such activities through a British governmental agency, the Crown Agents for the Colonies.[35]

Our conclusion, to avoid overstatement, is framed in the most modest terms. The systematic disparities in market performance analyzed above are explained by the colonial relationship. Consequently, the data at the very least warrant the inference that, in the absence of the colonial connection, Britain's economic advantages from trade with the territories of the new empire would have been less. In any case, given the formal and informal protectionism of Britain's industrial competitors, which included their colonial possessions, Britain would have derived economic advantages even from establishing colonies in which British exports merely competed freely with others.[36] The data undermine the notion that economic gains from trade with the new empire were "small" or "insignificant."

THE CAPITAL ACCOUNT

It remains to discuss the relationship of Britain's capital outflows to her new empire after 1870. The significant impact of Britain's foreign investments on domestic incomes and employment has been exhaustively studied and firmly established elsewhere.[37] What has continued to arouse controversy, however, is the role of the new empire as an outlet for such investments.

For some analysts, the simple fact that in 1913 less than 3 percent[38] of British foreign investments had been placed in new empire territories has seemed to destroy definitively the thesis that the new imperialism was in any sense "the product of economic necessity."[39] The appropriate criticism of these analysts is above all that their approach is unhistorical. Their penchant for judgments based on the juxtaposition of economic aggregates has led them, I believe, to a misreading of the importance of the new empire in terms of Britain's foreign capital position. That importance derived as much from the way in which outflows of British capital developed during the nineteenth century as from any particular characteristic of the new empire.

From the first beginnings of substantial capital outflows after the Napoleonic Wars, British foreign investment displayed two important aspects which continued to characterize it until 1914. The first was a close linkage between capital outflows and the foreign business connections of particular British industries and their bankers.[40] The second aspect was the linkage between capital outflows and the general system of political alliances currently being pursued by the British Government.[41] Until the 1850s British foreign investments can be readily subdivided according to which of these two aspects was most markedly in evidence. The loans to European and Latin American governments were clearly connected with general British political objectives, while other capital outflows, mainly to Europe, had close connections with the British textile industry.

The 1850s marked an important change. They followed a decade of intense railway investment inside Great Britain. A major iron and steel industry, largely oriented to railway supply, had grown up beside the hitherto predominant textile industry. As British railway construction slowed after 1850, the industries supplying it began to look to export markets to sell their rails, locomotives and other such goods. A hunt for concessions abroad began. British capital began to flow heavily into foreign and colonial railways, and by 1914 such investments accounted for over 40 percent of Britain's foreign assets, the largest single type of asset held.[42]

Initially, British foreign investments in railways went to Western Europe and the United States, where management was rarely left in British hands. Moreover, in France and Belgium after the 1850s and, toward the end of the century, in the United States as well, British investments in the overseas railways were steadily bought back by the nationals of the countries concerned.[43] The very speed and success of the British-financed railway networks in Western Europe and the United States rapidly propelled the economies of these counties toward industrialization (including the manufacture of railway components) and the internal generation of their own, ever larger investment funds.

Thus, as Jenks has pointed out, by the 1860s and 1870s, while British foreign investment in Western Europe and the United States continued to be important, the deceleration of orders to the United Kingdom for railway supplies once again served to turn the railway supply industries and their financiers toward new horizons. Thus, in India after the 1857 mutiny, successful political policy changes were made which, in effect, provided a very substantial subsidy to British railway construction there.[44] More generally, interest in railway investment spread to southern and eastern Europe, Latin America, Asia, and the colonies.

One might speculate that, in a world of free trade, the United States, Europe, Latin America, the old empire, India, and such nations as Japan and China would have provided ample territory before 1914 to satisfy the needs of the British railway industry for markets. However, free trade gave way toward the end of the century to protectionism, which soon closed off Germany and the United States, the two areas of most rapid growth in demand.[45] Protectionism also gave a further powerful stimulus to the industrial development of those nations which were increasingly competitive with Britain.

As outlined above, the competition from newly industrializing countries was forcing Britain's basic industrial exports increasingly toward empire markets. In the case of locomotive engines, to take but one example, British exports, which enjoyed the highest prestige in the world, demonstrate the course of change, as shown in table 1.26. Moreover, not only did such nations as Germany, the United States, and Japan begin to erode Britain's export position by entering the old empire—most markedly, the United States in Canada—but within the old empire demand was rising for some form of protection that would allow these countries to industrialize as well. By the turn of the century, Britain was facing appreciable competition in the old empire from manufactures produced in the British dominions.[46]

TABLE 1.26: British Sales of Locomotive Engines

Buyer	1860–1889	1890–1913
Home railways	5,891	3,711
Overseas railways	8,979	13,899
India	(3,418)	(5,542)
Europe	(2,480)	(770)
Rest of empire	(1,463)	(3,016)
Latin America	(1,037)	(3,090)
Other	(581)	(1,471)
Total	14,870	17,610

SOURCE: S. B. Saul, "The Engineering Industry," in Aldcroft, *British Industry and Foreign Competition*, p. 200.

The outflow of Britain's capital, as always, matched the flow and the interests of her merchants and was associated as much with political alliances as with changing trade relationships. As always, political and economic developments were mutually interdependent. The political movement in Great Britain toward closer ties with the empire was related to the realities of Britain's international economic position. Thus the flow of capital to colonial governments and investment in commercial ventures in the colonies had common roots.

The increasing tendency of British capital to flow toward the new empire in particular was part of a complex reorientation of Britain's entire foreign trade and international investment position. This reorientation was only beginning to reach statistically observable proportions in the last decade before World War I. Hence the absolute size of British capital flows to the new empire, if not seen in the appropriate historical setting, can mislead the researcher into an assumption that such flows were "unimportant and insignificant." The reorientation of British capital flows can be seen in table 1.27. In general the table indicates that the areas of largest absolute British investment had relatively slower rates of growth in investment. The exceptions to this generalization are Canada and Latin America, and they only further demonstrate the basic point. The flows to these areas were designed chiefly for railway construction in their outlying, undeveloped regions. Similarly, the far smaller investments in southern Europe, the Far East, and Russia were also heavily concentrated on railway construction.

TABLE 1.27: Size and Growth of British Foreign Investments, 1907–13 (Size in million £; growth as percentage of total in 1913)

	Size in 1913	Growth, 1907–13
Canada, Newfoundland	515	48.5
Australia, New Zealand	416	16.3
India, Ceylon	379	17.1
Rest of Empire	145	51.0
United States	755	21.7
Latin America	757	39.7
Russia	110	41.8
Other Europe	109	48.6
Japan and China	107	46.7
Other	78	26.9

SOURCES: G. Paish, "The Export of Capital and the Cost of Living," The Statist, supplement, 79 (14 February 1914): i-viii; and H. Feis, Europe, the World's Banker, 1870–1914, pp. 23–24.

The most rapidly growing field for British investments, however, was the new empire. By 1913 this growth, in absolute size, had made the new empire a larger factor in Britain's foreign investment positions than Russia, or "Other Europe," or Japan and China together. The new empire could reasonably be expected to absorb railway lines. And, most importantly, since the predominant investments in all colonies were those of nationals of the mother country, the exporters of British capital could foresee great opportunities to invest with security in railway and associated infrastructure construction. Moreover, as our previous discussion has indicated, men associated with the new empire railways could be reasonably expected to demonstrate a loyalty to British railway manufacturers that was not present elsewhere in the world.

Our argument here is not that British capital began to flow to the new empire instead of elsewhere. Rather, British investment continued along British lines of trade and political alliances as it always had throughout the nineteenth century. But the growth of foreign competition in manufactures and foreign protectionism, coupled with the internal response of British businessmen,[47] resulted in the reorientation of trade, investment, and political goals toward the acquisition and economic development of the new empire. Thus, in addition to certain flows of capital to Russia and Europe for "political reasons" and to the United States and Latin America along established British trade or investment patterns, the new element in Britain's international investment position was the new empire. Table 1.27 above justifies calling this the dynamic element with the surest chance of continued growth for Britain. Increasingly after 1870, the acquisition of the new empire commended itself to British statesmen as an economically reasonable course of action.

In conclusion, our examination of Britain's overseas investment in the period following the 1850s establishes as unacceptable the case made by some writers that the new empire was without significance to Britain's international capital position. This case, together with the Fieldhouse position on Britain's overseas trade, is unconvincing because its focus is on economic aggregates alone, without specifics as to underlying historically developed economic structures and patterns in trade and investment. I have also tried in this chapter to show how Britain's new imperialism emerged from and responded to genuine economic needs of the metropolitan economy. We can now move to the principal subject of this study, an investigation of the economic impact on one part of the new empire, Kenya, which resulted from British efforts to mold it into a profitable unit of an imperial economy.

2 British Imperialism and the East African Slave Trade

During the first half of the nineteenth century, Arab caravans traveling from the coast of East Africa as far as several
hundred miles into the interior were increasingly common
occurrences.[1] Generally quite profitable, they constituted the
backbone of a rich and complex Arab empire which included
Zanzibar, varying depths of the East African hinterland from
Portuguese Mozambique to the Somali region in the north,
and the territories of Muscat (Oman) and Aden on the Arabian peninsula. Slaves were the essential commodity of this
imperial economy.[2] Arab communities at Zanzibar and on
the nearby East African coast organized extensive slave-raid-
ing, slave-trading and ivory-gathering parties into the interior.
In this trade, the immigrant Arabs were assisted and joined
by a special population of coastal Bantu peoples intermixed
with and heavily influenced by the Arabs—the Swahilis. The
Arab and Swahili traders exported chiefly slaves and ivory
to dealers—including Europeans—in Zanzibar and Arabia.
Slaves and ivory captured or purchased in the interior were
normally transported to the coast, where both were sold.[3]

Slaves also worked on Arab plantations on the coast and
on Zanzibar, as well as being valuable export commodities.
The Arabs thus comprised a landlord as well as a trader
class. The British consul at Zanzibar in 1865, assessing the
role of slaves in Arab society, wrote:

> The whole fabric of Arab society is so interwoven with
> slavery that it is hopeless to expect that it will ever
> permanently abandon their [sic] pursuit of slaves. Their
> fathers have possessed them ever since Arabia was peo-
> pled, and they have no idea of a state of things in which
> slaves do not occupy a prominent place. The institu-
> tion is one sanctioned by their religion.[4]

This chapter has been published, in slightly altered form, in *Science and Society* 36 (Winter 1972): 443–62.

The sultan of Zanzibar was titular head of this Arab empire when the British and other Europeans first established their official presence in East Africa.[5] The sultan exercised real and effective power only along the coast of East Africa and parts of southeastern Arabia. Essentially ruling a sea oriented empire, his influence in the interior was stable and continuous only along some of the main caravan routes. What transitory power he could exert in the interior of East Africa tended to depend on struggles among feuding groups of Arabs and Swahilis, who often appealed to the sultan's authority merely as a tactic in their feuding. Even the Arab merchant community at Mombasa—clearly a coastal area—maintained a degree of autonomy and independence from the center of the sultan's power in Zanzibar and Muscat. At least until the last third of the nineteenth century, the sultan's modest financial resources and the physical obstacles of the countryside combined to undermine his capacity to develop a position of any real power in the East African interior.

The sultanate was financed by customs duties and also by taxes on the output of cloves from Zanzibar's slave plantations, the island's chief productive activity.[6] However, the credit essential to both the caravans and the clove plantations was advanced to the Arab community by British Indians resident in Zanzibar and on the coast. During the nineteenth century, the Arab and Swahili traders within the sultan's domain and beyond were increasingly financed by the immigrant Indians. By the 1890s British officials estimated that Indians possessed half the landed property in Zanzibar and had several million pounds sterling invested in East Africa.[7] British Indian subjects thus had a large stake in an East African economy based heavily on the slave trade, although they rarely participated in the trade directly.[8]

The economic ascendancy of the British Indian community introduced a unique complexity into the class structure of the sultanate. While gathering into their hands a near monopoly in the financial market and, as a result, holding extensive Zanzibar lands and a dominant position in the wholesale trade, the Indians remained British subjects, political aliens within the sultanate. Thus, while they had in fact taken over the dominant economic position from the Arab-Swahili slave-trading and landlord aristocracy, the latter retained formal political dominance under the sultan's leadership.[9]

For the first thirty years after the establishment of their consulate at Zanzibar in 1840, British authorities seemed quite content to rely on free trade and competition to maintain British merchants' interests in the East African trade. This confidence endured, despite frustration over American and German cotton cloth imports and the inability of British merchants to break the Indians' near monopoly position.[10] To some degree, official confidence reflected lack of official interest stemming from simple ignorance, as well as from the very small amounts of trade in the area. Little was known about the interior of East Africa and hence about its economic potential. It was the explorations of Livingstone, Stanley, Speke and others from the 1850s to the 1880s and the expansion of missionary activity—both especially stimulated by the opening of the Suez Canal in 1869—that served to inform and interest Englishmen.[11]

By the early 1870s the flow of information from explorers, missionaries and sportsmen began to provide images of East Africa to Europeans that prompted more active Belgian, French, and German, as well as British, interest. All reports spoke of the vast dislocation and suffering caused by the slave trade. For the British, long since committed to its abolition, these reports caused much public outcry in England, including demands made for immediate steps to halt all traffic in slaves.[12] Many reports described great wealth awaiting exploitation in the East African hinterland. A number of businessmen in Great Britain and elsewhere began to look more seriously into investment possibilities in East Africa.[13]

THE BEGINNINGS OF INTERVENTION

The period 1873 to 1887 defines a sharp transition in British official and private behavior toward East Africa. A progressively more active intervention replaced the earlier, relatively freer, trade and political relations.[14] Britain's consul-general in these years, John Kirk, made most of the day to day decisions that brought about this change.[15]

The change in British policy was first and foremost a response to two closely interconnected phenomena: the commercial interests of private European companies in East Africa, which had increased rapidly, and the simultaneous activity there of the major European powers. The complex economic ramifications of the opening of the Suez Canal in 1869 had drawn East Africa inevitably into the network of world trade. King Leopold of Belgium became very active in East Africa by 1877.[16] French activities along the coast were markedly intensified, especially after 1876.[17] In the interior, the work of Abbé Debaize resulted in a proposal to the sultan that he grant some Frenchmen a concession to develop parts of the Sultanate. Although the concession failed to materialize—in part because of Kirk's efforts—further French moves were made by the traveler Revoil in 1884. The very extensive efforts of German concession hunters and officials during the same period represented the most important of European challenges to the British position in East Africa. And finally, the British themselves deepened their involvement in East Africa after 1869 through the rapid expansion of the number and influence of their missionary stations, as well as through the expanding interests of British businessmen, above all a group of them led by William Mackinnon in London.

Facing this situation, the British government, operating through Consul Kirk, resorted to a strategy that had succeeded well for the previous half century. Put bluntly, the strategy involved the activation of serious anti-slave trade campaigns as a means of establishing British economic and political hegemony in an area.[18] For example, Britain had rescued the imam of Muscat in 1819, 1833, and 1839 from his disputes with Arab rivals. In return, Britain gained a treaty against slave trading, as well as a powerful position in the Persian Gulf, which was a strategic security objective for her at the time, and which led to her early special political influence in East Africa when the Muscat government moved its capital to Zanzibar in 1840. In 1820, 1838, and 1839, Britain made similar arrangements with several Arab sheikdoms on the Persian Gulf. Elsewhere, comparable arrangements were worked out in Madagascar (1817, 1820, and 1823), with the Persian Shah (1851), and with several southern Arabian sheikdoms (in the 1860s).[19]

By 1873, the British decided to launch a renewed and systematic campaign to stop the East African slave trade, a campaign designed to go well beyond their earlier rhetorical and largely ineffective measures.[20] The East African slave trade had reached huge proportions by the 1870s— relatively unhindered by the treaties and edicts enacted to stop it. A major purpose of the British campaign was to win broad political support in England for a policy of expansion in East Africa. In English politics, as well as for foreign consumption, British colonialism in Africa was generally manifest as an anti–slave-trade crusade. The Anglican and Nonconformist Churches were powerful influences with the electorate until the end of the century.[21]

However, the anti–slave-trade campaign also played a direct part in entrenching British political power in the sultanate far more firmly than ever before. Whatever Britain's original motives for such a campaign may have been, in fact, the outcome of the suppression of the slave trade represented at the least a major threat to, and at the most the ultimate negation of, the sultanate's economic base. The nature of British motivation is not at issue here. While the evidence suggests that Consul Kirk was well aware of the campaign's impact on the sultanate, the only matter of importance here is to assess that impact in terms of the interaction developing between the East African economy and British activities in the area.

As it happened, the British campaign influenced events in East Africa in two stages. In the first, running roughly from 1873 to 1883, the campaign caused considerable damage to the Arab-Swahili slave economy. The result was a split between the sultan and the Arab aristocracy which forced the sultan into a greater dependency on the British. This conformed precisely to British objectives at the time. In the second stage, from 1884 through the 1890s, the British finally subjected the slave trade to a systematic attack sufficient to stop it and to confront the traders with economic ruin. The coup de grâce followed, as Britain replaced both the sultan and the Arab-Swahili aristocracy with the direct economic and political hegemony of the British colonial administration.

Kirk became consul-general in 1873 and acted immediately to deepen British influence with the sultan. He pursued this course because he felt responsible to protect British commercial opportunities against interference from any other power and, even more, to advance them. "It is a disgrace that no British company should have stepped in before this time to share the chance of success and reap the advantage that must attend those who are first in the field."[22]

The problem was to prevent the sultan from inviting or permitting any other European power to establish a position in his domain that might harm British trade. Throughout this period, even after the attempt to set rigorous rules at the Berlin Conference of 1884–85, there remained a possibility that any European power might declare some form of control somewhere in the hinterland of East Africa. A few treaties with a few chiefs would suffice as a pretext. Such a power might then approach the sultan with an offer designed to divert his loyalty from his British friends. It was quite conceivable that the sultan might initiate such developments himself. So long as the sultan's position remained independent to any significant degree, his independence posed a potential danger to the objectives of British policy.

In 1873 and again in 1876, Consul Kirk used military and diplomatic pressure to force the sultan to enact strong new laws banning the slave trade by sea and then by land. British cruisers, as well as the sultan's agents, achieved some success in cutting down coastal slave trading. Of course, the sultan's policy struck sharply at the interests of the Arab-Swahili aristocracy.[23] This placed the sultan in an extremely unsure position, caught between the British and his local aristocratic power base. In 1875 Britain took steps to demonstrate the lengths to which she would go to support and defend the sultan's power. The result was a dramatically increased reliance on and confidence in the British on the part of the sultan.[24] In any case, neither the British nor the sultan moved so far as to outlaw the institution of slavery. Nor did either the British or the sultan have the power to stop slave trading in the interior of East Africa. Consequently, although Arab-Swahili slave-trading interests were partially damaged and anti-European sentiments given a strong impetus, there did not as yet develop the direct clash between Arab-Swahilis and Europeans which did develop in the mid-1880s.

Compared with developments on the coast, events in East Africa's interior built rapidly toward a crisis point. As has often been pointed out, legal restrictions on slave trading on the coast did not lessen, and in all probability increased, the hunt for slaves and trade in them throughout the interior of East Africa.[25] The supply being great, slave prices remained low.[26] One consequence of this in the late 1870s and 1880s was the increased use of the "interior slaves" by Arab-Swahili traders "to undercut the porter-carried ivory of European caravans."[27] Europeans were forbidden to use slaves as porters. This immediate pressure on European traders reinforced the already prevalent trader ideology of "legitimate commerce." This "theory"—popularized by Livingstone —held that the most effective policy against the slave trade was to supplant it by legitimate, that is European, commerce.[28]

As a result, the ever more frequent European commercial interest in interior trade after 1869 developed a rapidly intensified antislavery bias. The missionaries shared these feelings. "The missionary and trader thus became allies in a God-given task . . . a fusion of Manchester free-trade principles with evangelical piety."[29] The preaching of the missionaries against the slave trade and their practice of harboring runaway slaves were their contributions to this alliance.

Kirk moved slowly and carefully in the anti–slave-trade campaign. He clearly did not want to alienate the Arab-Swahili aristocracy too much too quickly. As one observer put it, "He made no unwise attempt to stop the slave trade. . . . One, perhaps, of the most remarkable of Sir John Kirk's feats was that he retained the goodwill and respect of the Arab slave dealers while he was known to be doing his utmost to restrict and stop their trade."[30] Kirk's policy sought to deepen British private and official power gradually in an increasingly dependent sultanate before precipitating a major confrontation with the Arab-Swahili community.

Besides the limited attack on coastal slave trading, Kirk made repeated attempts in the later 1870s to improve trading conditions for the Europeans. One method was to ally the sultan with certain powerful leaders in the interior who would protect and/or favor European traders over Arabs.[31] Of lesser yet significant impact was Kirk's introduction of the india rubber trade, which supplanted the slave trade in such major trading ports as Kilwa and indirectly provided a stimulus to British shipping.[32]

The third and final element of Kirk's policy involved his decision to enhance the military and thereby the political power of the sultanate, now tied quite closely to the British. Kirk wanted the economy of East Africa to be developed by British citizens under the political protection of the sultan.[33] By strengthening the dependent sultan's military power, Britain could exert force without any need for direct British military intervention. Thus Kirk arranged the appointment of a British naval officer, Lloyd Mathews, to establish, train, and command a standing army for the sultan.[34] The sultanate had previously lacked any significant standing military force. Taking his orders from Kirk at least as much as from the sultan, Mathews enabled the sultan to exercise more control, or at least more influence, over Arab-Swahili groups in the interior. The sultan thereby enhanced his power position on the coast and in significant portions of the interior. Yet the very continuance of the sultan's new power depended upon British favor, expressed through Kirk and Mathews.

Kirk followed this policy for reasons of defense, as well as to advance private British commerce. British apprehensions included the fear that another European power might bypass Zanzibar and the sultan's coastal holdings altogether and attempt to exert exclusive control directly over some portion of the hinterland. Kirk could perhaps prevent this if the British, through a powerful sultan controlling at least the Arab-Swahilis along the coast, could deny an outlet to the sea to any potential European possession in the hinterland.[35]

Increased private British merchant activities along the coast during the 1870s did little to change Kirk's basic

strategy. Several British capitalists, led by William Mackinnon, inaugurated regular commercial visits by their steamship line to Zanzibar. Then, in 1877, the growing economic
importance of East Africa and general European interests
there led Mackinnon to apply for an exclusive concession
to develop the sultan's mainland territory as a private company venture. He asked the British Foreign Office for support but received only a very mild, noncommittal form of
approval. In effect, London was not prepared to support
private enterprises abroad that risked diplomatic and costly military entanglements for objectives whose worth had
not yet been demonstrated.[36] Kirk had to continue to work
through the sultan to provide protection for British interests.

In the decade from the early 1870s to the early 1880s,
British policy had changed from a relatively limited, rather
passive involvement in East African affairs to a far more
active, extensive intervention. The causes were the opening
of the Suez Canal in 1869 and the consequent rapid increase in commercial, missionary, and official interest in
the area showed by many Europeans, not only the British.
The objectives of British policy under these new circumstances were explicitly described as the protection of present
and potential future British interests. There was also the
matter of stopping the slave trade. Britain moved directly
to boost British commercial interests, to make the sultan
increasingly dependent on Britain, and, finally, to give some
British-controlled military power to the dependent sultan.
In this context, the anti–slave trade campaign takes on its
historic significance as a process which, whatever the motives of those involved, made the sultan less dependent on
the wealthy Arab aristocracy and more dependent on the
British.

By the early 1880s, British activities had achieved mixed
results. Kirk could take satisfaction in the fact that British
power over the sultan was nearly absolute and beyond
serious challenge. Kirk could also note that British economic
interests in the sultanate were larger and more extensive in
1883 than in 1873. On the other hand, British policy had
badly shaken the dominant class in the sultanate because
of the attack upon the slave-trading interests, especially

those of the Arab-Swahili aristocracy. Consequently, a powerful group, possessing considerable wealth and influence, found itself increasingly threatened by and opposed to British policy. Finally, Kirk's policy failed to block the establishment of a competitive European power, Germany, on the East African mainland. This failure set in motion the further changes in British policy that led directly to the final, total destruction of East Africa's nineteenth century economic and social structure and the concomitant British decision to build a new economy in its newly annexed East Africa Protectorate.

British Imperialism and the Slave Trade

The Liberal Gladstone Ministry of 1880–85 maintained an official position of minimal direct support for the commercial activities of Britons in such places as East Africa. Gladstone simply could see no "adequate reason for our being 'dans cette galère.' "[37] Gladstone's broader imperial strategy did not mesh for a while with Kirk's narrower focus in Zanzibar and thereby undermined the thrust of Kirk's efforts to forestall the establishment of any other European power in East Africa. Consequently, during these years, despite the efforts of Kirk and merchants from the Manchester Chamber of Commerce in particular, an energetic group of Germans intensified their activity in East Africa and acquired a definite foothold by 1884.[38] Germany validated her claims in a London-approved agreement with the sultan in 1885. Finally, Germany signed a delimitation of spheres of influence with Great Britain in 1886 and a treaty in 1890. These developments produced the division of the area into British and German East Africa that was to last until World War I.

In the face of German activity, and with rare assistance from London, Kirk's efforts emphasized salvaging the British position. Only the return of Lord Salisbury to power in 1885 finally permitted a more active London-supported official policy to establish a British sphere in East Africa that would halt further encroachment by Germany or any other power.

With the German penetration an accomplished and threatening fact, British policy began an intensive search for ways to acquire a nonnegotiable sphere in East Africa. In practice, British policy in Africa changed from an effort to help the dependent sultan of Zanzibar keep control of his lands and his power to a concerted drive to make the entire Arab-Indian economy directly subordinate to British policy.[39] To ensure the freedom of British trade and economic opportunity, Britain changed course to exercise a more direct, explicit and comprehensive rule over the areas that had not yet been ceded to other Europeans.

British policy after 1885 changed, in the first instance, toward the sharpest, most determined drive so far to stop the slave trade. After Germany's arrival, Britain's assessment of the situation emphasized the unreliability of the sultanate as a means to forestall the other European powers. So long as the Arab empire was maintained, no matter how influential the British consul-general was, it always remained possible for another power to buy or force concessions from the sultan. Pursuing the full abolition of the slave trade, and ultimately of the institution of slavery itself, meant welcoming the collapse of the sultanate of Zanzibar. The well-known 1890 partition of the sultan's dominions between Great Britain and Germany followed from Britain's lack of interest in the territorial integrity of the sultanate.[40]

The British decision to intensify the anti–slave trade campaign reflected a desire to overcome the failures of British policy during the previous decade. Rule through the sultan had not stopped German efforts when they were based in Germany, and it would probably be even less effective when the German base was moved to East Africa. Moreover, the growing anxiety and hostility of the Arab-Swahili slave traders throughout the interior might increase their receptivity to German or other propositions for treaties, alliances, or other political arrangements with an anti-British bias.[41] The sultan, under continual Arab-Swahili pressure, and dismayed by the territory Britain had effectively passed to the Germans in 1886, was also formally still a sovereign power, liable to make embarrassing deals with Europeans. Such considerations probably sufficed to confirm a hardening British cabinet policy summed up in one minister's firm understatement: "We ought, I think, to do our utmost to prevent any foreign power supplanting us at Zanzibar."[42]

Private British economic interests added pressure for fur-

ther official measures which, if implemented, would tend
toward the disintegration of the independent sultanate. Growing European trade interests in East Africa produced competitive frictions with the Arab-Swahili traders that reached
a full crisis in the mid–1880s.[43] European explorers, missionaries, sportsmen, and merchants were managing growing
numbers of caravans during the 1880s and 1890s. These
Europeans, mainly British, complained bitterly about Arab-
Swahili competition. One on-the-spot observer summarized
their views:

> Any European proposing to establish a house at Zan-
> zibar, for the purpose of trading direct with the interior
> . . . would discover that the cost of transport independent
> of risk, would render his efforts to compete with the
> Arab trader, who pays in slaves and deals in slaves by
> the way, futile.[44]

Complaints of Europeans and demands for official action
on their behalf intensified rapidly after 1880.[45] European
traders saw and demanded the advantages that would accrue
to them if official measures reduced the slave trade and in
general undercut the ability of the Arab-Swahili-Indian trading networks to best the Europeans in competition.

Thus, official considerations on positions of global power
were buttressed by private interests demanding official assistance. The result was a general British offensive against
the limited independence of the sultanate and the Arab-
Swahili trading networks in general. Arabs and Swahilis
throughout East Africa reacted in the late 1880s with a general counteroffensive against Europeans.[46] Repeated and
often violent clashes resulted from the interior lakes to the
coast. British military campaigns against Arab power continued well into the 1890s, as exemplified by the final clash
which established British rule over the coastal Arab-Swahilis,
the Mazrui War in 1895. At about the same time, German
private interests and officials moving toward the establishment of German economic and political supremacy in their
sphere encountered similar resistance, which they also crushed
militarily.[47]

While fighting Arab-Swahili power militarily, the British

undertook parallel diplomatic moves to undercut the Arab-Swahili social and economic position in East Africa. Britain declared a protectorate over Zanzibar in 1890. The next year, the new British agent, Portal, carried out a coup d'état, which put Britons in charge of state administration, replacing the sultan's Arabs. This proved to be the "decisive step in the gradual loss of Arab political control."[48]

On the economic front, Britain supplemented her attack on Arab-Swahili political power with strong support for private British interests working to establish economic predominance in the area. In 1887–88 the Foreign Office granted Mackinnon the support and official backing it had denied him a decade earlier. The Crown issued a royal charter to the Imperial British East Africa Company (IBEA), empowering it to penetrate, open, and administer East Africa from the coast inland through Uganda. IBEA received nearly complete political authority, as well as exclusive economic privileges. From its inception IBEA concentrated on the twin goals of establishing a safe trade route from the coast to Uganda and constructing a railroad along that route.[49]

Achievement of these goals involved several key economic changes in East Africa. First, the cost of freight from the coast to the interior would decrease sufficiently to stimulate what was expected to be a large and profitable trade.[50] Second, the railway, by expanding trade possibilities throughout the area, would offer the Arab-Swahilis and their Indian creditors certain albeit restricted fields of commercial activity different from their traditional slave-trading and other caravans. In this manner, British-Indian investments would not be totally lost, and the Arab-Swahili trading community would not be totally ruined economically.

However, the railroad, as a purely British-owned, British-financed, and British-run enterprise, actively shifted the locus of economic power in the interior for the first time from Arabs to Europeans. Lugard summarized the purpose of building a railway explicitly: "to restrict the Swahili to the main arteries of traffic established by the Administration [British], and to those methods of transport which he could obtain along those main trade routes . . . it would result in compelling him to settle down and trade under the protection of the Administration."[51]

By 1895 British policy had committed itself to building the Uganda Railway. It had purposefully eliminated the independent economic and political position of the Arab-Indian empire. The existence, growth, and direction of economic development henceforth depended almost completely on the British. British political hegemony began formally with the declaration of the East Africa Protectorate in 1895.

In the 1890s the British achieved their objective of firmly securing a large portion of East Africa against the inroads of any other European power. Zanzibar and its sultan were completely and formally subordinated to British rule. Similarly, the Arab-Swahili aristocracies of most of both the coast and the interior had been subordinated. Official British rule on Zanzibar, combined with chartered company rule on the mainland, typified the new, dominant political and economic forces exercising direct power in the British area.

The interpretation of the British anti–slave trade campaigns suggested by the foregoing differs from the two general kinds of interpretation that run throughout the literature. One view holds that purely internal British humanitarian, religious, and political impulses led to a worldwide crusade which, while concurrent, was basically unconnected and uncoordinated with other objectives and tactics of British foreign policy. The other basic view holds that the anti–slave trade campaign was merely a cloak to disguise or give spurious justification to the economic and political objectives and strategies that were the core of British imperialism.

The evidence on the campaign against the East African slave trade, however, warrants the conclusion that, at least in East Africa, the campaign played a role coordinated with other tactics to further the objectives of British imperial policy. But neither was that role limited to being merely a cloak. Rather the anti–slave trade campaigns were sincere and serious efforts whose results were both anticipated by British officials and in line with their general policy objectives. Moreover, the British attack upon the slave trade in East Africa con-

tributed to results more complex than the mere achievement
of British supremacy.

BRITISH POLICY AND THE ARAB-SWAHILI COMMUNITY

The first result of the attack upon the slave trade, as we
have seen, was the reduction of Arab-Swahili power. Yet it
is important to note that the British were careful to save
the Arab-Swahili-Indian communities and their trading connections from complete ruin. British officials repeatedly
blocked, postponed, diluted and retarded moves toward what
struck them as too rapid or too complete actions against
the slave trade or slavery as an institution.[52] "Nor was the
British Government anxious to undertake experiments in
social revolution."[53] Thus, while British policy damaged the
interests and diminished the overall social position of the
Arab-Swahili community, it did not choose to ruin it totally
or to render it propertyless. As one good reverend moaned:
"Our government has been urged again and again to compel
the Sultan of Zanzibar to abolish the status of slavery . . .: but
rather than interfere, [it prefers that] this hideous loss of
life must go on."[54]

Rather than destroy the Arab-Swahili community, Britain
kept it with its trading and plantation interests at least partially intact. The first Commissioner of the East Africa Protectorate expressed the essence of British objectives in solving
the Arab-Swahili problem:

> I would endeavor . . . to enlist the rising generation of
> Arabs and Swahilis (of the better class) in the service
> of government, . . . [their] interests with [British officials]
> would thus become identified, and so [we would] grad-
> ually create throughout the territory a body of men
> which could serve as a useful intermediary between the
> British ruler and the native population.[55]

Slave trading and Britain's anti–slave trade campaigns had
far-reaching consequences for the majority African population of East Africa. Nearly every historical record that exists
testifies to the immense damage caused among most East
African tribes by the slave trade.[56] It disrupted the economic
structure and activities of African society. The removal of

tribespeople often denied the tribe the labor power and security necessary for the agricultural output essential to survival. The weakening of the defensive potential of some
tribes in some regions led to increased intertribal raiding
and warfare.[57] The spread of traffic in slaves made guns
increasingly available to tribes whose proclivities toward
raiding and warfare became far more damaging than before
as a result. The profitability of supplying slaves and provisions to Arab and then to European caravans shifted the
economic activities of some Africans toward raiding and the
activities of others toward a degree of dependence on purchases from caravans.[58] Traditional African trading and agriculture gave way to newer economic activities geared to the
slave trade economy. The pre-1850 patterns of limited household slavery in certain African areas "slid disasterously" under
pressure from traders "into competitive slaving for export."[59]

As of the 1890s, the social disruption occasioned by the slave
trade had fostered among some Africans a kind of economic re-
gression from higher levels of development to more primitive,
locally self-sufficient economies,[60] while for other Africans providing slaves and/or supplies to slave caravans had become
an economic necessity. Then the intensified campaigns against
slave trading gave the African economy yet another shock
by sharply reducing the caravan trade. The coast and hinterland lay in disarray with population, agricultural production, and trading in a depressed and dismal state. As Kirk
himself once observed about East Africa, "its capacity for
development could not be realized until the slave trade and
its attendant atrocities were abolished, for apart from the
moral point of view, this human traffic was steadily denud-
ing the continent of its population."[61] In essence, both the
slave-trading system in East Africa and Britain's sudden abolition of it in the 1880s and 1890s were major contributions
to the bleak economic situation there at the century's close.

The political economy of the slave trade and its abolition
in East Africa form a chapter in the economic history of
British colonialism in Africa. The British anti–slave trade
campaign contributed both to the establishment of British
colonial hegemony and to the further economic disorganiza-

tion—or, perhaps, reorganization—of the local Asian and African populations that had already been so profoundly affected by the slave trade. Having secured the area from the inroads of foreigners, the new protectorate's first and fundamental task was to organize the disarrayed local Africans and Asians it had subordinated into a profitable economic unit of the British Empire. This became the purpose and guiding theme of British policy in the protectorate, later renamed Kenya Colony, for the next several decades.

3 The Colonization of Land in Kenya

British policy totally transformed the economy of the East Africa Protectorate in the years between 1895 and the First World War. Why, where, how, and with what results the British acquired the land, labor and capital to effect the transformation will be examined in the next four chapters.

MAKING THE PROTECTORATE SELF-SUPPORTING

The views of British officials toward East Africa were strongly colored by the vast differences they saw around 1900 between the economic conditions in the neighboring Uganda Protectorate and the East Africa Protectorate respectively. In Uganda, the agricultural activities of the African tribes—above all, in the Buganda state—seemed well-organized. They were clearly prosperous. Indeed, the economic rationale for the Uganda Railway was the rich trade envisioned between Europe and Uganda. Consequently, it was generally thought prudent to interfere as little as possible with the economic institutions and practices found there except for slavery and the slave trade. By contrast, economic conditions in the East Africa Protectorate were seen as dismal and hopeless.

Commissioner Charles Eliot collected the views of his officials, forwarded them to London, and frequently added his own observations on the protectorate's economic situation.[1] He reported that around 1900 the large and important Kikuyu people were badly disorganized as a result of severe famines in 1897. From agricultural production, they had turned to cattle raiding and, according to Eliot, came increasingly to depend upon warfare for their livelihood. Eliot's appraisal of the sizable agricultural population living around the western end of the Uganda Railway and along the Gulf of Kavirondo, an extension of Lake Victoria, noted their occasional industriousness, but termed their love of alcohol and leisure a major barrier to sustained productive activity. The nomadic Masai people were called "utterly non-productive"; they received only scorn from Eliot, who demanded

47

that they be prohibited from roaming in areas they would
not usefully cultivate.[2]

However biased his preconceptions, Eliot was expressing
the prevailing British view of the differences between the
Uganda and East Africa Protectorates when he remarked
that "to cross the lake [separating the two territories] is
like visiting another continent."[3] Thus by 1904 the commissioner of the Uganda Protectorate could predict very con-
fidently that "Uganda will never be a white man's country."[4]
A few years later, Winston Churchill echoed these sentiments
in giving an overall impression of his talks with East African
officials in 1907.[5]

The Arab slave trade and its consequences certainly explain more of whatever real difference there was between
the economic situation of the two protectorates than the
specific characteristics of the various tribes or families—
which were themselves affected by slave trading. In any case,
the perceptions of the officials provide the background for
their policy choices. Buganda was seen to possess a politi-
cally centralized kingdom with a prosperous agrarian economy. In the East Africa Protectorate, on the other hand,
British authorities expected to have to create and maintain
viable economic institutions and patterns of productive activity.

British officials saw as a prime task the search for agents
to make the East Africa Protectorate productive. Having
blamed the Africans for the economic disarray in which they
pictured most African tribes, these officials tended to look
to other races to play the key role. As Commissioner Eliot
phrased it, Bantu peoples "are somewhat low on the scale
of civilization, with no inclination to trade, and not much
disposition for work of any kind."[6] The officials also operated under growing pressure from London to move—and
move quickly—to recoup imperial outlays on the defense, administration, and railway (construction and maintenance)
costs incurred in adding the protectorate to the empire. Table
3.1 presents the picture of developments in the first years of
the protectorate as they appeared in London and in East
Africa.

Debates in the House of Commons on the issue of imperial

TABLE 3.1: Protectorate Trade and Administrative Budget Data
(In thousand £ sterling, at current prices)

Year	Imports	Exports	Receipts	Expenditures	Grants[a]
1895–96[b]	177	74	—[c]	—	51
1896–97	262	78	39	148	
1897–98	268	73	30	134	[d]
1898–99	472	71	—	—	
1899–1900	447	122	—	—	110
1900–01	450	71	64	193	87
1901–02	421	96	68	278	93
1902–03	443	135	96	311	314
1903–04	437	134	109	419	256
1904–05	742[e]	123	155	303	251
1905–06	974	125	270	419	214
1906–07	1,227	164	461	616	164
1907–08	1,217	157	475	692	193
1908–09	1,774	140	486	703	138
1909–10	1,166	191	503	669	133
1910–11	1,607	276	610	682	130
1911–12	2,070	333	729	772	190
1912–13	2,892	421	953	961	23
1913–14	3,397	444	1,124	1,116	0

SOURCES: GB *CP* CO, "Annual Blue Books," in CO 543; GB, *Statistical Abstract for the Several British Oversea Dominions and Protectorates, 1903–1917*, Cmd. 664, 1920, pp. 16–19; Max Salvadori, *La Colonisation Européene du Kenya*, pp. 54, 71, 83, 86; GB *PP*, "Report on the British East African Protectorate for the Year 1897–98," C. 9125, 1899, p. 2; GB *PP*, "Reports Relating to the Administration of the East Africa Protectorate," Cd. 2740, 1905, p. 44; GB *PP*, "Statistical Tables Relating to British Colonies, Possessions and Protectorates," pt. 27, Cd. 2629, 1903, p. 815.

NOTE: The above figures for the protectorate budget exclude the accounts for the Uganda Railway through 1905. For 1905–06, only the profits for the railway are included (£68,835). For later years, figures are for full accounts, not just profits.
[a] The Imperial Treasury extended imperial grants-in-aid to the East Africa Protectorate through 1912–13.
[b] Nine-month period, 1 July 1895–31 March 1896.
[c] Dash indicates data not available.
[d] Annual average = approximately 140.
[e] Prior to 1904–05, import figures exclude imports for administrative, railway, telegraph, and military purposes, as well as imports of bullion and goods-in-transit. After 1905, these imports are included.

grants-in-aid introduced several statistics which were universally deplored. From 1895 to 1903, annual grants to the East Africa Protectorate totaled £1,200,000. One speaker noted that, in the six years before March 31, 1900, Britain's trade with the protectorate amounted to £540,000, while imperial grants totaled £566,675. In ponderous phrases, Lloyd

George bemoaned the seeming absence of economic progress in the East African Protectorate.[7]

While the costs of administration and railway maintenance were as anticipated, the charges for defense were the basis for bringing severe pressure to bear on officials to make the colony pay. The large number of punitive military expeditions undertaken had resulted in both enormous extra expenditures and the further disorganization of the economic and social structure of the tribes punished. Military expenditures were 30 percent of total expenditures in 1897–98, falling to 7 percent in 1910 and further thereafter (see table 3.2).[8]

TABLE 3.2: Early Military Expenditures
(In £ sterling)

Year	(A) Military Expenditures	(B) Total Expenditures	Col. A as Percentage of Col. B
1897–98	40,000	133,723	30
1905–06	104,981	418,839	25
1910–11	49,736	682,041	7
1913	74,555	1,115,899	6

SOURCES: GB *CP* CO, "Annual Blue Books for the East Africa Protectorate," CO 543/5, 10, and 13; and GB *PP*, "Report on the East Africa Protectorate for the Year 1897–98," C. 9125, 1899, p. 5.

These extraordinary outlays prompted Secretary Lansdowne at the Foreign Office to write to Eliot in 1901, making the pregnant point that such high military spending made it impossible for London to make money available for economic development purposes.[9] The economic problem for protectorate officials was to make the new imperial acquisition pay for extraordinary expenditures at the very time that those expenditures denied them the funds from London that were needed to solve their problem.

British policy has, of course, also been described—not to say rationalized—in terms of its contribution to pacification, and to providing thereby the essential preconditions for the prosperity and happiness of Africans. The validity or relevance of this interpretation is not of concern here. The discussion has been confined to the more strictly economic goals of British policy in order to set the stage for an analysis

THE COLONIZATION OF LAND IN KENYA   51

of the steps taken to achieve these goals and their economic
consequences.

THE CHOICE OF SETTLERS

The British organized entirely new land tenure and land
use systems for East Africa after 1900. In the process, they
dealt simultaneously with the questions of *who* would use
the land and *how* it was to be used. The decisions on how
and who were, of course, interdependent. However, before
examining their interdependence, these questions must be
separated and treated distinctly.

British policy makers under Hardinge, Eliot, Stewart, and
Sadler[10] concerned themselves with the issue of who was
to own the productive land and thus directly manage agricultural development as perhaps the task with the highest
priority in colonial administration. (Agricultural—as opposed to industrial—development and economic development
were synonymous in the minds of all officials.)

The official desire to make the newly acquired East Africa
Protectorate a self-supporting and valuable part of the empire led directly to disputes over which group of local people
could best implement development policies. In 1885, the
Charter of the IBEA Company had clearly indicated the
directors' assumption that East Africa would be colonized
chiefly by natives of the Indian subcontinent. East Africa
was envisioned as playing somewhat the same role for major
nations bordering on the Indian Ocean that America played
for those bordering on the Atlantic.[11] In 1900 British officials (who were largely former IBEA Company employees)
could still have arranged for the Indian community to play
the key development role in the protectorate. Indians had
come to East Africa as commercial traders and, more recently,
as British military personnel and as laborers.

Some officials argued strongly in favor of assigning the
Indians the function of managing economic development
along lines to be established by British authorities.[12] In 1901
Commissioner Eliot, reacting to mounting pressure for concrete steps toward economic development, approved the immigration of Indian agricultural settlers.[13] Sir Clement Hill,
head of the Africa Department at the Foreign Office, sec-

onded Eliot: "We are looking to India for our East African
system and for development."[14] In 1902 Eliot supported land
grants, free seed distribution, and agricultural loans to Indian settlers in the Highlands of the protectorate—universally recognized as the choicest land available for farming.[15]
As late as 1906, an official mission went to the Punjab to recruit Indian families for settlement. The effort failed, largely
because the potential settlers were only interested in immigration if whole Indian villages could move together, a course
London deemed too expensive.[16]

While British officials pondered and explored the possibilities of encouraging Indian settlers to become the chief
agents of development, private British citizens and companies sought to establish themselves advantageously within
the protectorate. By 1900 there were perhaps a few dozen
Europeans who either were, or planned soon to become, permanent settlers in the protectorate. They opposed any idea
of Indian settlement in the choice agricultural areas, mainly
the Highlands. In 1902 European settlers founded a Society
to Promote European Immigration. Besides their prejudices,
these settlers and the Europeans interested in commerce had
a fear of the competition expected from Indians willing to
operate in both agriculture and commerce at lower incomes
and hence at lower profit margins. The Europeans also saw
the Indians as established in tightly knit communities closed
to European interference, especially to economic competition.[17]

The relatively few Europeans who had come to the protectorate by 1902 appealed successfully to Eliot to end the
policy of officially sponsoring Indian immigration for settlement purposes.[18] Instead, Eliot sent a mission to South
Africa to recruit Europeans as settlers. Many South Africans
responded, and from 1904 until 1912 South African immigrants outnumbered immigrants from Britain.[19]

While Eliot struggled, amid the constraints imposed by
local conditions, to find the best agents of economic development, the Foreign Office in London explored other possibilities. Proposals were made to settle Finns in the protectorate.[20] Joseph Chamberlain, after a visit to East Africa,
apparently suggested to the Zionist Congress the possibility

of a Jewish National Home in East Africa, but after some consideration the Zionists refused.[21] The Foreign Office did have some success in negotiating concessions with large British companies interested in sizable investments in the protectorate. Large syndicates of merchants and investors in England received tracts of land at little or no cost.[22] They were encouraged and subsidized to search for minerals and to experiment in cultivating such crops as rubber and cotton. Finally, individual wealthy Englishmen also used their influence in London to acquire huge tracts of farm land at little or no cost. Chief among these, Lord Delamere ultimately accumulated over one million acres.[23]

Officials at the Foreign Office and later at the Colonial Office, as well as Eliot and his successors in the protectorate, confronted a rapidly changing economic situation, which was only in part the result of their separate actions. European immigrants and the syndicates moving into the protectorate increased the prospect of having Europeans rather than Indians play the key role in enabling the colony to pay for its administration, defense, and railway. Eliot's initial success in importing South African settlers made him turn increasingly toward a policy of actively recruiting additional European settlers. By 1905 he had induced numbers of British settlers and over 700 South African farmers to immigrate (see table 3.3).

Eliot eagerly supported a policy of granting large concessions. Both concessions and immigrants brought capital—the factor London had refused to supply—into the protectorate. Local officials increasingly echoed the European settlers'

TABLE 3.3: European Population in the East Africa Protectorate

Year	Number of Europeans
1902	506
1903	596
1904	886
1905	954
1906	1,814

SOURCES: R. R. Kuczynski, *Demographic Survey of the British Colonial Empire*, 2: 156–170; and R. A. Remole, "White Settlers or The Foundation of Agricultural Settlement in Kenya" (Ph.D. diss., Harvard University, 1959). See his painstakingly researched study of European population growth in the appendix and graph, pp. 384–395.

views and demands. By 1906 John Ainsworth, one of the protectorate's highest and most influential officials, summarized the converging position of settlers and officials on economic development as it took shape: "White people can live here and *will* live here, not . . . as colonists performing manual labor, as in Canada or New Zealand, but as planters, etc., overseeing natives doing the work of development."[24]

London officials looked at these early developments in East Africa with hope, but also with some anxiety. While they shared the local authorities' commitment to finding the best agents to manage economic development, they were increasingly uneasy about the motivations and capacities of both the European syndicates and many of the individual immigrant settlers. The fear in London hinged on the suspicion—increasingly confirmed—that the syndicates had no real commitment to genuine development, but were simply speculators in protectorate lands. Such fears grew in the face of appeals from some medium-sized farmers in Kenya, who claimed that monopolies of large land areas threatened their economic activities and therefore their continued presence in the protectorate.[25]

The influx of settlers with modest resources from South Africa and elsewhere also troubled London. At first these settlers seemed to be the solution to the great problem of finding agents of economic development.[26] But not long after the arrival of larger numbers of settler immigrants, reports from their settlements gave rise to great skepticism over their capability to develop the protectorate. In the Foreign Office one high official commented:

> I do not at all believe in the present race of small settlers who are coming into East Africa and taking free grants which they neither have the money, the knowledge or the energy to develop. If we could get 100 good men with £500 a piece, it would be worth our while to do so.[27]

Such reports continued until it became clear that a large proportion of the early settlers were unproductive and had failed in terms of both making their own living and developing the protectorate. Their only achievement, it seemed, was to make money for the speculators. Another official at the Colonial Office, with a long experience in East African affairs, went so far as to recommend complete repatriation of the European settlers in the protectorate: "It would probably pay the British taxpayer to repatriate all the whites and forbid their entry except on payment of a heavy poll tax."[28] Governor Sadler even wrote to the high commissioner of South Africa at one point to inquire about possible measures to stop further immigration into East Africa.[29]

It is no exaggeration to conclude that, from London's point of view, the task of long-run economic development seemed beyond the capacity or the intentions of all the available agents, African, Asian, or European. However, despite London's worries on this score, the immediate problems demanded at least temporary solutions. *And, as it happened, the temporary solutions became more and more permanent, as temporary arrangements led to vested interests on the part of persons intent upon consolidating their own positions.*

Thus, to get capital for development, London supported Eliot's policy of encouraging small, European settler immigration, including the settlers who came from South Africa. For the same reason, large European syndicates were given grants; the Foreign Office and the Colonial Office hoped thereby to stimulate further investment.

The first demand of the settlers was for exclusive land rights for Europeans in the Highlands. With some hesitation, London acquiesced, shortly after the local officials did. Some Indians were to be permitted to enter and remain as retail traders or laborers and to settle in lands deemed unsuitable for, and unwanted by, Europeans.

After 1905 the question of who would play the key role in economic development had been decided. How development proceeded remained the great question. The answer depended chiefly on the interaction of settlers, concessionaires, and local and London officials on the one hand, and on the role of the African population on the other.

THE CHOICE OF LANDS FOR ALIENATION

The initial expediency of promoting European settler immigration and granting concessions of lands, temporary and experimental as it was, nevertheless presupposed the ability of the local authorities to provide good land. In the *Report of the Land Committee* of 1905, the settlers argued that, since the profitability and viability of the protectorate depended upon them, the administration should give European agriculture every freedom and assistance that the European settler community deemed necessary.[30] From his travels and interviews in 1908, Winston Churchill came to a similar conclusion: since the protectorate government either could not or would not fund the development of the "natural economic strength" of the country, it must allow and assist the Europeans there to do the job.[31] In 1922 the Land Tenure Commission declared: "every scrap of land to which the agricultural development of the country could be extended should be earmarked and made available for future alienation."[32]

A dominant concern of the East Africa Protectorate's economic policy in its first thirty years was the provision of land to the European settler. Since the administration agreed that the prosperity of the territory was linked to the settlers, it acted—sometimes willingly and at other times with misgivings—to provide the optimum economic environment for the European settlers.[33]

The land given to the European settlers was situated in the region of Kenya generally most favorable to agricultural production. The elevation is, with few exceptions, over 4,500 feet above sea level. As figures 1 and 2 indicate, the areas alienated for European settlement were among those with the highest and most advantageous levels of precipitation. The 35,000 square miles called the Kenya Highlands—under 15 percent of Kenya's area—supported over 75 percent of the population—black and white—throughout the period under consideration. The route of the Uganda Railway suggests the further reasons for settling Europeans in the Highlands area. Such land was quite simply the most fertile and the best watered, and the railway made its location ideal for the area's exports and its imports of agricultural implements. Probably as good an estimate of the situation as any was Lord Hailey's remark that "about half of the land in Kenya worth cultivating lay in what came to be called the White Highlands."[34]

A few Europeans settled in the Highlands along the railway's projected path even before the railway reached the Highlands. After 1903, with Commissioner Eliot's efforts, settlement proceeded quite rapidly. Table 3.4 presents statistics on land alienation to Europeans.

TABLE 3.4: Land Alienated to Europeans in Selected Years

Year	No. of Holdings Allocated	Acreage Allocated				
		Agriculture[a]	Pastoral	Fibers	Other[b]	Total
1903	89	3,991	1,000	0	0	4,991
1905	263	14,520	193,645	96,000	6,400	368,165
1907	208	26,126	329,219	214,400	1,623	571,368
1909	222	18,394	350,988	3,362	826	373,670
1911	382	7,370	601,382	0	0	608,752
1913	447	14,052	494,276	63,831	0	572,159
1914	312	9,635	630,005	0	0	639,640

SOURCES: GB *CP* CO, "Annual Blue Books," CO 543, sect. BB for each year indicated.
[a] This designation means crop cultivation other than fibrous crops.
[b] Land used to provide forest and fuel.

While World War I interrupted the inflow of settlers and the alienation of land to Europeans, the end of the war offered new opportunities to stimulate immigration. Officials in London and Nairobi, with the enthusiastic support of settlers already established in East Africa, prepared a Soldiers Settlement Scheme in 1919. Some 2.5 million acres were parceled out into essentially free farms.[35] Ultimately, a group of 545 families, mostly families of low-ranking commissioned officers, occupied lands made available under the scheme.[36] Originally 1,245 farm plots were allocated; but sales among the original grantees and between the grantees and already established settlers resulted in actual occupation of their farms by only 545 of the original grantees.

Speculation in land accompanied every step in the process of white settlement. The first settler plots were intended to cover the traditional 640-acre homestead. The basic charge

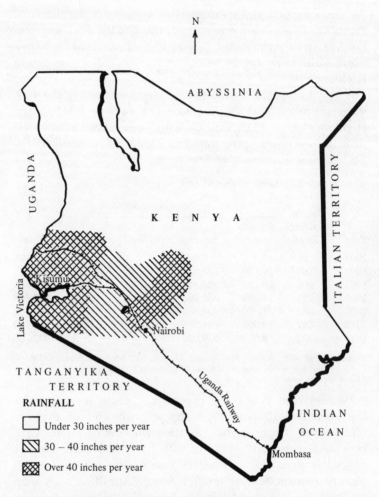

Figure 1. Patterns of Rainfall in Kenya

was two rupees per acre, or £80 in all, payable over sixteen years. Pastoral land was leased at rates which made the cost of the typical 5,000-acre farm something over £10 per annum. Such extremely low prices made speculation in land possible not only for the rich, but even for the average settler, who often purchased or leased land in excess of his anticipated needs simply as a good speculative investment.

Expectations of profits from speculation proved well-found-

Figure 2. Patterns of European Farming Settlement in Kenya
in the 1920s

ed in the decade before World War I. At times the value
of land rose so fast that various official reports gave the issue
specific attention. In 1911–12 officials noted the spectacular
gains made as new settlers purchased the undeveloped parts
of "pioneer estates."[37] Speculative profits went hand in hand
with the concentration of holdings. By 1912 five owners together held over 20 percent of all land alienated to Europeans
in the protectorate. In the most fertile, centrally located

Rift Valley of East Africa, over 50 percent of all alienated
land was owned by two syndicates and four individuals.
Farms in the Rift Valley which sold for sixpence per acre
in 1908 were resold for 10 shillings per acre in 1912. In
1914 the same land changed hands on the market at £1
per acre.[38] Top quality land became relatively scarce.

Whatever the Colonial Office's original intentions, its
policy of charging so little for land led to speculative activity generally. Insofar as they speculated in land, the established settlers had a vested interest in further immigration of Europeans interested in buying or leasing land. *Thus,
through this mechanism encouraging speculation, the original commitment of London to European farming generated
independent pressures from earlier settlers for ever more immigration and settlement by Europeans with the means to
pay.* Individually and through formal organizations, the settlers fought for policies that enhanced the profitability of
both their farming activities and their ventures in land speculation. By 1930, 64.8 percent of the land available to Europeans was not in any form of agriculturally productive activity
(see table 3.5).

TABLE 3.5: European Land Uses

A. Land Development, 1920–30		*1920*	*1930*
Land occupied (acres)		3,157,440	5,111,161
Land cultivated (acres)		176,290	643,644
Proportion under cultivation		5.6%	12.3%
Land used for livestock (acres)		1,137,354	2,054,001
Number of European occupiers		1,183	2,097

B. Land Use in 1930

Land Available to *Europeans* (acres)		*Land Not Used by* *Europeans* (acres)	
Land alienated	6,766,080	Land alienated	1,654,900
Surveyed land avail-		Land occupied	2,413,500
able for alienation	892,800	Land available	892,800
Total	7,658,880	Total	4,961,200

Land not used, in proportion to land available   64.8%

SOURCE: A. Holm, "Memorandum: A Decade of Agricultural Progress in Kenya,"
in GB *CP* CO, Kenya Land Commission, "Evidence and Memoranda," 3: 3057–59.

As indicated earlier, the settlers' activities in this regard did not always find official approval. The dynamics of settler and official interaction in making policy for the East Africa Protectorate on matters of fiscal policy, labor supply, and aid to European and independent African agriculture will be discussed in the chapters to follow. But first, in this chapter I will analyze briefly some of the specifics of protectorate land policy respecting Europeans and the effect of this policy on the location of the African population.

THE CONSEQUENCES FOR AFRICANS

The details of land alienation laws and procedures and the specifics of settler agitation on these subjects are among the few topics of East African economic history that have received close scholarly attention.[39] The important aspect of land alienation that is pertinent here is the length to which British policy makers were willing to go in order to give Europeans land on the most favorable terms. In 1891 and again in 1894, the Imperial British East Africa Company forbade categorically all dealings in land between Africans and Europeans. The reason may well have been the company's knowledge of the tenuous character of such transactions. The Africans were often misled regarding just exactly what they had sold or leased and came soon to resent it angrily.[40]

While also aware of the dangers inherent in permitting land transactions between "natives" and "non-natives," the Foreign Office issued regulations in 1897 allowing, first, 21-year leases, and then, in the same year, 99-year leases on land to be granted to immigrant settlers by the commissioner of the protectorate—presumably at his own discretion. The Foreign Office took this step under mounting pressure to make the protectorate pay its way, despite the opinion of the legal department of the Colonial Office that: "It is . . . advisable to avoid making grants or leases or other dispositions purporting to be an alienation of land by the British authorities, *to whom in fact it does not belong.*"[41] The Foreign Office continued to press in London for legal reinterpretations to make possible the aliena-

tion of land in the protectorate which policy dictated. The
Foreign Office pleaded for "jurisdiction over waste and un-
cultivated land in places where the native Ruler is incom-
petent, whether from ignorance or otherwise, to exercise that
jurisdiction."[42] The Law Officers of the Crown responded
favorably to the plea, and the result was the Crown Lands
Ordinance of 1902. This enactment enabled Commissioner
Eliot and his successors to dispense land "on such terms and
conditions as he may think fit, subject to any directions from
the Secretary of State." The only real limitation on the
commissioners was the proviso that forbade the sale of more
than 1,000 acres to any one applicant without the specific
approval of the secretary at the Foreign Office. The ineffectiveness of this limitation in fact was discussed above.

Between 1902 and 1915, the settlers were engaged chiefly
in trying to make their farms and their land speculation
yield profits.[43] These objectives drove them to seek longer
leases than the 99 years stipulated in the 1902 ordinance.
They also pressured the administration to reduce the requirements of various commissioners and governors between
1902 and 1915 that settlers make physical improvements of
specified minimum values on alienated property. Clearly, the
limited tenure and costs of the required improvements
worsened the prospects for profits from both agriculture and
land speculation.

The year 1915, however, was a turning point. The Crown
Lands Ordinance of 1915 provided for the conversion of 99-
year to 999-year leases. It reduced the rents. It reduced the
minimum values of the required improvements. The ordinance was generally acceptable to the European settler community. It signaled the fact that the European settlers had
transformed themselves and their interests from temporary
concerns of British policy into the guiding light and main
purpose of that policy. The choicest land of the East Africa
Protectorate was in the hands of Europeans under terms favorable and satisfactory to them (see table 3.5).

In the last analysis, the lands given, sold, or leased to
Europeans had to be withdrawn from the sphere of African
economic activities. In his report on the state of the East
Africa Protectorate in 1902–03, Commissioner Eliot specif-

ically listed the areas he foresaw as sites for European settlements:[44]

Lumbwa territory
Nandi territory
Southern part of the Rift Valley
Settima territory
Laikipia plateau
Kenya Province (entirely)
Kikuyu territory
Ukamba territory as far east as Makindu ("probably")

A comparison of figures 2 and 3 will indicate the accuracy of Eliot's prediction.

Throughout Kenya's twentieth-century history, Africans have raised the issue of these lands, which they claim were taken from them illegally.[45] The argument often turns on the question whether the Africans were "beneficially using" the land over which they may have had certain customary rights.[46] The point to be made here, however, is not to evaluate the justice, but to understand the process and the consequences of shifting effective control of land from the indigenous to the immigrant population. The Nandi, Kikuyu, and Masai tribes may serve as examples, since they are among the larger tribes and also comprise both pastoral (Nandi, Masai) and settled agricultural (Kikuyu) types of African peoples.

The Nandi tribe proved a troublesome obstacle to the security of the British administration, the Uganda Railway, and the establishment of European settlement for several years after the protectorate was declared. In 1895, 1900, 1902, 1903, and finally in 1905, British authorities mounted punitive raids against the Nandi. The last expedition, in 1905, required twelve companies of the King's African Rifles, along with 1,000 Masai levies. The defeated Nandi lost many lives, a large proportion of their livestock, and the greater part of the land in the southeastern section of the territory that they had come over the years to consider their domain. They also lost lands used for grazing in the Uasin Gishu area. The lands left to them within their original domain were

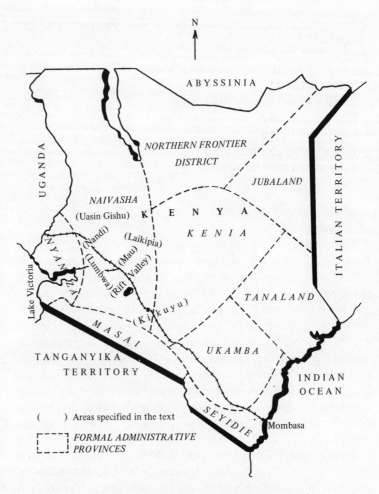

Figure 3. Early Administrative Subdivisions in the
East Africa Protectorate

provisionally set aside as a Nandi reserve—explicitly exempt
from any further encroachment.[47]

British officials sold enough captured Nandi livestock to
European settlers to recover the full cost of the punitive
expeditions, returning any remaining animals to the Nandi.[48]
A decade later, however, the post–World War I Soldiers Settlement Scheme required new lands. Some 64,000 acres of
the Nandi's best lands were then appropriated by the ad-

ministration. The Nandi received compensation at the rate of slightly over 6 shillings per hut in each Nandi village that had to be abandoned.[49]

The Kikuyu people first confronted forced dispossession—albeit through the mechanism of hastily concocted new land laws—in 1903 and in 1904, when approximately 5,000 people left land subsequently parceled out to perhaps as many as 200 European settlers. Some Kikuyu remained as squatters on alienated land.[50] The procedure for originally alienating Kikuyu land involved the dispatch, in September 1903, of a low government official to Kikuyu territory with instructions to draw a line through southern Kikuyu territory to divide alienable from nonalienable land. This he did without benefit of either survey or consultation with the Kikuyu. The lands he marked for alienation were later described as "the richest coffee belt of Kenya, and every available foot is cultivated."[51] Again, in 1920, several thousand Kikuyu a few miles west of Nairobi were removed when Europeans sought land that was so advantageously close to the Nairobi market.[52]

The Kikuyu protested their loss of control over lands they deemed their own and finally carried their case to the protectorate's highest court. Confronted increasingly by piece-meal appropriation of their land, they were more concerned by that time with preventing further encroachments than with recovering lands already lost. Hence they sought above all else to obtain absolutely firm guarantees of the security of their tenure over lands still under their control. In 1921, the court's judge, Sir Jacob Barth, ruled, however, that regardless of native land tenure systems, all land—even that which was "reserved for natives"—remained Crown land. All natives remained tenants-at-will of the British Crown.[53]

The case of the Masai has received the largest amount of scholarly attention of all examples of expropriation of African lands.[54] The Masai were quite probably the richest pastoral tribe in the protectorate. In 1904 they possessed over 50,000 head of cattle and over 600,000 sheep and goats. Europeans arriving in 1903 and 1904 cast covetous eyes on the fertile Masai grazing areas of the southern Rift Valley. After long negotiations, the Masai agreed late in 1904 to move out of large tracts of the Rift Valley onto the Laikipia plateau. The conditions that they set included strict observance of the agreement's language: that the settlement would be valid and final "so long as the Masai as a race shall exist."[55] The British authorities signed the agreement. Nevertheless, in 1911 the Masai inhabiting the Laikipia plateau were moved again—the evidence points to an involuntary move—to a position far to the south of the Uganda Railway, away from land sought by Europeans.[56] In 1904 Eliot had written:

> Your lordship has opened this Protectorate to white immigration and colonization, and I think it well that in confidential correspondence at least, we should face the undoubted issue—viz., that white mates black in a very few moves. . . . There can be no doubt that the Masai and many other tribes must go under. It is a prospect which I view with equanimity and a clear conscience.[57]

The Masai moves served to establish firmly an administrative policy of setting precise limits on European "areas" and native "reserves" as theoretically exclusive domains. This pattern was gradually extended to other areas and tribes, notably in the regions of the protectorate bordering on Lake Victoria, but losses of land by African peoples in these regions were generally smaller than those of the Kikuyu.

Not all transfers of land from African to European control concerned land for agricultural uses. After World War I, the growth of many cities and towns in the protectorate generated severe problems of urban crowding. Increasing numbers of Africans surrounded urban centers in very dense "villages." Simultaneously, the growing European and Indian populations sought to expand outwards from the inner cores of these areas. A conflict arose. The Europeans wanted the land of the Africans, which had become valuable urban property. They also claimed that they feared the contagion of plagues, which were thought constantly to beset the overcrowded African areas.[58] At Nairobi, Eldoret, and other cities, Europeans soon brought about the removal of Africans to specified "locations" further removed from the urban center.[59]

The land for European agriculture and the land to support the urban European population, which handled the agricultural output, the commerce, and the overall administration of Kenya, had to be withdrawn more and more from African control.

The choice by British authorities of immigrant European settlers as the chief agents of economic development in East Africa and the transfer of the choicest lands from African to exclusive European control suggest the emergence of a conscious settler economic interest dependent upon the property and the environment the British administration made available.

In the broadest terms, one may say that British authorities, bent on deriving economic benefit for Britain and Briton, boldly rearranged the geographic distribution of black, brown and white populations within the East Africa Protectorate and movement into it from overseas. They shifted control of land resources much as they moved populations—and all with a view to the economic betterment, they claimed, of all involved.

In Kenya, a fundamental dimension of the economics of colonialism was the transfer of land from African to European control. Other dimensions were (a) the creation of a wage-earning class and the conditions necessary for its employment, (b) the creation of an elaborate program of state aid to European agriculture, and (c) the creation of a fiscal system to maintain the whole economic structure. These are examined in later chapters. Chapter 4 deals with government policies on crops for European cultivation.

4 The Determination of Crops for East Africa

Shortly after World War I, a group of British businessmen and publicists decided to prepare an elaborate, comprehensive study of the current and anticipated resources of the British Empire as an economic unit. The guiding purpose of the series of published volumes was expressed succinctly by one of the editors:

> It will not have escaped attention that the object of this series on the Resources of the British Empire is to cater for the needs of the businessman . . . and the Imperialist (included, it is to be hoped, in the former) who seeks to assess the various resources of the Empire at their proper value, actual and potential, from a desire to tackle from its foundations a problem which is much to the front in the councils of the Empire, namely: How best to utilize Empire assets for Imperial ends.[1]

In fact, British colonial officials had been "tackling" just this problem in East Africa from the founding of the protectorate in 1895. Having made the complex of decisions that established European immigrant settlers as the chief agents of economic development, the problem remained to find and successfully produce a mix of commodities that would best utilize the protectorate's assets for imperial ends.

The decisions on what to produce were made in the years from 1905 to 1910 through an interdependent sequence of official and private acts. However, the European settlers and, to a greater extent, the British officials responded not only to concrete and immediate circumstances and demands. They also acted in conformity with some more general notions developed in the preceding decade about the desired structure and role of the protectorate as part of the empire.

THE CHOICE TO DEVELOP AGRICULTURE

As early as 1893, British experts had made very confident predictions based on their travels: British East Africa could generate profitable exports. Francis Parry inspected East Africa systematically and, from his observations of the German organization of cotton and coffee production, published several glowing estimates of possibilities in the neighboring British territory.[2] In 1895 Sir John Kirk, at a major international conference, delivered a paper devoted entirely to the assessment of prospects for profitable European colonization in Africa.[3] He found East Africa eminently suitable for permanent European colonization, in large part because of the prospects for agricultural exports.

Another well-known and highly respected British scientist-explorer, G. Scott Elliot, traveled to East and Central Africa with the explicit objective of evaluating the possibilities for profitable trade. His report in 1896 was extremely favorable.[4] In addition to observing German activities, he made a point of studying native cultivation, most particularly native cultivation of wild rubber. He sent samples of the rubber back to England to get expert estimates of its worth. Elliot made the further comment that plantations, as the basic unit of production, seemed by far the best way to develop East African agriculture. This bias toward plantation agriculture emerged directly from his observations of the African economy and of the German experience in the 1890s. Elliot's findings were delivered as a paper to the Royal Society of Arts, where they elicited excited agreement and equally optimistic comments from the other specialists who had been designated by the society to respond to his paper.[5]

A climate of opinion developed in London—especially among official specialists interested in colonization and the empire—that favored European plantation agriculture. This climate could not but influence policy makers. In 1902 and 1903 three specialists were officially dispatched to look more closely into the precise opportunities for European agriculture. Whyte's travels along the coast of East Africa led him to entertain high hopes for the cultivation and export of indigo, rubber, and coconuts.[6] More importantly, his general impression is suggestive of developing official attitudes on the East Africa Protectorate's future: "We know from experience the wonderful productiveness of Ceylon and can thus draw fairly correct conclusions as to what may be ex-

pected of the East African coast-belt from an agricultural
point of view."[7]

Whyte's travels on the coast were complemented by the
expedition of R. N. Lyne, director of the Department of
Agriculture of Zanzibar, to the plateau in the interior along
the Uganda Railway. Again, his prognosis after exhaustive
research pointed to a bright future for European farming.[8]
In a separate journey, R. B. Buckley, a professional geographer, visited the protectorate to ascertain the suitability
of the climatic conditions, chiefly the rainfall, for the kinds
of agriculture which were then generally assumed to be appropriate for the area.[9] His findings were entirely favorable,
with the conclusion that no large irrigation projects would
be needed. In addition, a government geologist's comprehensive survey of possible mineral resources proved to Commissioner Eliot's satisfaction that no future in mineral exploitation existed.[10]

In the dozen years before 1905, the conception of British
East Africa as essentially the next New Zealand-type colony
became a generally held belief. Perhaps the most widely read
book on the subject, by Lord Lugard, made this point best:

> The time is not distant when the teeming populations
> of Europe will turn to the fertile highlands of Africa
> to seek new fields for expansion. It is probable, therefore,
> that British Central and British East Africa may be the
> embryo empire of an epoch already dawning—empires
> which, in the zenith of their growth and development,
> may rival those mighty dependencies which are now the
> pride of the Anglo-Saxon race.[11]

The only major modification of Lugard's vision that emerged
during the period was the recognition of the need to find a
place in the model for the African population. Some observers therefore suggested Ceylon as an example of a plantation economy, not necessarily as an alternative to Lugard's
vision, but, rather tentatively, as perhaps an interim solution until enough Europeans arrived. In any case, officials
and knowledgeable settlers shared a conception of the protectorate's economic development which was based on a feel-
ing of near certainty that they could achieve prosperity

through plantation exports. Moreover, they saw their task, at least implicitly, as one of learning from the experience of New Zealand or Ceylon, or both, to choose the right mix of export commodities vis-à-vis the demands of the empire and the world market.

THE DECISION TO GROW STAPLES

Imperial goals in the protectorate included (1) making the colony pay its way, which meant finding exportables for the European settlers; (2) getting the best possible return on the capital invested to produce the exportables; and (3) producing those commodities whose availability for import into Britain would lessen or remove what British business-men and authorities deemed a dangerous dependence on foreign sources of supply. Of course, as discussed above, the empire as a whole also served as an outlet for British manufactured exports and capital, but this was of less im-portance to the economic history of Kenya than the three goals enumerated above.

The decisions on what to produce in the East Africa Pro-tectorate were made jointly by the settlers and the imperial authorities in London and Nairobi.[12] The chief role lay with the government, which not only conducted the great bulk of experimental research but also encouraged or dis-couraged other activities of the settlers according to the of-ficial conception of the general needs of the protectorate.

The immediate goal of finding exportables to relieve the British treasury of the financial burden imposed by the protectorate in its early years prompted several different choices on just what to produce. In the first few years of settlement, when very little was known about soil properties and general climatic conditions, most settlers planted rela-tively small acreages of several crops. This practice spread the risk of crop failures, but, more importantly, it imitated the brief experience of the few missionaries, railway per-sonnel, and scattered early settlers, who had discovered that various garden vegetables and grains could be easily and successfully grown (see table 4.1).

At first some officials in the protectorate administration contributed to this scattered pattern of mixed farming. In

TABLE 4.1: European Planting, 1905

Crop	Acres
Maize	800
Beans (several varieties)	700
Potatoes	700
Coffee	80
Wheat	150
Oats, barley	110
Ramie fiber	90

SOURCE: GB *PP,* "Report from the Director of Agriculture on the Government Farms at Nairobi and Naivasha in the East Africa Protectorate for 1904," Cd. 2410, 1905, p. 45.

NOTE: This table excludes the many personal vegetable plots which amounted in total to several hundred acres.

1903 an officer of the newly established Department of Agriculture undertook research which led him to recommend strongly the cultivation of groundnuts in the protectorate.[13] In 1905 the *East Africa Quarterly* published a report from the Imperial Institute in London which described the excellent market for ostrich feathers—another crop suggested for the East Africa Protectorate.[14]

Before very long, however, the desperate financial straits of the protectorate and the Ceylon model of development, which focused on only one or two crops for export, coalesced in the minds of many administrators to bring about some "agonizing reappraisals" of the mixed farming pattern. John Ainsworth, the official who founded the East Africa Agriculture and Horticulture Society, began the process with a very influential article in 1906.[15] His thesis was simple: for too long the settlers in the protectorate had produced small amounts of many different commodities. The result had been that the prospects for a prosperous agriculture, for making the protectorate pay, and for recouping the outlays on the Uganda Railway were not good. Looking at market realities, Ainsworth was "absolutely convinced" of the need to produce basic staple products, instead of the diversified crops then grown. He went further and argued that production of fibers could and should be the basis of agriculture in the protectorate.

Ainsworth's recommendation was not entirely new. The occasional early efforts of the administration to promote the production of staples for export had simply not worked.[16] The administration's determination not to impose conditions on new settlers that would in any way discourage further immigration was probably the chief cause of failure. In any case, the overwhelming pressure of insufficient exports and lagging railway income forced a renewed and this time successful insistence on production of staples. The consequences for Kenya proved clear and profound. By 1930, of something over 600,000 acres cultivated by Europeans, four major staples accounted for over 520,000 acres (see table 4.2). The more important indicator of Kenyan de-

TABLE 4.2: European Crop Acreages

Crop	1905	1920	1930
Maize	800	30,846	223,973ᵃ
Wheat	150	4,999	63,217ᵃ
Coffee	80	27,813	96,042
Sisal	—ᵇ	30,698	138,012
Barley, oats	110	—	14,539ᶜ
Tea	—	—	8,331
Sugar cane	—	—	11,161

SOURCES: GB PP, "Report on the Government Farms at Nairobi and Naivasha," Cd. 2410, 1905, p. 45; GB CP CO, Kenya Land Commission, "Evidence and Memoranda," 3: 3059; GB CP CO, "Annual Blue Book for Kenya Colony, 1928–29," in CO 543/19, sect. 22, pp. 3–6.

NOTE: Acreages of crops not listed are relatively unimportant.
ᵃ Figures for 1929.
ᵇ Dash indicates data not available.
ᶜ Figure for 1929; includes only barley.

pendence on basic staple exports, the value of exports in pounds sterling then showed coffee and sisal together providing over 50 percent of all domestic exports (see table 4.3).

COFFEE

The systematic move after 1905 toward production of special staples demonstrates some dimensions of the process whereby the structure of a colonial economy is determined by reference to the economic needs of the metropolitan power. London, as described above, undertook rather exhaustive research into the kinds of commodities that were most likely to maximize returns on the capital invested in the protectorate. More importantly, London sought to encourage

TABLE 4.3: Exports of Crops

Crop	1913		1920		1930	
	Quantity	£ Value	Quantity	£ Value	Quantity	£ Value
Coffee[a]	3,032	11,071	106,386	392,507	310,088	1,426,869
Sisal[b]	—	—	4,196	122,558	15,947	437,269
Maize[a]	226,438	53,920	145,554	51,491	2,222,528	565,517[c]

Above 3 crops
as percentage
of total domes-
tic exports: 16   47   72

SOURCE: GB *CP* CO, "Report of the Commission Appointed to Enquire into and Report on the Financial Position and System of Taxation of Kenya," Colonial Office Paper no. 116, 1936, app. 2, pp. 254–55.
[a] Quantity in cwts.
[b] Quantity in tons.
[c] 1930 was an exceptionally good year for maize exports. The average annual value of maize exports for 1926–30, inclusive, was £392,800.

production of commodities that would lessen the vulner-
ability of the British metropolitan economy when exposed
to fluctuations in the quantities and prices of foods and raw
materials imported from outside the empire. The complex
of decisions leading to the establishment of coffee as Kenya's
major product and export illustrates this process.

In the 1870s and 1880s, Ceylon and, to a lesser degree, India
had produced most of the coffee imported into Britain.
Ceylon often exported as much as 100 million pounds of
coffee per year. Most of these exports went to London, from
which they were re-exported (see table 4.4), mainly to Western

TABLE 4.4: British Coffee Trade
(In £)

Year	Imports	Re-exports
1884	127,400,000	109,100,000
1894	81,800,000	60,000,000
1904	118,200,000	78,700,000

SOURCE: GB *PP*, vol. 73 (1905), Board of Trade, "Memorandum on Coffee and Tea," 4 August 1905.

Europe. Throughout this period, Brazil was by far the world's
largest supplier of coffee. As Ceylon's ability to export van-
ished with the disastrous coffee leaf disease—exports falling
from 100 million to 18,000 pounds between 1874 and 1913—
Britain had to turn for coffee increasingly toward Brazil and

toward the United States, which controlled and re-exported increasing proportions of the Brazilian coffee crop (see table 4.5).

TABLE 4.5: British Coffee Imports by Area of Origin
(In thousand £)

Year	British East Indies	USA	Latin America
1884	1,817	77	548
1894	820	489	1,346
1904	611	486	1,217

SOURCE: Same as for table 4.4.

Brazil's coffee production and exports grew at a pace as impressive as the pace of Ceylon's decline (see table 4.6).

TABLE 4.6: Brazilian Coffee Exports
(In million £)

Year	Exports
1870–71	427.4
1880–81	764.9
1890–91	739.7
1900–01	1,504.4
1906–07	2,699.6
1907–25	{ 1,300.0 } 2,000.0 } [a]
1927–28	3,425.0
1930–31	3,881.0

SOURCE: W. H. Ukers, *All about Coffee*, pp. 502–03.

[a] As a consequence of Brazilian interference to protect export values in the coffee market, Brazilian coffee exports fluctuated between these figures during the period 1907 to 1925.

The growth of output in other Latin American coffee-producing countries paralleled that of Brazil, especially during and after the 1890s. The chief reason for the rapid expansion of coffee acreage in the 1890s was the high price level.[17] But the response to high prices clearly threatened the maintenance of such levels. In addition, the activities of speculators— chiefly at the New York Coffee Exchange—further endangered the prices coffee producers could expect. The twin problems of over-supply and speculation took on crisis proportions in the 1890s.[18]

In 1902 representatives of every Latin American coffee-

growing nation met with representatives of the chief coffee
consumer in the world, the United States, for a first major
conference on the crisis. The meetings, held during October
in the offices of the Coffee Exchange in New York, took
the title International American Coffee Commission. The
key report of the conference on the crisis occurring in coffee
concluded its analysis of the central problem as follows:
"Due to the absolute control of the market, the monopo-
lists can maintain a stationary relatively high price to the
consumer and a low price for the producer. . . . [T]heir gain
depends on the disparity of prices."[19] All participants agreed
that their main response to the situation had to be a limitation of the supply of coffee. They hoped thereby to limit
and control, if not eliminate, the extent and effects of speculation.[20]

Even before this conference, voices had been raised in
Latin America in favor of restricting the supply in order to
achieve high producer prices. A Venezuelan diplomat in 1898
had made such proposals.[21] In 1902 the Brazilian State of
Sao Paulo, which alone accounted for 70 percent of Brazilian output, called a convention of planters with the object of systematically controlling the planting of trees.[22] The
call represented the Brazilian reaction to the clearly exces-
sive plantings of the 1890s. Market analysts in Brazil had
calculated that the plantings of the 1890s would produce
20 million bags of Brazilian coffee for export by 1906–07,
while demand for Brazilian coffee at that time was expected
to be only 14 million bags.

The Sao Paulo convention decided to raise a loan of £15
million to finance systematic interference—buying of excess
supplies—in the coffee market. Unable to raise the money
on their own, the Brazilian coffee planters turned to the
largest coffee merchant in New York, Herman Selcken. In
1907 and 1908, Selcken and the National City Bank of New
York arranged loans in Germany, France, Belgium, and the
United States to finance the Sao Paulo scheme. While they
had considerable difficulty borrowing from London, part
of the £15 million eventually was raised even there. The
scheme succeeded. The figures in table 4.6 demonstrate the
consequent movement in quantities of Brazilian coffee ex-

ported. Coffee prices never again fell to the depths reached from 1900 to 1908 until the Great Depression of the 1930s.

British merchants, trade officials and policy makers were hardly unaware of these developments. In a special report presented to the House of Commons in 1900, the Board of Trade commented, rather candidly:

> The United States holds a very similar place in the coffee trade to that held by the United Kingdom in the tea trade. . . . The coffee trade of the United States therefore may be said to virtually control the trade as well as to a certain extent the price of coffee throughout the world.[23]

The British economy could only lose either by an artificial control of coffee supplies at their source or by speculation in New York, or by both. The British were also concerned about their opportunities for coffee re-exports to Continental Europe that were threatened by these possibilities. The report to the House of Commons pointedly charted the impressive increases in European coffee consumption (see table 4.7). Britain's increasing imports of manufactured

TABLE 4.7: Continental European Coffee Consumption
(In million £)

Nation	1884	1894	1904
Germany	244.4	269.2	400.4
France	149.4	153.6	245.6
Austria-Hungary	78.1	82.1	103.8
Total	471.9	504.9	749.8

SOURCE: Same as for table 4.4.

goods from Western Europe and the consequent threats of balance of payments deficits (see above, chapter 1), could not but give any concerned Englishman aware of the coffee market a strong interest in developing empire sources of coffee.

In perhaps the first systematic economic survey of the potential of the East Africa Protectorate, Francis Parry discussed the possibilities of coffee production. He was impressed with the German experiments in coffee cultivation in German East Africa. His conclusions embodied a strong

recommendation to try growing coffee in British East Africa:
"Since the blight destroyed the Ceylon coffee plantations
. . . England has been driven out of her important and
lucrative position as a grower."[24] He also noted the remarkable rates of return realized on investments in Brazilian coffee production and predicted comparable opportunities in British East Africa.

From 1905 to 1907, the Department of Agriculture in the
protectorate sent several samples of locally grown coffee to
London for expert evaluations of both the beans sent and
the general marketability of coffee from the protectorate.
As a result, a pamphlet issued by the department in 1907
strongly endorsed the efforts of coffee planters. London
expert opinion had only the best to say about British East
African coffee and noted specifically that it compared favorably with the best imports from the British West Indies.[25]
London coffee prices for empire imports were turning upward. Coffee production in the protectorate developed very
rapidly, as shown in table 4.8.

On the occasion of the founding of the Coffee Planters
Association in 1909, its first honorary secretary concluded
a speech by reminding his audience that

> it may be said with confidence that the coffee planters
> are, with hardly an exception, the only body of settlers
> who have not suffered bitter experiences during the
> term of their settlement. . . . The plantations are doing
> well and the trees yielding large crops.[26]

From 1910 to 1915, the Department of Agriculture reported
steady improvement in the already profitable levels of coffee
prices.[27]

In 1922 the coffee growers of Kenya Colony held a conference. They noted proudly the existence of 700 coffee estates employing an average of 35,000 African laborers. Kenya
already ranked as the second most important supplier of
coffee to Britain after Costa Rica. British imports of coffee
from Kenya amounted to twice the value of coffee imports
from India. Demonstrating a clear awareness of the special
opportunities for empire-grown coffee in the markets of the
United Kingdom, the governor of Kenya, Sir Edward Grigg,

TABLE 4.8: East Africa Protectorate Coffee Exports

Year	Tons	£ Value
1907–08	—a	69
1908–09	—	235
1909b	8.5	236
1910	31.5	1,086
1911	61.0	2,995
1912	104.5	5,765
1913	151.5	11,071
1914	275.0	18,502
1920	5,329.0	392,507
1925	7,363.0	823,901
1930	15,504.0	1,426,869

SOURCES: GB CP CO, "Report of the Commission to Report on the Financial Position and System of Taxation," app. 2, p. 254; and M. F. Hill, *Planters' Progress*, p. 22.

a Dash indicates not available.
b The time span for which data were collected changed in 1909; this explains the wide difference between the 1908 and 1909 figures.

addressed the conference: "East Africa should soon become the largest supplier to the British market, and we should aim at capturing the market *so freely open to us*."[28] In 1924 shortages of coffee supplies from Costa Rica were offset by added British imports from Kenya.[29]

OTHER STAPLES

The concern of British policy makers for empire sources of foods and raw materials became more deeply and widely felt as the twentieth century progressed. Two statements made by members of the first full-dress parliamentary commission sent to British East Africa on a general fact-finding mission illustrate these prevailing views. The first, made by a Liberal member of Parliament sitting on the commission, expressed worries over the high prices and related unemployment in Britain resulting from too costly food imports: "The increased demands for foodstuffs, due to the growth of the world's population, is seriously affecting the cost of living."[30] In the commission's final report, the following appears:

Britain possesses a rich potential heritage in tropical Africa. From it, with wise capital expenditure, she can

expect to receive in ever-increasing quantities supplies
of those raw materials and foodstuffs for which she is
at present so dependent on foreign countries.[31]

The choices for and against the systematic cultivation of
other crops important to the protectorate's economic history
besides coffee were further influenced by the economically
defensive concerns of merchants and bureaucrats in London.
Such crops included cotton, rubber, sisal and wheat. The
history of raw cotton imports into the United Kingdom
had led British policy makers in Egypt to encourage extensive cultivation of cotton during the third quarter of
the nineteenth century. However, the growth of cotton production in Egypt was increasingly offset by declines in British
cotton imports from other empire sources (see table 4.9).

TABLE 4.9: United Kingdom Cotton Imports
(In thousand £)

Origin	1870	1880	1890	1900
Foreign countries	700	1,261	1,371	1,410
Egypt	144	153	181	312
Empire (except Egypt)	366	214	241	37

SOURCES: GB, *Statistical Abstract for the United Kingdom,* no. 32, C. 4463, 1885,
pp. 68–69; and no. 52, Cd. 2622, 1905, pp. 118–19.

The economic dangers of the growing dependency on non-
empire sources of raw cotton were appreciated particularly
sharply during the 1901–03 cotton crisis. Lancashire experienced very costly cotton shortages, whose harmful effects
were exacerbated by speculation in the United States. A
subsequent parliamentary enquiry determined that the cash
loss to Lancashire amounted to over £2 million. Long established market relationships beneficial to Lancashire collapsed as a direct result.[32] This affair, coming after earlier
and similar incidents, led quickly to the founding of the
British Cotton Growing Association in 1902. The British
government granted this Lancashire group a royal charter.
Its explicit purpose was to foster cotton growing inside the
empire. It tried with impressive thoroughness in each territory listed in table 4.10. The table demonstrates the association's efforts, successes, and failures.

TABLE 4.10: United Kingdom Cotton Imports from Colonies
(In thousand £)

Territory	1903	1914
India	73,044	79,271
Ceylon	—	118[b]
Australia	—	84[c]
Fiji	—	4
Cyprus	14[d]	849[e]
Union of South Africa	18[f]	38
Northern Rhodesia	12[g]	28[d]
Nyasaland	57	2,597
Gold Coast	10	24
Uganda	20[h]	8,241
East Africa Protectorate	—	125[c]
Egypt	280,655	242,162
Sudan	—	1,784
Nigeria	573[h]	5,641
Sierra Leone	1	88[f]
Gambia	1	59[h]
British West Indies	412	2,642[c]

SOURCE: GB, *Statistical Abstract for the Several British Overseas Dominions and Protectorates for 1903–1917*, no. 54, Cmd. 664, 1920, pp. 378–85.

a Dash indicates no exact data available, but quantity is very small or insignificant. b 1912. c 1913. d 1911. e 1916. f 1906. g 1908. h 1904.

Despite the early findings of geographer G. S. Elliot, that prospects for growing cotton in East Africa were poor, both private interests and officials occasionally sent samples of cotton taken from mission or African plots to England for evaluation.[33] The first issue of the *East Africa Quarterly* carried a lead article reporting on the British Cotton Growing Association's assessment of the quality and prospects of cotton samples from Uganda and the East Africa Protectorate. Besides the report, the author, a high official, discussed Britain's need to be free of U.S. "corners" and "trusts" active in the raw cotton markets.[34] He pointed to the cotton-growing efforts of the Germans and Belgians in their African colonies. He explained that London was so eager to stimulate cotton production that all potential planters were offered free transport on the Uganda Railway for up to 4 million pounds of raw cotton. Finally, he calculated the profit per acre available to growers as a result; it approximated £3 per acre.

Also in 1904, a specially arranged report on selected agricultural districts in the East Africa Protectorate extolled the virtues and the promising potential of cotton production.[35] The British Cotton Growing Association donated two cotton gins, a baling press, and 1,000 pounds of prime Egyptian seed for distribution by the protectorate authorities.[36]

However, the attempt to establish extensive cultivation of cotton in the East Africa Protectorate failed as totally as it succeeded in the Uganda Protectorate.[37] As early as 1904, a special study presented to Parliament of the possibilities for cotton cultivation cast serious doubts on the whole idea.[38] The study found that African cultivation required a very high degree of expert supervision by Europeans, which the authors surmised would be "unprofitable." European cotton production, on the other hand, seemed an unlikely prospect because of the problems of finding an adequate labor supply. Nor did the authors foresee any quick solution to the labor problem. Nevertheless, local authorities offered every inducement to Europeans to produce cotton during the next five years.[39]

By 1910 the European farming community had quite definitely rejected cotton. They had found the return simply too low, given the difficult and uncertain conditions of labor supply, transport, and so forth in the protectorate. Authorities in the protectorate then once again took up consideration of African cultivation with the necessary European supervision.[40] A full explanation for the failure of African cotton cultivation will emerge in the next chapter. Suffice it here to note that the central problem was the labor supply. The European community opposed any systematic governmental aid to African agriculture for fear that such pursuits would make the Africans unavailable for wage labor on European plantations.[41] Equally important, they opposed using the scarce personnel of the Department of Agriculture—which European farmers needed so desperately and so constantly—to assist African cultivators.[42] Before 1930 African cultivation never provided any significant output of raw cotton.[43] Thus, even as late as 1925, Lancashire was still trying to get cotton going in East Africa, impressing this need on the commission sent that year to study Africa: "Lancashire also is anxious about the future supply of its raw material—cotton—and the increased demand for foodstuffs due to the growth of the world's population, is seriously affecting the cost of living."[44]

The concerns which so influenced the decisions about coffee and cotton were also evident in the consideration of other possible major export crops for the protectorate. Rubber attracted the attention of merchants, investors, and imperial officials toward the end of the nineteenth century, as its uses, and hence the demand, began to outstrip available, mainly wild, sources of supply.[45] Discussing rubber production in the East Africa Protectorate in 1896, Elliot remarked, "as the demand is now increasing, and the supply is diminishing, it is perhaps the most important problem in commercial botany to find what plants can be cultivated."[46] He and others sent rubber samples to London for evaluation.[47] The sharp fluctuations in rubber prices around the turn of the century, a consequence in part of speculative hoardings, stimulated great interest in empire rubber production. Authorities in East Africa encouraged rubber cultivation in hopes it might become a staple export.[48] However, the rapid expansion of rubber production in British-controlled parts of Southeast Asia, together with price reversals, especially the downturn in 1912–13, drove the few companies interested in rubber to turn their properties in the protectorate to production of sisal fiber.[49]

Fibrous plants caught the attention of protectorate authorities very early in the search for staple exports. The *East Africa Quarterly* published original articles and reprints on all aspects of the cultivation and marketing of ramie and sanseviera (sisal) fibers.[50] One such reprint, from the *Anglo-Indian Review* of March 1905, bemoaned the fact that London quotations for sisal fiber depended on the New York market, which induced fluctuations harmful to British interests: "English fiber brokers would be glad to see imports coming to London direct in order that the centre of quotations might be changed."[51] Such directness presupposed and implied sources of sisal fiber imports inside the British Empire. The Department of Agriculture's experimental farms distributed young fiber plants at little or no cost to European settlers.[52] Ainsworth calculated the expected profits of sisal cultivation at £3 17s. per acre.[53]

Sisal continued to be a favored crop in the general promotional literature of the protectorate government after World War I.[54] Unlike rubber, sisal production in other British colonial possessions did not combine with world market conditions to saturate or ruin the market. London's anxiety about sources of sisal continued. Thus in 1925 an East African planter, writing in praise of the excellent market for agricultural twines manufactured from sisal fibers, had as his main purpose to emphasize that Mexican henequen, a fiber alternative to sisal, "is entirely controlled and financed by a collection of banking syndicates in Mexico, New Orleans and New York who fix prices." Their "pernicious monopoly" he maintained, had to be broken, and Kenya sisal, being of better quality than the Yucatan fiber, both could and should do the job.[55]

The expansion of wheat acreage in the protectorate occurred during the 1920s. Wartime grain shortages in East Africa and in Great Britain had combined to stimulate great interest among the protectorate's Europeans in wheat as an import substitute and quite possibly as a favored export to Great Britain.[56] The protectorate government intervened directly to subsidize wheat production and control prices from 1919 to 1922. In 1924 a 30 percent ad valorem duty on wheat imports took effect. In 1925 the Department of Agriculture widely distributed a document whose message was "Grow wheat." To suggest bright prospects for wheat exports the document cited the cessation of wheat exports from East Asia to the United Kingdom and certain other colonial territories, notably the Union of South Africa, as well as the expected decline of the United States as a source of wheat.[57]

Maize growing by Europeans seems to have developed largely in response to local demand in East Africa, rather than in response to the wider market factors affecting British imports of coffee, cotton, rubber and fibers.[58] Finally, a brief spurt in flax cultivation in the early 1920s was a response to the unusually high prices caused by the wartime interruption of flax exports from Russia and Belgium. As these wartime dislocations passed, prices fell again, ruining almost all the Kenya flax farmers.[59]

THE CHOICE OF LANDS FOR EUROPEAN AGRICULTURE

Finally, it was not only the question of *which* crops to concentrate on but *where* to grow them that agitated both London and the local administration. The official desire to make the Uganda Railway financially profitable affected the location of agricultural production, just as other financial concerns determined the mix of crops produced. The documents on early agricultural policy in the protectorate usually display a marked bias against production by Europeans along the coast. Officials and settlers argued frequently that the coastal temperature and humidity made it physically impossible for Europeans to function productively. This assertion was never proved. In fact, the successful work of European railway personnel, soldiers, and administrators—and even a few stray settlers—constantly cast doubt on its veracity.[60] The other argument against European agriculture along the coast was that the sparse African population there would provide an inadequate supply of labor. Yet the ease and thoroughness with which protectorate authorities moved masses of the Masai, Kikuyu, Nandi, and other Africans suggests that an *initial* scarcity of Africans was not the determining factor preventing European settlement.

The explanation lies—beyond the simple preference of Europeans for the climate of the interior—perhaps most importantly in the recognition in official circles that the protectorate needed not only an agricultural export economy but also one whose input and output would use the railway as much as possible. The most explicit expression of the importance of this factor in choosing the crops to be produced occurred in 1906 when, during an official inspection tour of the East Africa economy, Sir Alfred Lyttleton, then Secretary of State for the Colonies, told local officials, "I want traffic for the railway—something that the world wants and which will be a staple, reliable and increasing traffic."[61]

THE HAND OF GOVERNMENT

The choice of what and where to produce in the East Africa Protectorate resulted from interaction between the needs felt by private interests and government circles in London, on the one hand, and the conditions of soil, climate, transport, protectorate finances, and so forth, under which European settlers functioned, on the other. The colonial administration acted as the intermediary between the needs of the empire and those of the local immigrants. It suggested, promoted, and financed experiments with specific, carefully selected exportable crops. Rather widespread British fears about Britain's economic future determined which crops were selected.

In any case, the local administration provided every feasible kind of direct assistance to the economic activities of the European settler community, especially—but not solely —where it concerned crops favored by the administration. The major forms of such assistance, the creation of a cheap and sufficient labor supply and the provision of elaborate expert agricultural services at very low cost through a remarkable fiscal system, are examined in chapters 5 and 6. I turn now to some of the other forms of government assistance provided to European farmers.

The first systematic demand of the settlers was for military security throughout the territory. Besides guaranteeing freedom from African interference, the military measures taken often made new lands available for alienation (see above, chapter 3). The punitive raids also involved sizable transfers of captured livestock from Africans to Europeans. The normal procedure was to sell to Europeans, at low prices, the cattle captured from offending tribes; this was a way of reimbursing the protectorate authorities for the military costs incurred.[62] Importing livestock was always an extremely expensive and a risky transaction. Therefore, the generally accepted rule for stock farmers was to "breed up" African livestock. The punitive expeditions provided quantities of African livestock which could have been obtained in no other way, since self-preservation, custom, and religion prevented most Africans from selling any of their livestock.[63] One of the larger and costlier of early administrative divisions of the protectorate government, the Veterinary Department, was kept constantly busy protecting the livestock of Europeans from innumerable diseases and pests, while developing resistant strains.[64]

Throughout the first twenty years of the protectorate, settlers complained about the absence of comprehensive surveys of land and water resources. This lack, they argued, inhibited and complicated both alienation of land and proper estimates of crop and livestock prospects. The Survey Department was perhaps the largest division of the administration, employing eighteen Europeans and five Indians to make extensive surveys of the protectorate, especially during the period 1905–25.[65]

In 1905 the Colonists Association—the chief organization of the European settlers—requested the local administration to lower rates on the Uganda Railway, thus subsidizing its use by planters for both imports needed for agriculture and exports of produce.[66] They also requested inclusion of the East Africa Protectorate in the South Africa common market in order to obtain special, favored access to that economy, and they asked London to offer subsidies to a British steamship company as an inducement for regular shipping to and from Mombasa harbor. The protectorate government reduced Uganda Railway rates as requested, but inclusion in the South Africa common market did not occur. In August 1905, Colonial Secretary Alfred Lyttleton wrote to the British India Steam Navigation Company asking for lower freight rates for East Africa Protectorate settlers. He offered in return to cut railway rates in the Union of South Africa, thereby stimulating trade there, which would benefit shipping.[67]

In 1904, when a general import duty of 5 percent ad valorem was raised to 10 percent, the protectorate government specifically exempted all agricultural implements used by European settlers; by thus enhancing the profitability of farming the administration provided an inducement to Europeans to settle.[68] At the same time, export taxes on likely European exports were reduced.

During his tenure of office, Commissioner Eliot established the Departments of Trade, Agriculture, Forestry, and the Veterinary Department. He managed to obtain relatively generous treasury appropriations for them, even though the protectorate accounts showed large deficits at the same time.[69] These government departments, particularly the Department of Agriculture, were given a huge task, to ascertain the resources of the protectorate and to develop profitable farming in the crops chosen for cultivation. In 1908 in measuring the activities of these departments, the Government came to the following conclusions: "As an accessory branch of farming, coffee should pay well, but settlers are not recommended to depend solely on coffee, owing to the many diseases to which it is liable."[70]

This advice could be as totally ignored as it was only because of the comprehensive research and other efforts of the Department of Agriculture. The Department established several experimental farms; distributed equipment, seeds, seedlings, and stud animals; and published innumerable articles, both original studies and reprints from other sources. The department designed all its activities to inform Europeans and improve their farming.[71] In addition, it provided absolutely essential supervision, grading, and certification of crops for export. Certified grading of protectorate exports was indispensable to their acceptance by the London merchant houses and ultimately by the final consumers. "In fostering the agricultural industry, the Department has introduced grading regulations for the improvement of the marketing of produce. Few countries have the same provision and organization as that obtaining in Kenya."[72] It is no exaggeration to conclude that the quantity and quality of official assistance to European agriculture in Kenya were among the highest in any colonial experience.

The fact that physical and social conditions in the protectorate still made European agriculture a precarious economic affair in the late 1920s in no way detracts from the impressive level of agricultural services supplied by the administration.[73] The failures of smaller farmers and the sizable turnover of settlers simply remained as a constant problem and challenge to the entomologists, mycologists, agronomists, plant virologists, and others, working in the Department of Agriculture and to the other officials that were occupied with marketing and with the financial aspects of European farming.

5 The Reorganization of African Labor

Anthropologists interested in East Africa seem to agree that fully integrated economic structures existed within and, to a far lesser degree, among the African tribes before the British arrived.[1] Based everywhere on agriculture and/or livestock, these structures comprised a complicated pattern of economic activities specifically distributed among the clans, sexes, and age groups of the tribe. Religion and custom sanctified this distribution. To indicate, on the one hand, the necessity for and difficulties in developing a wage-earning labor force in Kenya and, on the other, the magnitude and significance of doing so, I must first sketch briefly the pattern of work activities in the African population before British settlement was firmly established.

European travelers in East Africa often concluded that "nature" was so bountiful there that Africans had to do barely any work to live comfortably. Moreover, whatever productive effort proved unavoidable was observed and reported to be the special responsibility of women, not men.[2] In fact, the tasks assigned to male Africans by tribal custom included agricultural labor, trading, handicrafts, and defense, or a warrior function. Women had responsibilities for certain other handicrafts, trading activities, and domestic chores, as well as specified kinds of agricultural labor.[3] By all accounts, the early European observers' conclusions were inaccurate both in terms of the large amount of heavy work actually performed by men and women and in the distribution between them of all kinds of work.

Four basic industries supplemented direct agricultural production among many, although not all, tribes in East Africa.[4] Iron work was fairly well developed in several tribes. Special clans of these tribes divided their male members into smelters and forgers. They produced varieties of spears, knives, swords, hoes, wire, jewelry, arrowheads, chains, tongs, and so on. These craftsmen often attained a degree of skill that impressed Europeans who had the chance to observe them and occasionally to employ them as well.[5] The importance of these manufactures in hunting, defense, and religious observances conveyed a high status on the clans within the larger tribe who made them. African women were the exclusive producers of pottery. As with iron manufacture, special clans produced finished pottery, mainly for trading, but also, of course, for general use within the clan and the tribe. Basket-making and the tanning of skins to provide clothing complete the list of the four basic kinds of crafts supplementing agriculture. The latter two activities were apparently allocated to specific members of a family group rather than to a clan or sex. Thus most African family units probably possessed some craft, as well as agricultural, skills.

Early trading in surplus food products, iron ore, and handicrafted items expanded later to include goods imported by Somali, Arab, and Indian traders and slave dealers, and by European merchants.[6] Some tribes developed specialized clans to do the tribe's trading, as other clans did the iron work. Large and more or less regular gatherings of African traders were known to occur at various special locations.

While the slave-trading period of East African history shook and changed the economic structure sketched above, no new pattern of economic activity and division of labor emerged which could be described as fundamentally different. African economic structures more or less sufficed for African societies—insofar as they ever had done so—before the British came. European settlers and administrators eventually discovered, however, that to obtain sufficient numbers of Africans for labor, they would have to coerce Africans out of their existing economic structure by transforming the structure totally.

Perhaps their first and foremost object lesson in this regard emerged from the near impossibility of utilizing African labor to construct the Kenya and Uganda Railway in the 1890s.[7] Frustrated with the great scarcity and low quality of African labor, the construction management looked to Indian and, failing that, Chinese immigrants for workers.[8] Basically, the issue was one of cost. Expenditures in the territory allowed by London from 1895 to 1902 were barely adequate to secure minimum pacification of the countryside and protection for administrative outposts. There was at that time no possibility of undertaking the actions—military, educational, and so on, with their attendant costs—that would have been necessary to find and maintain an African work force for the Railway. The assumed inefficiency of African workers—at least in comparison with their Indian counterparts—added yet another unfavorable dimension to the cost problem. Indian coolies for railway construction flowed into the East Africa Protectorate in large numbers during the first decade of the protectorate's history.

The evidence gathered by travelers, ethnographers, and anthropologists on the pre-British economic structure in East Africa, seen in the light of early difficulties in securing African labor for railway work, suggests one possible path of economic development that the protectorate's authorities might have pursued. A "dual" economy might have evolved, with Europeans and Asians occupying one economic sphere completely distinct from that of the African tribes except, perhaps, for some minimal trading between the spheres.[9] In fact, British policy in the East Africa Protectorate charted a very different course of development. In 1898, amid the most acute awareness of the difficulties of securing African labor, Colonial Secretary Joseph Chamberlain envisioned Britain's task in the protectorate in these words: "I think that something in the nature of inducement, stimulus or pressure is absolutely necessary if you are to secure a result which is desirable in the interests of humanity and civilization."[10]

Chamberlain's assessment of the interests of humanity and civilization coincided nicely with the spreading European attitude toward the African population as the labor base for economic development. Chamberlain and the British officials working under him were moving steadily toward a vision of a development process—colonization—for East Africa which depended upon African labor as the protectorate's key asset. One official specifically rated East Africa as superior to South Africa for colonization purposes precisely on the grounds of the greater abundance of relatively cheap labor.[11] An official report prepared in 1902 recommended strongly that Africans from the East Africa Protectorate be prohibited from going to South Africa to work in the mines of the Rand. The argument turned on the assumed need of prospective settlers in the protectorate for all the African labor that was available.[12] By 1906 a leading official could write with certainty that the development path for the protectorate would definitely emerge from "planters overseeing natives doing the work of development."[13]

Given the economic structure of pre-British African tribal society, the development pattern implied by Chamberlain and expressed explicitly by Ainsworth presupposed a fundamental transformation in the life of every African. From more or less self-sufficient peasant proprietors in common, the African population was increasingly transformed into wage laborers on European farms.* From a position in which they were owners in common of their land, animals, and agricultural implements, Africans were compelled to adopt a way of life in which they derived an increasing portion of their sustenance from land and equipment owned legally by others, namely by immigrant European settlers. The ways in which British policy produced these changes and their economic consequences are examined in chapters 5 and 6.

GENERATING A SUPPLY OF LABOR

The transformation of the African population into an African wage labor force passed through three quite distinct stages. The first stage, covering the first twenty years of the protectorate's history, involved several experiments with alternative methods of development. Once the British authorities had committed themselves to European immigrant settlement with emphasis on a plantation-type economic structure, experimentation focused on finding a solution to the problem of an inadequate supply of labor. Deciding on a means of generating an adequate supply proved to be a difficult problem with complicating political overtones. In addition, implementation in practice of decisions made in

---

* Marx's celebrated analysis of the "primitive" (or "primary") accumulation of capital in Europe involved a transformation of the peasantry with some strikingly similar and hence suggestive characteristics. See *Capital*, vol. 1 (Moscow: Foreign Languages Publishing House, 1959), pt. 8, pp. 713 ff.

theory took time at best, and at worst proved impossible. Consequently, the first stage in creating an African labor force was a time of experimentation, accompanied by frustratingly irregular supplies of labor. Settlers and officials cooperated, with frequent and bitter frictions, to establish a set of priorities and institutions to overcome the irregularity and inadequacy of supply.

The second stage coincided with the mobilization for war and the actual hostilities in the East African theater in World War I. The exigencies of war heightened immensely the official sense of urgency about the labor problem. The war provided the impetus for a mobilization of African labor that served both to demonstrate its potential availability and to guide the postwar labor policies of the British authorities.

The third stage, from 1919 to the Great Depression, saw the establishment of a regular labor supply. Many experiments made before the war were fully implemented and coordinated during these years. British officials applied lessons learned in the experience of wartime mobilization. During this decade, the labor situation demonstrated the completion of the transition from the pre-British economic structure of the African tribes to a more or less smoothly functioning colonial plantation economy. From peasant proprietors in common, Africans increasingly became hired laborers, dependent on regular wages earned on European estates. While this was to the greatest degree true for the Kikuyu tribe, dependence on Europeans for wage labor spread steadily, though in varying degrees, to many other tribes.

The steady flow of immigrant European settlers that began in 1903 and accelerated after 1908 caused almost immediate concern about the supply of labor for work in the settled areas. Complaints about the quality and quantity of available Africans began in 1903. Perhaps the most condensed summary of the settler position from 1903 to 1930, and even after, appeared in a letter from the principal settlers' organization to the then Governor Sadler:

We must point out, your Excellency, that it is grossly unfair to invite the settler to this country, as has been done, to give him land under conditions which force him to work, and at the same time to do away with the foundation on which the whole of his enterprise and hope is based, namely, cheap labor.[14]

The letter exaggerates the settlers' case. The British authorities were by no means denying labor to the settlers. What the settlers sought was far more active, persistent, and direct official intervention to provide sufficient labor. The settlers understood from the beginning that only the colonial administration had the power to produce a labor force, or, to be more precise, a cheap labor force.

Reports of labor shortages occurred during most years before World War I.[15] In several instances, a particular shortage prompted demands for imported indentured laborers. The shortages hit the coastal planters especially severely. In consequence they talked increasingly about the need for indentured Indians to do their plantation work. Thus sisal producers met with the governor in 1908 and 1909 and pleaded with him to allow Indian immigration. The Colonial Secretary, however, decided against such immigration.[16]

Indian Immigration?

There was one basic concern behind the Secretary's decision. Europeans owning lands in the Central Highlands greatly feared the advent of Indians who might possibly seek to settle there. The Europeans had early received official assurances that the Highlands would always remain "white territory." However, a large growth in the Indian population anywhere in the protectorate always appeared to them as a distinct threat. Before the war, European agriculture was neither firmly established nor prosperous enough to keep officials from raising questions about the basic commitment to plantations owned by Europeans.[17] The European settlers had to fight strenuously to restrict the influence of the Indian community, which clearly sought to obtain settlements in the Highlands.[18] One way to minimize such influence, and consequently the attractiveness of Indian rather than European settlement to colonial authorities, was simply to control the size of the Indian population through limits on immigration.

The European settlers also opposed Indian immigration that could lead to the agricultural settlement of the immigrant *outside* the Highlands. Lord Delamere, the leading settler politician, explained this position:

> In all new countries the backbone of the country is the small man, the white colonist with small means, but there is no place for him in a country when once the Asiatic is there. . . . All the vegetable growing for the towns is done by Indians, all the butchers with one or two exceptions are Indians, all the small country stores are kept by Indians and most of the town shops, all the lower grade clerks are Indians, nearly all the carpentering and building is done by Indians. *They thus fill all the occupations and trades which would give employment to the poorer white colonists, especially those arriving new in the country.*[19] [Emphasis added]

Lord Delamere's concern lay with the long-run effects of allowing *any* Indian immigration. His theory of colonization in the protectorate envisioned implicitly the growth of agricultural settlement built on personnel drawn from nonagricultural or, at least, non-land-owning pursuits. The security of Europeans as landowners in the Highlands thus depended indirectly on having Europeans fill just the types of jobs that Delamere deplored having fallen to the Indians.[20]

In sum, Europeans feared Indian competition, tried to keep the Indian population in the protectorate to a minimum, and thereby linked the prosperity of the European even more closely to the supply of cheap African labor. Nor did the Europeans look favorably to African laborers drawn from neighboring territories. The one relevant possible source of labor at the time, Nyasaland, drew a sharply negative response from the settlers. They based their opposition on one fact of predominant importance. Nyasaland labor was accustomed to wages that were too high and would, the settlers feared, "tend to raise the price of other native labor."[21] European agriculture in the East Africa Protectorate thus was based on the productive utilization of Africans resident within the territory.

The labor problems of the prewar period in the protectorate created difficult and complex tasks for European settlers and officials. The obstacles in their way were huge. Methodically, they moved to establish institutions and laws intended to ensure a steady flow of cheap African labor.

African Shortcomings

Africans were simply not experienced in, or amenable to, the kind of work discipline demanded by their European employers. The reminiscences of settlers, newspaper accounts, official reports—all such sources are filled with accounts of the "incompetence" of African laborers, especially agricultural workers. The seeming impossibility of finding sufficient numbers of minimally efficient African workers absorbed the attention of Europeans to the exclusion of almost all other concerns: "[it is] . . . the constant theme of every discussion at every hotel, at every club, in the train, and on the boat, round every dinner table and on every verandah. . . ."[22]

In addition to the problem of inefficient labor, the settlers faced other related and costly manifestations of the Africans' distaste for wage labor under prevailing conditions. Africans came for very short periods of work only. At first, the average span of work for an African agricultural laborer was less than two months. From 1902 to 1906, for example, the usual working period for such a laborer was about one month, for which he received an average wage of 3 to 5 rupees.[23] New taxes were a determining factor. The Hut Tax on African dwellings (1902), supplemented by the Poll Tax for African adults other than hut "owners" (1903), touched the lives of an increasing number of Africans. Such Africans thus faced a new obligation to work for wages in order to obtain ready cash to fulfill their annual tax obligation of 3 rupees.[24] However, these early taxes soon proved ineffective in solving the labor problem—even when supplemented by higher wage offerings. In essence, European settlers confronted a backward-bending supply curve for labor. With the tax rate unchanged, higher wages would mean less rather than more labor time offered by Africans. "To raise the rate of wages would not increase, but would diminish the supply of labor."[25]

These conditions gave rise to many bitter complaints from

settlers. Every one or two months, the European farmer had "to take on a fresh batch of the rawest and most ignorant of youths when ground has to be cultivated, seeds sown, and crops harvested."[26] The time and effort consumed in training Africans promised to persist as a perpetual extra cost. Africans who worked only one month in twelve had to be retrained again each year. Moreover, settlers quickly observed that Africans chose to work during those months when sowing or harvesting chores were not pressing them to work on their own lands. Since sowing and harvesting seasons for African and European coincided, the need of European farmers for Africans was at its maximum just when the supply was most constricted.

The labor situation, by confronting the settlers with recurrent major difficulties and crises, became the chief obstacle to the success of the colonial administration's development plans. In the early period of experimentation with European coffee culture, the limited labor supply (coffee is relatively highly labor-intensive) proved a serious impediment. "The uncertainty . . . of obtaining sufficient labor for the picking of the berries has deterred many from extending their plantations beyond a very limited extent."[27] The development of another crop of vital importance to the protectorate economy, sisal, was so hampered by labor supply difficulties that one promising syndicate ceased its activities by 1908. In early 1909 the sisal producers who met with the governor urged the importation of indentured Indians at wages as much as five times what they were prepared to pay African laborers.[28]

European settlers and officials sought to formulate plans to produce enough African laborers at the wages the settlers deemed necessary. The alternative was failure of the British program of economic development through European colonization. Beginning in 1902 with the basic commitment to, and first arrivals of, European settlers, British officials began to evolve a labor policy.

A GOVERNMENT POLICY

The two earliest and most basic acts of the officials actually were originally designed to fill other pressing needs.

First, the process of allocating to Europeans land that Africans had utilized previously—however irregularly—reduced the productive area available for African agriculture (see above, chapter 3). The relocation of tribes and the steady progress toward strictly delimited "reserve" areas for specified tribal groups undercut an African agricultural system that was based on land-intensive, shifting-cultivation methods of production. The consequence of giving land to Europeans thus indirectly included stimuli to Africans to derive their income from wage labor on European farms. These stimuli were later recognized and integrated into a comprehensive labor policy. Second, the enactment of hut taxes in 1897 was initially a response to the officials' need to find revenue for the protectorate rather than to any explicit land policy.[29] The official view was that taxes levied on Africans represented only their fair share of the costs of abolishing the slave trade and guaranteeing general peace in the territory. In any case, sorely needed revenue at that time could only have come from either the British treasury in London or the native African. British officials chose the latter.

Land policies and revenue taxes formed the basic but not the only dimensions of early labor policy, intentional or otherwise. Subsequently, officials shaped other government policies and the government's own practices as a major employer of African labor to conform to and merge with an evolving general labor policy.

THE NATIVE RESERVES. In 1905 a group composed mainly of influential settlers, the Land Committee, proposed that the geographic boundaries of African reserved territories be set in terms of the minimum area required by the specific tribal groups. The criterion for determining African land requirements was to be the current physical needs of the current African population. The Land Committee explicitly forecast that normal growth would result in an African population in excess of the physical carrying capacity of the reserved areas. Such persons would then be available to enlarge the labor supply of the European farmers.[30]

In 1908 during testimony before the colonial government, the chief settlers' organization contended that one way to se-

cure more labor lay in further limiting the quantity of land
held by Africans. One settler's testimony developed the old
theme of the African's industriousness ruined by a too bountiful nature: "The natives live under such easy natural conditions that there is little in these conditions to induce them to
overcome the natural tendency of the African to avoid manual
labor."[31] Consequently, "the land set aside for Native Reserves
should be limited to the present requirements of the natives. . . . The existence of unnecessarily extensive reserves
is directly antagonistic to an adequate labor supply."[32]

The proposals to constrict more and more the lands allotted to Africans were repeated regularly throughout the
prewar years. While it is impossible to prove finally exactly
how much the consideration of the labor supply influenced
the choice of boundaries for the African reserved areas, the
general responsiveness of officials to the needs of settlers
suggests the importance of such influence. By the 1920s, in
any case, many African reserves were notably congested and
overcrowded. A senior official in the protectorate reviewed
the state of the reserves and concluded that their land area
was physically able to, but did not in fact, support the existing resident African population. The explanation, he
argued, rested with the outdated and extremely inefficient
agricultural methods of the Africans. He criticized the protectorate officials for having done nothing to improve these
methods in the reserves.[33] By limiting the land and the
knowledge available to Africans in the reserves, protectorate
land policies induced them to leave the reserves for employment as wage earners on European farms.

TAXES. The hut tax legislation of 1897 and 1902 quite soon
became a vehicle consciously used by officials to draw a labor force out of the African reserves. No better summary
statement exists of the official view on the purposes of African
taxation than a dinner speech of the then governor of the
protectorate: "We consider that taxation is . . . compelling
the native to leave his Reserve for the purpose of seeking
work. Only in this way can the cost of living be increased
for the native, and . . . it is on this that the supply of labour
and the price of labour depends."[34]

The possibilities, suggested by experiences with the hut
and poll tax, of using revenue taxes and fees for purposes
other than revenue, namely, to create greater supplies of
wage labor, resulted in some specific proposals. In 1907,
Lord Delamere proposed a tax of 1 rupee per palm tree.
His reason: Africans used the sap from palm trees to manufacture their beer. At a meeting of European settlers with
government representatives in 1908, one settler made yet
another suggestion:

> There certainly appears to be no need for them [the
> Akamba tribesmen] to work as they were able to buy
> their blankets, wire and beads so cheaply owing to the
> absence of any import duty on those articles. . . . these
> would be an additional inducement for them to work
> for the white man.[35]

In March 1911, Lord Delamere proposed, and the *East Africa
Standard* seconded, increased freight rates on the Uganda
Railway for *Amerikani,* the unbleached white calico textile
worn by Africans, and blankets, a basic commodity consumed
by most Africans in the protectorate.[36] In 1912 and 1913,
a formally instituted Labour Commission heard and published evidence from at least 284 witnesses. Large numbers
of settler witnesses endorsed higher taxes on Africans to obtain more workers. Some witnesses urged the taxing of lands
used by Africans within the reserves. A very popular idea
among witnesses was the proposal that the protectorate administration offer to remit a portion of taxes due if and
when an African could prove that he had done wage labor
for some minimum time period during the year prior to
the tax collection date.[37]

During the protectorate's first two decades, the general
European support for goals and concepts of taxation such
as these provides the background to the taxes that were
finally levied. In 1901 Colonial Secretary Lansdowne sanctioned the levy of no more than 2 rupees per African dwelling (the Hut Tax). Between 1901 and 1903, the actual rate
charged was increased by the appropriate enabling legislation from an average of 1 to an average of 3 rupees. Before

1903 collection touched a very small proportion of the African population. However, administrative officers had already noticed that African villagers were crowding into ever fewer huts to lessen their tax burden. The officials moved quickly to adjust the tax. In Ordinance No. 19 of 1903 they introduced the poll tax principle by making all adults in a dwelling liable either to hut tax (the owner and his wife) or poll tax (all other persons in the dwelling over 16 years of age). The steadily increasing number of Africans paying taxes led officials to a further readjustment of the law in Ordinance No. 2 of 1910, whose basic provisions remained in effect until 1934. According to this ordinance, tax payments in the form of specified amounts of labor-time on public works were permitted in lieu of cash. Taxes on individuals could be paid by entire villages or even larger tribal groupings. Penalties for nonpayment included confiscation of huts and/or imprisonment.[38]

A general import duty of 4 percent ad valorem was increased to 10 percent in 1904. The main categories of commodities specifically exempted from tariffs included all agricultural implements, livestock for breeding purposes, and commercial seeds and seedlings—all clearly items of special importance to Europeans rather than Africans.

These steps in taxation, while in accord with the European settlers' needs, fell short of their demands for a comprehensive, all-purpose taxation system. Neither the constriction of the Africans' landholdings nor the imposition of various taxes sufficed in the prewar period. To get labor regularly and cheaply, the settlers had to try yet other means. They sought to influence further decisions of the government toward their objective of pushing out greater numbers of African laborers. In 1904 and again in 1908, several settlers lodged a formal complaint that the government paid wages in excess of what they wished to pay Africans in their region.[39] In 1907, the long list of settlers' complaints resulted in the formal establishment of a Department of Native Affairs, which was "specifically instituted to deal with the labor supply."[40] In essence, the settlers wanted government administrators to include as a definite routine task recruitment of labor for private farmers.

GOVERNMENT RECRUITMENT AND OTHER MEASURES. The administration sometimes balked at outright recruitment for European settlers. In doing so, it reflected an anxiety among some Europeans about the long-term wisdom of active government recruitment. First, given the combined military, police, and taxing functions performed by most individual administrative officers, their "suggestion" to an African that he do wage labor had the force of a command. This served the purpose of the settlers quite admirably, but some officials argued that "a system of forced labor is never a success and is apt to alienate the confidence of the natives."[41] Such officials feared that the association of work with compulsion might later prove to have made provision of an adequate labor supply even more difficult and costly. In his visit during 1907, Colonial Undersecretary Winston S. Churchill added to the government's hesitation and anxiety by his remark that officials had to avoid possibly "shocking scandals" in the labor situation that might embarrass London. Churchill was clearly linking government recruiting with a serious possibility of scandal.[42]

In 1908 the protectorate administration, in view of the known abuse of African laborers by certain European employers, apparently decided to direct its officials to minimize their role as recruiters for private employers. This directive provoked the sharpest clash between settlers and officialdom in the East Africa Protectorate's history. The settlers uniformly demanded that officials continue to "aid" Africans seeking work by giving all possible assistance to them. The settlers argued that

> there was certainly an unpleasant sound about the word compulsion, but after all the majority of people throughout the world had to work from compulsion, and often take up work that is distasteful to them in order to obtain the necessaries of life.[43]

The issue was finally "settled" much as the tax and the African land restriction issues had been—that is, in a partial and irregular fashion. Much depended on the individual official, who had fairly wide latitude in interpreting the limits of his "suggestions" to potential African wage laborers. The influence of settlers and settler opinions on middle and lower echelon officials was rarely insignificant.

There were yet other avenues for settlers and officials who sought to mold various government policies to solve their labor problem. Indigenous African leadership and communal social structures might, they thought, aid the search for secure supplies of cheap labor. Chiefs and headmen were often appointed by British authorities to replace unfriendly tribal leaders, especially in the earlier years of the protectorate. The administration often commissioned them informally to help obtain labor. The position and powers of such headmen were granted formal recognition and authority in the Native Authority Ordinance of 1912.[44] Documents of the time frequently mention complaints by Africans against headmen who used compulsion in recruiting labor for private employers and for themselves.[45] Related complaints cite the frequent absence of any payment for such work.[46] The chiefs and headmen also apparently appropriated directly a percentage of the taxes they collected. By improving overall tax collection, these leaders indirectly enhanced the pressure on Africans to do wage labor.[47]

Initially, British administrators regarded their tasks vis-à-vis African authority systems from a simple military standpoint: "We cannot however hope to succeed in adjusting and controlling large native populations without some form of native civil administration."[48] Such an administration, once established, offered an obvious focus for pressure from settlers and officials intent on meeting the needs of Europeans for labor. Government policy regarding African reserves sought in general to shore up the communal tenure systems there, although a few officials did advocate introducing European notions of tenure. One official explained the prevailing belief in the desirability of continuing communal tenure in the reserves in terms of the problem of the supply of labor. He felt the primary task of British policy was to avoid the emergence of a completely "landless proletariat" of African wage earners. In his view, the communal tenure system provided a kind of necessary social insurance for the new African wage workers who, when unemployed and without income, could fall back on their communal rights and resources.[49]

Thus, government policies on indigenous leadership and structures in the African reserves had, beyond other objectives, the goal of enhancing the flow of African labor to Europeans while simultaneously supporting institutions which could reabsorb laborers more or less temporarily unemployed.

Lastly, three further developments of the prewar period deserve mention as additional dimensions in the process of transforming the African population into a steady, inexpensive wage labor force. The continuing difficulties with the quantity and quality of the labor supply prompted observers, settlers and officials to search for remedies beyond the devices of taxes, land restrictions, and manipulation of indigenous leaders and structures. In 1909 Governor Girouard declared that "squatting" offered the solution.[50] Squatting was a practice which involved Europeans in the Highlands giving Africans the right to settle on their land in exchange for a specified number of days of paid labor for the European landowner rendered by the African. Europeans in the protectorate had experimented with squatting since 1903. Many apparently found it a workable arrangement. It was thought the wisest alternative to offer squatters' rights to Africans as a privilege.[51] Beyond the chief advantage to Europeans of having a ready source of labor permanently settled nearby, squatting enabled the European farmer to control the seeds used and crops produced by Africans. Europeans could also expect opportunities to cross-breed their stock with African cattle and obtain cheaply the highly desirable progeny. Thus, European farmers sometimes arranged with squatters to permit the latter to graze and cultivate unused land in return for a payment in money or in kind, rather than in paid labor.[52] Given the low cost of land to the European, squatting afforded him an inexpensive way to secure labor and perhaps a little extra income on the side. Officials generally condoned squatting, while maintaining doubts about the potential in the system for abuses. They gave squatting a full legal status only in 1918 with the Resident Natives Ordinance.

A second device designed to develop the labor supply had its origin in the South African experiences of many settlers in the protectorate:

> A great many gentlemen present were South Africans who knew that for a hundred years the question had been studied and the result of the hundred years' experience is the *pass system*. Under that system you get a disciplined native; you know where every native is, what his wages are and his employment.[53]

Little transpired along the lines of this proposal until 1915, when a Native Registration Ordinance was passed. The war intervened and postponed enactment of universal adult male registration until the end of hostilities.

A third device, about which very little is known in detail, demonstrated yet another aspect of the development of an African labor force. Shortages of funds in the protectorate's treasury led officials to decide against any expenditures for the training of Africans in labor skills. However, regarding the years before the war, one study concluded that "the prison industries carried on in Nairobi and Mombasa were the chief means at this time of providing industrial training for Africans."[54]

THE CONTINUING SHORTAGE

British policy on African labor in the protectorate reflected strongly pressed settler interests. Whatever immediate concerns prompted early official policy on land, taxes, African leadership, or African land tenure systems, within a short time the need for a labor supply became the dominant factor determining that policy. Shortly after European settlement began, settlers sought and increasingly were conceded official actions specifically designed to make cheap African labor more available.

Yet the labor situation before World War I never satisfied the settler community for any significant length of time. The Africans persistently resisted the changes in the whole economic and social pattern of their lives which was demanded by the policy transforming them into regular wage earners. The evidence of the difficulties of the change for Africans is sobering in its proportions. It also suggests the profundity and violence of the alterations in the lives of the African population brought about by the British settlers and officials, despite the efforts of a few local missionaries to soften the impact.

The physical effects of wage labor on the African population in the prewar period were extreme. In 1911–12, among plantation workers counted at Mombasa, 140 per 1000 were seriously ill and had never been treated.[55] "Physique deteriorates so rapidly among up-country labourers that few can serve for as long as three months and many cannot earn their pay after the first few weeks." Neither the European settlers nor the officials directed any attention or expenditure to the dietary, housing, and sanitary conditions provided for African wage laborers while they worked. Mortality rates among African laborers were recorded at 80 per 1000.[56] Accurate measurement of the larger true mortality rates proved impossible chiefly because of difficulties encountered in ascertaining mortality rates among African laborers after they returned to their reserves.[57]

Culminating in the number of deaths connected with World War I and the immediate postwar conditions, the first thirty years of the protectorate's history appear to demonstrate a sharp decline in the African population. From perhaps four million Africans in 1902–03, the population fell to under three million by 1912 and to below two and a half million in 1921. Not until about 1923–24 did a reverse, upward trend begin to establish itself, probably the result of the relative social stability of postwar, vis-à-vis prewar, Kenya.[58]

Unwilling to pay for the facilities necessary, if not sufficient, for a healthy, vigorous work force, the European settler community could only expect the difficulties in securing sufficient workers which resulted, constant training and retraining, and gross inefficiency in workers. At least implicitly, the settlers seemed to assume that the supply of African laborers could and would be augmented enough to offset losses incurred through disease, death, and any other disablements, psychological and otherwise, which followed the transformation of tribespeople into wage earners.[59]

The settlers' assumption of a steady labor supply proved

TABLE 5.1: Population

Year	Africans	Europeans[a]	Indians, Arabs, and Others
1897	2,500,000	391	13,434
1901		506	35,000[b]
1902	4,000,000[c]		
1905		954[d]	
1910		2,654[d]	
1911	3,000,000		20,986
1914		5,438[d]	
1916			22,118[e]
1920		7,660[e]	30,685[e]
1921	2,483,500		
1924		11,002[e]	34,524[e]
1925	2,549,300		
1929	2,930,604	16,663[e]	55,891[e]

SOURCE: R. R. Kuczynski, *Demographic Survey of the British Colonial Empire*, 2: 144–48.

NOTE: It is difficult to understand the evasive treatment of these data in J. Middleton, "Kenya: Administration and Changes in African Life, 1912–1945," in V. Harlow, E. M. Chilver and A. Smith, eds., *History of East Africa*, 2: 337.

[a] This category includes a very small number of Eurasians.
[b] This sharp increase is explained by the large number of Indian laborers imported to work on the Uganda Railway.
[c] This figure includes a corrected estimate plus the increase of 1,000,000 in the population due to the transfer of the provinces of Kisumu and Naivasha from Uganda to the East Africa Protectorate in 1902.
[d] As of 31 March of that year.
[e] As of 31 December of that year.

to be incorrect, or rather premature, in the prewar years. The supply of African laborers then was persistently irregular, uncertain, and inadequate. The continuing labor problem outweighed all others in the minds of officials and settlers. The ceaseless search for new, additional ways to draw Africans into wage labor led to a proliferation of policies designed to do this. The authorities restricted African reserves, manipulated hut and poll taxes, structured indigenous leadership and tenure systems in the reserves, facilitated squatting, moved toward a South African type of pass system, and even utilized prison terms to give prisoners some minimal training in work discipline. These and other, less developed, less generalized programs of similar intent were all attempts to meet the goal of a cheap, regular labor supply.

Individually, none proved sufficient. Together, they had a marked impact; yet the labor supply remained irregular.

Settlers and officials could not avoid a growing skepticism and doubt about the possibility of ever securing enough Africans. Settlers had several times demanded forced labor, but, as the officials had pointed out to them, when Africans experienced and then mentally connected wage labor with compulsion, they would do all in their power to avoid it. Moreover, the colonial government could not afford the supervisory and military expenses entailed in maintaining the type of force that would be needed to keep Africans working.

World War I brought hostilities to the East African mainland. The preparations for and conduct of the military campaigns involved the authorities and the total African population in ways that demonstrated conclusively that enough Africans did exist who could, if they had no alternative, be mobilized for labor. The compulsion that was too costly and dangerous before the war was required and justified by the war. World War I in East Africa demonstrated for the European settlers some definite and reassuring possibilities.

WORLD WAR I CHANGES

German and British armies clashed repeatedly on the East African mainland. The pattern of life of Europeans, Africans, and Asians changed sharply for the duration of hostilities. Moreover, the war and the associated mobilization of men and resources had important and far-reaching consequences, which define an important step in the development of a regular labor force in the East Africa Protectorate.

Faced with the outbreak of war in Europe in 1914, British officials in the protectorate began to plan for the military campaigns assumed to be imminent. They immediately confronted a fundamental tactical problem, namely, how to move the equipment and supplies needed for military operations. The absence of any adequate road system made motor vehicles useless. The prevalence of the tsetse fly made the use of oxen impossible. The only solution lay in the mobilization of Africans into a mass carrier corps. A total of 150,000 Africans from the East Africa Protectorate served in the unarmed Carrier Corps. Approximately 14,000 participated as part of the armed forces. The war resulted in a mobilization of Africans which was far more extensive than any previous recruitment of Africans for public and private labor.[60]

Throughout 1914 and 1915 government recruitment efforts encountered tribes that had previously resisted successfully the prewar pressures to provide wage labor for Europeans.[61] The Kamba and Giriama people were the object of repeated military operations by government expeditions before recruits for the formal Carrier Corps came forward in sufficiently large numbers to satisfy the military commanders.[62] Africans generally feared service in the Carrier Corps. Individually, they made every effort to avoid it both before actual recruitment and/or through desertion. The sufferings of Africans touched by the war in all ways reached enormous proportions. Of the total of about 164,000 Africans formally engaged in the British campaigns, at least 46,618 died in combat or from one or more of the many prevalent corps-connected diseases: "It is sad to read, in the earlier reports, of how great a boon we bestowed by stopping inter-tribal war. Since then our own War has destroyed more life than a generation of inter-tribal wars."[63]

European settlers, called by the imperial authorities to lead and support the military campaigns, systematically exploited London's dependence upon them to wring further beneficial enactments regarding supplies of African labor from all levels of protectorate officialdom. In 1915 they secured passage of the Native Registration Ordinance, which introduced a version of the South African pass system. Angered by the fact that the wages at first being offered to potential African carriers by the government were higher than those the settlers paid, they successfully pressured the protectorate administration into making Carrier Corps wages conform to the average wage level—set by the settlers—in the district where carriers were present or sought. The most effective agitation of the settlers led to a government policy of conscripting any African who did not have proof of current employment. Thus fear of conscription produced a supply of African labor that was ready and sufficient; this had not occurred in any earlier period.[64]

The resistance of European employers to conscription from among their employees focused conscription on the reserves as a source to be exhausted before employed Africans would be tapped. The Native Followers Ordinance of 1915 vested extraordinary powers of conscription and powers of punishment for its evasion in the headmen of the reserves.[65]

The settlers claimed consistently that these measures were essential to military effectiveness. They also argued that official support on the issue of labor supply was the least the government could do to maintain the value of European land holdings while Europeans fought. In fact, the measures taken during the war had consequences more far-reaching than support for military operations and maintenance of European estates.

Notwithstanding all the difficulties, mobilization had clearly demonstrated that Africans could be put to work in numbers far exceeding the requirements of European settlers. The need to monitor and control the movements of all African adult males to make these numbers available was recognized in the Native Registration Ordinance. All Europeans agreed, at least implicitly, that, after the war, conditions of life for the Africans should be regulated so as to provide incentives as effective as fear of conscription to induce Africans to provide wage labor. The scattered and nonintegrated efforts to create such conditions before 1914 had thenceforth to be streamlined in the light of the lessons of wartime experience. The "right" conditions created and administered outside the reserves by the government, complemented with the beneficial exercise of authority by compliant headmen, would solve the labor problems in the postwar East Africa Protectorate, newly named in 1920 the Colony and Protectorate of Kenya.

6 The Development of a Kenyan
Wage-earning Class

The role of the African Carrier Corps in World War I provided ample evidence of the size and quality of the labor
force potentially available to European settlers. What both
settlers and officials observed during the military campaigns
reassured them about the prospects for prosperous colonization in the protectorate. African labor as the basis for the
plantation economy that they had organized in the previous
decades indirectly proved in the war that it was suitable to
perform its assigned functions. Or so it seemed, in any case,
to the European community after the war. In 1919 the
administration directed a land settlement commission to inquire into the practicability of an extensive scheme for settling discharged soldiers in the protectorate. Referring particularly to the question of an available labor supply, the
commission found conditions adequate and encouraging. It
added, however, the cautionary remark that the continued
adequacy of the African labor supply presupposed a proper
organization of the laboring population.[1]

THE LESSONS OF WORLD WAR I

Wartime experience strongly influenced the settlers' conceptions of the proper organization of the African population for supplying cheap labor. The partial implementation
and only partial success of the various measures taken before the war to encourage Africans to provide wage labor
stood in sharp contrast to the efficacy of their mobilization
for the Carrier Corps and for labor on European farms
during the hostilities. Mobilization for the farms had been
given high priority and was fully justified by the settlers as
essential support for the military campaigns. It was but a
natural and logical next step in settler thought and agitation
to equate the desirability of victory in war with victory in
the effort to make the protectorate a prosperous member
of the British Empire. Hence, the techniques of mobilization

111

which had proved so successful in war should properly be applied during peacetime to provide adequate, cheap labor for the settlers.

The two most important dimensions of wartime mobilization were "total" pressure and complete organization. The only real alternatives facing most African adult males consisted of carrier corps service with a high probability of disease and/or death, on the one hand, and agricultural labor for Europeans, on the other. As the reality of their situation impressed itself progressively on the African population, the supply of workers available to Europeans exceeded the settlers' demands, despite the drain of manpower to the Carrier Corps. The lesson seemed clear: postwar conditions had somehow to maintain equivalent "total" pressures to achieve equivalent results. Records kept during the war, although far from fully accurate or complete, proved their value in achieving heightened efficiency in the shifting deployment of manpower. Thus wartime experience reinforced settler demands to institute the South African pass system in the protectorate as an essential control and efficiency measure.

The severe labor shortages that suddenly materialized in 1919 and 1920 served to confirm settler attitudes and to point up the lessons of the war. The end of mobilization conditions combined with an African realization that there was a wider range of possible alternatives for them; the result was a curtailment of the flow of laborers to the European farms. Simultaneously, worldwide postwar dislocations brought a period of extreme financial difficulty to the accounts of both European governments and the settlers in Kenya.[2] The externally imposed commitment to settle discharged soldiers and to establish a new currency system (replacing rupees by shillings) only further aggravated economic conditions in the colony. In these circumstances, the settlers simply increased their determination to reconstruct their economy around a cheap, steady African labor supply.[3] One European settler summarized his group's position:

> Short of compulsion, direct or indirect, the main mass of Africa's inhabitants will never take part in the development of their country. We can never develop their

country without their cooperation, because where negroes are, white men will not do manual work. And
the negroes will not disappear, as have savages of other
lands.[4]

During the 1920s, the colony's labor supply situation improved steadily, reaching levels of available labor that were
satisfactory to European employers but for the brief, tran-
sient exceptions of 1920 and 1925–26 (see table 6.1).

TABLE 6.1: African Labor Force

Year	Average Labor Units per Month on European Farms
1920[a]	53,709
1921	67,388
1922	61,649
1923	70,957
1924	87,092
1925[a]	78,527
1926[a]	84,611
1927[b]	102,074
1928	114,320
1929	110,697
1930	125,885
1931	120,210

SOURCES: Agricultural Censuses and Annual Reports of the Department
of Agriculture of Kenya, quoted in M. R. Dilley, *British Policy in
Kenya Colony*, 2d. ed., p. 235.

[a] Years of insufficient labor supply according to the testimony of European settlers.
[b] Casual labor included for the first time.

The European community achieved this much desired result by applying the lessons of wartime experience to the
haphazard partial measures of prewar years. The various
kinds of direct and indirect pressure placed on the African
population during the 1920s had all been applied to some
extent before the war, with the one significant exception of
the pass system. The difference after the war lay in the
far more complete, systematic, and fully coordinated way in
which partial measures strengthened and complemented one
another to produce a labor supply in peacetime that matched
the supply drawn out during the war. The evolution of the
laws governing the African population offers clear evidence

of this difference. This chapter turns to the labor situation of the 1920s, as perhaps the key element in the working of mature British colonialism in Kenya.

ESTIMATING THE LABOR SUPPLY

As administrators faced the task of organizing a labor supply in a systematic way, an initial requirement was a careful estimate of the total numbers they could expect ultimately to have available. The first detailed inquiry on this matter fell to the Labour Bureau Commission in 1920-21. The purpose of this commission was to determine whether overcoming the problem of shortages in the labor supply necessitated direct government intervention in the form of a bureau to recruit, transport, and otherwise similarly service the African laborers potentially available for employment by Europeans.[5] The commission made its estimates of the available African labor supply by using assumptions borrowed from South Africa.[6] First it calculated that 15 percent of the African population comprised males between the ages of 16 and 30. This group of adult males then became the prime target of public and private labor recruitment. Poor medical conditions in African reserves required a further deduction of 20 percent of such males as physically unfit. Lastly, an additional deduction of 2.5 percent was made to allow for those African males engaged in successful small scale trading on their own account and consequently uninterested in wage labor.

In the commission's judgment, at any given point in time, 50 percent of the able males between 16 and 30 years of age could be expected to "come forward and work."[7] Thus, according to table 6.2, Kenya authorities could and did establish an initial target size for the regular African labor supply, namely, about 88,000 men working at any one time. In the year of the commission's report, the average monthly labor force on European farms slightly exceeded 67,000 of which an unknown but in all likelihood sizable number were women and children. The clear implication of the report was that the commission foresaw and proposed an increase approaching 50 percent in the farm labor supply.[8]

Perhaps the most significant aspect of the commission's

TABLE 6.2: African Labor Supply, c. 1921

Total male population, 16–30 years of age, in areas near to European employers	218,000
20 percent deducted as unfit	−44,000
2.5 percent deducted, traders	− 6,000
Subtotal	168,000
Total male population, 16–30 years of age, in other areas	75,000
90 percent deducted as generally unavailable or unreachable[a]	−68,000
Subtotal	7,000
Total male population available for labor	175,000

SOURCE: GB CPK, "Report of the Labour Bureau Commission," 1921; see especially table 2, p. 12. Areas near European employers, above, are Kisumu, Kavirondo, Lumbwa, Nandi, Kiambu, Fort Hall, Nyeri, Voi (Teita), Embu and Meru.

[a] The figure of 90 percent was used by the commission. It reflects chiefly the administrative impracticability of obtaining in any way more than 10 percent of eligible males from these thinly populated border regions.

work lay in its working assumption that the African population's sole economic function was to provide wage labor. Thus, in addition to its proposal to squeeze more labor out of existing sources, the commission endorsed, as a corollary of this assumption, the necessity of a systematic campaign to increase the number of source areas, that is, to bring more of Kenya's African population within the range of the complex of pressures which resulted in Africans providing wage labor for Europeans. The success of the effort outlined by the commission, in addition to the growth of the African population, led after 1923 to the labor situation depicted in table 6.3 (all data are, of course, very rough).

TABLE 6.3: African Labor Supply, c. 1927

Total male population, 16–40 years of age, in areas near to European employers	489,000
20 percent deducted as unfit	−98,000
Subtotal	391,000
Total male population, 16–40 years of age, in other areas	40,000
100 percent deducted as beyond the lure of, or pressure for, wage labor	−40,000
Subtotal	0
Total male population available for labor	391,000

SOURCE: GB CPK, Department of Native Affairs, "Annual Report for 1927," p. 92.

NOTE: These figures include all African workers, not only those involved in agricultural labor as in table 6.2. The figures also reflect increased population and, more importantly, upwardly revised estimates of the relevant population base.

Table 6.3 and the original data from which it is derived illustrate the direction of Kenyan labor policy through the 1920s. First, the upward figure for the age of males in official eyes eligible to work advanced from 30 to 40 years old between 1921 and 1927. Second, a large proportion of the African population whose geographic location had earlier enabled it to escape the pressures to accept wage labor found itself increasingly under official administration and thus increasingly considered to be economically oriented toward wage labor. Third, the Native Affairs Department dropped the practice used by the Labour Bureau Commission of deducting 2.5 percent from the number of eligible males to allow for those who earned sufficient income from trading activities in the reserves to make wage labor unnecessary. It is at least a fair hypothesis—to be discussed further in the next chapter—that such activities supported progressively fewer Africans during the 1920s.

In 1926 and 1927, the average number of African males actually employed monthly on European farms was about 44 and 39 percent respectively of the total number calculated to be eligible.[9] Something approaching half the adult male population calculated to be eligible worked on European land holdings.[10] When to this is added the very sizable squatter ("resident native") population, the African women and children laboring on European farms, and the very many Africans working for non-farm-connected Europeans (official and private), only one conclusion is possible.[11] European officials and settlers in Kenya intended to use the African population as a cheap wage labor force. In this, they succeeded. By the late 1920s, they had forced the African population as a whole to play its assigned role in their plantation-based economic structure. The methods responsible for their success will be outlined in the remainder of this chapter.

THE ROLE OF TAXATION

The tax system was a basic element in the complex of pressures driving the Africans to wage labor. Ordinance No. 2 of 1910, the Native Hut and Poll Tax Ordinance, remained in force throughout the 1920s, until 1934.[12] Its provisions made every male over 16 years of age liable to tax.

It prescribed alternatives to cash payment: either payment in kind, or labor on public works at the rate of one month's labor for each 3 rupees due. Needless to say, the value of payment in kind exceeded the cash tax due, while one month's labor for a private employer returned more than 3 rupees. Refusal to pay taxes in any form was punishable by confiscation of an African's hut, other property, and/or imprisonment.

In 1910 the yearly rate generally applied was 3 rupees, the legal maximum. An enactment of 1915 raised this maximum to 5 rupees. By 1919 the rate for almost all Africans was 5 rupees. In 1920 the maximum was again raised, this time to 10 rupees, while a fixed penalty of two months' labor for nonpayment was established. During the 1920s most Africans paid at an annual rate of about 8 rupees. The changes are reflected in table 6.4. The wartime mobilization, which

TABLE 6.4: African Tax Revenue
(In £)

Year	Total Native Hut and Poll Tax Revenues
1901–02	3,328
1905–06	44,541
1909–10	105,000
1914–15	175,000
1919–20	279,000
1920–21	658,414
1926	558,000
1930	591,424

SOURCE: Governor E. P. C. Girouard, "Memorandum," 25 May 1910, in GB *CP* CO Confidential Print, Item No. 39400, CO 879/105, p. 108; and G. Walsh and H. R. Montgomery, *Report on Native Taxation*, pp. 11–12.

increased the number of persons taxed, and the tax rise of 1920 accounted for the large jumps in revenue from direct taxes on Africans. In the 1920s, under the new British currency system which replaced the rupee, these taxes averaged around 12 shillings per adult African taxpayer except for the Masai tribesmen, who paid 20 shillings per adult male.

Between 1912 and 1927 the only comparable direct tax on non-Africans was set at 30 shillings per adult male over 18 years of age. In 1926 assuming 5,000 eligible Europeans, their contribution to direct tax revenues totaled £7,500, compared to £558,044 contributed by the eligible Africans. The Asian community, with perhaps 14,000 eligible direct taxpayers, contributed £21,000. In 1927 another 30 shilling tax per capita for educational purposes, for European and Asian children only, was levied on the non-African male population over 18 years of age.[13]

Customs duties provided the major source of revenue from indirect taxation. The general 10 percent ad valorem tariff in effect from 1904 to World War I, which exempted agricultural implements, breeding stock, and commercial seeds for Europeans, rose to 20 percent in 1921, with specific adjustments thereafter. This increase, by raising the cost of all imported commodities, was a regressive tax on the African consumer. Imported commodities purchased heavily by Africans included chiefly cotton goods, cigarettes, certain household goods, beads, and wire. In 1922 customs duties were estimated to come from the different ethnic communities as follows:

Europeans	£222,300
Indian	£ 96,900
African	£218,900[14]

Finally, Kenya's government obtained revenue from game, gun, motor vehicle, liquor, and other licenses, gasoline tax, a very small estate duty, and a few other small miscellaneous items which fell upon the non-African population. However, all these imposts together produced much less revenue than either the African Hut and Poll Tax or the customs duties. In 1925, for example, revenue from all the secondary imposts plus the non-African poll tax (30 shillings per adult male) was less than 20 percent of the revenue from direct taxation of the Africans and less than 15 percent of the customs duties.[15]

To sum up, direct and indirect taxes on Africans rose dramatically after World War I and provided the major share of internal revenues in Kenya. This increased burden of taxation sharply reduced the real purchasing power of money received by African laborers in wages. The dimensions of this reduction in purchasing power appear in the report of a 1927 Labour Commission.[16] According to its findings, the total money earnings of a typical African family living in a reserve varied from 90 to 110 shillings per annum.[17] The average direct tax payable by the head of such a family for all its members amounted to about 28 shillings. With a direct tax bill in the neighborhood of 30 percent of earnings, and indirect taxes on imported goods averaging 20 percent ad valorem, it is safe to say that African laborers only very rarely had anything left of their earnings after outlays for taxes and minimal living expenses.[18]

Increased direct and indirect taxation in Kenya after the war did more than merely increase the flow of labor to European employers. It also served to inhibit the accumulation of funds in African hands that might have enabled them to withhold their labor from Europeans and find other ways to pay their tax bills. With an average wage of 12 shillings per month in the 1920s, the direct poll tax of 12 shillings per head meant that the African laborer worked one month for each poll tax responsibility he carried, which was typically more than one. Wage labor for Europeans remained the chief and almost the sole manner of earning money throughout the 1920s, a situation to be examined in the next chapter.

THE PASS SYSTEM

What the tax system made necessary, the pass system organized and regulated. The original enactment of 1915 was implemented after July 1920 and formally promulgated in the Native Registration Ordinance No. 56 of 1921 (see table 6.5). Every adult male African received and was required to carry a certificate, called a pass. In this certificate each employer recorded the time worked, kind of work performed, the wages earned, and general comments on the individual. Loss of the certificate rendered the loser liable to severe punishment. Exemptions from the obligation to carry it were extremely difficult to obtain and in any case cost £4, which placed them out of reach of almost all Africans.

The agitation and rebellious attitudes which developed among Africans in the years immediately after World War I focused on two main issues: the loss of land to the Euro-

TABLE 6.5: The Pass System

Year	Cumulated Number of Africans Issued Certificates
1920 (December)	194,750
1921 (December)	389,632
1922 (May)	435,584
1924 (October)	519,056
1928 (December)	675,000[a]

SOURCE: W. M. Ross, *Kenya from Within*, pp. 189–93; and R. R. Kuczynski, *Demographic Survey of the British Colonial Empire*, 2: 140–43.

NOTE: All figures in this table are liable to significant error because of problems of double and triple counting inherent in the conditions of issuing certificates.
[a] The total number of certificates outstanding, 737,936, was reduced by Kuczynski to 675,000 to account for deaths, desertions, and so on.

peans, and the pass system.[19] The hostility grew from a realization by the Africans that the pass system gave the Europeans enormous control over the African population. And the Europeans had every intention to use that power as far as possible. For example, ordinances in 1920 and 1921 essentially outlawed vagrancy. Police were empowered to arrest without warrant any African apprehended without visible means of support, the latter fact being determined by the African's certificate. In fact, almost every official enactment concerning African labor involved the certificate and the information entered upon it. Employers could note there an unruly worker, thereby forewarning other possible employers. Similarly, ordinances enabling authorities to conscript labor for public works stipulated that exemptions could be secured only on the basis of labor performed elsewhere within the preceding year. Only the certificate could establish the African's liability or exemption. Another purpose of the pass system, greatly praised by the settlers, was to provide a means of identifying deserters who had broken their labor contracts.[20] In 1932 evidence was presented to a special governmental committee indicating that the pass system was used by plantation owners to keep wages down.[21]

In essence, the power of the employer to write almost anything he chose on the certificate implied the power to control his African employee far more thoroughly than before the establishment of the pass system. It made possible the rigorous enforcement of nearly every past and future measure taken to affect the labor supply. Having learned how useful it proved in South Africa and how helpful it would have been during the mobilization of World War I, Europeans after the war were resolutely determined to establish it immediately.

GOVERNMENT "ENCOURAGEMENT"

The postwar government actions, raising taxes, making the tax system more comprehensive and efficient, and firmly establishing the pass system, affected the supply of African labor somewhat indirectly. In theory, that is, Africans were legally free to respond to these measures by not doing wage labor for Europeans. There are indications that a small, struggling group of Africans was able in fact to escape wage labor.[22] No doubt another small proportion of eligible Africans evaded taxes and/or the certificates and perhaps wage labor, as well.

Some officials dismissed the problem of Africans who were capable of wage labor but able to avoid it legally or otherwise. These officials were consoled by the increasing availability and popularity among African consumers of imported European, American, and Japanese manufactures. Growing demand for imports was expected to prod Africans further to provide wage labor for Europeans. The chief native commissioner noted the progress of these imports among African purchasers, who were, he observed, passing "from practically primitive nudity or a few rough skins, to a complete European costume."[23]

However, the prevalent official attitude favored a program to increase the labor supply which would supplement the pressures of taxation and certificates with direct government intervention in the labor market. In 1925 the governor of Kenya expressed this view with a strong sense of urgency: "some measure of compulsion is necessary, as the only alternative is letting matters drift until the natives consider that they require more money."[24] Throughout most of the 1920s officials performed functions which alternated between outright recruitment and "encouragement" of Africans to work for private and public European employers. The British authorities not only undertook these tasks themselves, but they also arranged to have the chiefs and headmen among the Africans do likewise.

The labor shortage immediately after the war forced the colonial officials to decide quickly just how far they would interfere directly to expand the labor supply. Meeting in 1918 and 1919 the Land Settlement Commission made explicit recommendations, in anticipation of the expected settlement of discharged soldiers.[25] It proposed the establishment of special government operated African labor camps. Their purpose was to provide Africans with information, advice, and assistance in finding employment. The commission further explicitly recommended that the government actively recruit African adult males for public works as an indirect way of encouraging Africans to work for private employers. The commission opposed any direct government recruiting for individual private employers.

On 23 October 1919, Kenya's Governor Northey issued a special labour circular.[26] The key element of this document was its clear set of instructions to regional officials of the British administration regarding the labor supply. These officials were directed to "actively encourage" Africans to engage in wage labor and to place heavy pressure on chiefs and headmen to give Africans similar encouragement.

While the labour circular did not describe "active encouragement" as actual recruitment, it raised an enormous storm of protest in England on the grounds that Kenya seemed to be adopting a policy indistinguishable from government sanctioned forced labor.[27] Colonial officials in London and Nairobi denied that their policies had such intentions or implications. They issued a second labour circular on February 17, 1920, which did not retreat in any important respect from the first but couched every point in humanitarian language clearly designed to mollify the critics.[28]

The Northey Circulars, as they came to be known, in essence reinstituted the wartime system of encouragement to Africans to engage in wage labor. Since regional officials had powers of taxing, rendering binding legal judgments, imposing punishments, and so on, their encouragement could not but appear to Africans more like command than encouragement. The Africans feared the consequences of resisting such encouragement.[29]

The complexities and contradictions connected with British policy on direct labor encouragement and recruitment were brought into view most sharply in the brief labor shortages of late 1924 and 1925. Between May 1923 and October 1924 the number of Africans coming forward to work for the government on railway construction fell from 17,426 to 2,719.[30] This situation caused immediate concern. Officials were planning to build a new branch of the Uganda Railway to the Uasin Gishu area, thereby providing a fresh stimulus to European settlement, trade, and so forth. The governor requested the secretary of state for the colonies to approve forced labor for the railway construction work. He also proposed specifically that wages paid to such workers fall below the rate obtainable by Africans from private employment. Always mindful of the basic task of government, he argued that otherwise "the lesson would be lost."

While Colonial Secretary Amory ultimately granted his approval, he also added a revealing series of cautionary remarks.[31] He expressed anxiety that the association of compulsion with wage labor in the African mind might lead to greater labor problems subsequently. He expressed the fear that by permitting compulsion when supply was short, British policy would have the effect of discouraging use of laborsaving devices and procedures, which he implied would be a preferable response to labor difficulties.

In fact, the urgency of the railway construction project and the loud clamorings of European settlers forced immediate action on the officials, who opted for recruitment and, when necessary, direct compulsion to draw out labor for both private and public purposes. However, Secretary Amory's concerns were shared by other officials to such an extent that an implicit bias against direct and in favor of indirect methods of securing laborers can be found throughout the 1920s. Taxes, certificates, and other indirect forms of encouragement were intended to create adequate supplies of labor. Direct encouragement became a last resort, although one not infrequently applied.[32]

LOCAL GOVERNMENT AND FORCED LABOR

British officials also pressured chiefs and headmen in the African reserves to use forced labor for public works. The power of the European regional administrator over his African counterpart grew out of two underlying facts of life in Kenya. First, the Africans holding leadership positions had often obtained them directly from the British. "The British . . . did not want leaders in whom the people had confidence. . . . When the people objected, saying 'We have our Chief, the man you appointed is his messenger and interpreter,' the British would not listen, and there was trouble during which the real Chief and some of the elders were sent to prison."[33] Such leaders owed their positions only to the pleasure of the local British official. Second, the superior military and police power of the British quite simply left even the most recalcitrant African leader with no real choice. If the regional official ordered him to recruit forced labor, he complied, no matter how unpopular his fellow tribesmen found the order.[34] The Northey Circulars had specifically instructed British officials that headmen and chiefs were to be "repeatedly reminded that it is part of their duty to advise and encourage all unemployed men to go out and work." Under such pressure the headmen could and did use both the threat and the reality of forced labor to aid the "encouragement" process.

The Native Authority Ordinance of 1912 empowered appointed headmen to make legal arrests and compel attendance by Africans within their jurisdiction at "native tribunals." The headman's judgment when countersigned by the local British official possessed the force of law.[35] Each headman could require 24 days per year of labor for the "community benefit" from each African male under his control. Such work could, but did not need to receive any remuneration. Headmen also possessed vaguely described powers to recruit additional forced labor without pay for "emergencies."

Then, in 1920, an amendment to the 1912 ordinance was passed which specified that headmen could require as much as 60 days of forced labor from adult male Africans (see table 6.6). The latter could claim exemption only if their

TABLE 6.6: Labor Called for Compulsory Government Work

Year	Number of Men	Number of Man-Days
1923	12,809	95,972
1924	13,228	56,781
1925	15,240	76,264
1926	19,323	151,064
1927	25,501	241,196

SOURCE: GB CPK, Department of Native Affairs, "Annual Report for 1927," app. D, p. 99.

NOTE: Major users of this labor were the colonial administration and the King's African Rifles (the Kenya military).

certificates showed either that they were currently employed or that they had worked for wages for at least three of the directly preceding twelve months.[36]

As with most other policy measures designed to augment the labor supply, the British actions regarding their head-men demonstrated the sharp intensification of pressure from the settlers after World War I. Similarly, their purpose consistently was to drive Africans to perform wage labor as an alternative preferable to public works at less or no pay from the central authorities and/or the headmen.

The problems of labor supply in Kenya led also to the intensification of government policies other than those concerned with taxes, passes, and forced labor for public works. While all of these other policies had been discussed and at least partially implemented before the war, it was only after 1918 that most of them took effect in a manner both comprehensive and complementing one another. Colonial Secretary Lord Milner explained the underlying imperial motivation as support for "settlers who have embarked on enterprises calculated to assist not only the Protectorate itself but also this country and other parts of the Empire by the production of raw materials which are in urgent demand."[37]

SQUATTERS AND THE LABOR SUPPLY

The official policy of supporting and partially regulating squatting reveals another dimension of the process of transforming African peasants into wage laborers.[38] Squatters differed from monthly contract workers chiefly insofar as they lived with their families on the property of their European employer. There they built their huts from materials furnished by the employer, who assigned them specific lots of land for their own use. Squatters entered into contracts with Europeans for between one and three years. In return, the European employers had the right to 180 days of paid labor from each adult male African per year. The wage rates stipulated usually paralleled those prevailing in the immediate area.

During the 1920s Kikuyu families found themselves increasingly drawn to seek positions as squatters. Three main problems of life in the reserves explained their increased interest in squatter status. First, the growth of population in the African reserves, whose boundaries were fixed, resulted in considerable pressure on the land.[39] During the decade 1921–31, for example, while the overall Kikuyu population increased at an average rate of 1.5 percent per year, the comparable figure for the Kikuyu squatter population was 6.2 percent.[40] Second, soil erosion within the reserves reduced the return from reserve lands, and hence their attractiveness relative to the land, usually virgin land, offered as part of a squatter contract.[41] Finally, increasing population density was matched by rapid growth in the number of livestock maintained by Africans in the reserves. Increasingly scarce inside the reserves, available grazing land was an important attraction of squatter status.[42] Statistics for the early 1930s indicate a total squatter population of roughly 110,000, including families who managed over 550,000 animals on the European owned property they occupied.[43]

European settlers often preferred squatters to monthly contract workers. Their basic reason was quite simply that squatters offered "the most certain form of labour."[44] An African squatting for one to three years tended to become detribalized. Since not only his wages, but his food-producing land and his hut could be taken from him, he was far more docile and tractable in meeting the demands of his employer. European settlers could make more efficient use of labor since it was immediately available precisely, and only, when and where they required it (up to 180 days per year). During emergencies other members of squatter families could be impressed into labor. Finally, growing families were readily accessible recruiting grounds for yet more laborers.[45] An ordinance of 1924 illustrates the expectations for the future entertained by many Europeans concerned with African squatting. The ordinance granted Kenya's governor the power "in a state of emergency" to waive the plantation owners' obligation to pay their squatters for the mandatory 180 days of work. The ordinance further stipulated that, when a squatter's son reached the age of 16, he would automatically become subject to the squatting contract then binding upon his father. On appeal, the secretary of state for the colonies disallowed this ordinance.[46]

There were still other reasons for Europeans to favor squatting. As most European settlers had acquired more land than they were cultivating during the 1920s, they gave unused land to squatters, who often had to clear it before beginning to work it.[47] Also, the possibilities for African squatters to raise their own food probably mitigated any potential upward pressure on wages.[48]

The economic conditions in which the squatter population lived, together with its size, made it represent an important contribution to the general social solution of the labor problem. The key factor explaining the growth and significance of squatting was probably the overcrowded state of the reserves. By the late 1920s official and unofficial reports indicated that "the people are more thick on the land than is suitable to their present degree of skill in methods to combat soil erosion and exhaustion."[49]

OTHER GOVERNMENT MEASURES

By the mid-1920s officials concerned with the labor problem broadened the scope of their efforts in yet another direction. Until then their programs had sought chiefly to draw out local adult male Africans for agricultural wage labor on extremely labor-intensive European plantations. In the mid-1920s they began to seek to augment labor supplies with both non-Kenyan Africans and Kenyan women and children. At about the same time they made a few efforts to reduce the private demand for labor by supporting the use of equipment, crops, and organizational schemes that were laborsaving.

In 1925 European farmers from all parts of East Africa assembled at Tukuyu to discuss their mutual problems. One of their concluding recommendations was that "voluntary movements of the Natives in and between territories should . . . be unrestricted."[50] The governor of Kenya officially sanctioned the encouragement of labor to enter Kenya from neighboring territories.

The use of women and children for European farm labor became increasingly widespread and important throughout the 1920s. This is shown by the data in tables 6.7, 6.8, and 6.9, which demonstrate that by 1927 women and juveniles, at the peak season, comprised over 20 percent of the labor force. Their work was chiefly cultivation of coffee, above all picking the ripe coffee berries. Within the purely agricultural labor force, women and children accounted for as much as 35 to 40 percent of total employees at the peak coffee-picking

TABLE 6.7: Agricultural Labor Employment, 1927–1928

	Number of Workers Employed	
Crop	April–Sept. 1927	Oct. 1927 to March 1928
Coffee		
In bearing	26,400	46,640
1–3 years old	4,500	4,500
Clearing, planting	1,000	1,000
Sisal	19,880	13,916
Maize		
General	13,200	21,120
Clearing, preparation	3,000	3,000
Wheat		
General	3,000	2,700
Clearing, preparation	500	500
Sugar	2,070	1,760
Tea		
In bearing	125	32
1–3 years old	1,050	630
Clearing, planting	450	360
Coconuts	1,040	832
All other crops	2,000	2,000
Livestock	5,500	5,500
Total employed	83,715	117,155

SOURCE: "Report of the Labour Commission," 1927, app. 6, table 5, p. 49, in East Africa Pamphlet no. 217 (fol.).

TABLE 6.8: Average Monthly Employment, 1927

	Adult Males	Women and Juveniles	Totals
Activity: April–September			
Agriculture	61,700	22,015	83,715
Other	85,923		85,923
Totals	147,623	22,015	179,638
Activity: October–December			
Agriculture	70,940	46,215	117,155
Other	85,923		85,923
Totals	156,863	46,215	203,078

SOURCE: GB CPK, Department of Native Affairs, "Annual Report for 1927," pp. 90–91.

season. While there is some evidence of forced labor required of women and children, the general attitude of the British authorities seems to have favored having women and children recruited privately by European employers.[51]

In 1925 the East Africa Commission made a strong and emphatic recommendation for the introduction of labor-saving mechanical devices for use on European farms.[52] By 1926 the chief agricultural official in Kenya could report: "To reduce the number of labourers required and the risks consequent upon a shortage of labour supply, laboursaving machinery and appliances are being introduced, and used to an increasing extent." He noted the success of officially encouraged reorganization of farm procedures, which had resulted in significantly increased output-per-laborer ratios.[53] Another approach to the problem of the labor supply focused on an adjustment of the agricultural-output mix. Its advocates forecast escape from costly labor shortages "in the

TABLE 6.9: Average Monthly Agricultural Employment, January–July 1927

Type of Worker	Total Engaged
Adult males	76,838
Women, juveniles	20,230
Casual laborers (mostly adult males)	5,006
Total	102,074

SOURCE: GB CPK, Department of Agriculture, "Annual Report for 1927," quoted in Department of Native Affairs, "Annual Report for 1927," p. 91.

increasing development of crops and industries which make
the least demand for native labour."[54] For example, whereas
cultivation of coffee and tea required over 100 men per
100 acres, cultivation of wheat and maize needed only about
3 and 10 respectively. Through exhortation backed up by
experiments at government agricultural stations, the administration encouraged European employers to grow alternative crops that were less labor-intensive.

THE CONSEQUENCES FOR AFRICANS

The combined effect of government and private measures
designed to overcome the labor shortage—comprehensive and
high taxes, an all-inclusive pass system, government "encouragement" of Africans to work, forced labor, support of
squatting, measures leading to overcrowded reserves, encouragement of Africans to immigrate from neighboring territories, the use of the labor of women and children on farms,
and carefully promoted laborsaving innovations—taken together these measures proved successful, perhaps even oversuccess-
ful. For the most part the 1920s saw an abundance of African
labor seeking employment at the low wage rates prevailing.[55]
"While the Protectorate can be assured of its present cheap
labour—*probably the cheapest in the world*—the advantages
over other countries . . . are enormous."[56] In this, the 1920s
stood in marked contrast to the prewar period. The first
unsuccessful, haphazard gropings had been given impetus
by the war and were transformed after it into a coordinated
economic structure imposed on the African population in
order to procure labor for the settlers. By the 1920s the
European community had seen its labor problem solved.

However, the very abundance of Africans seeking work
left unchanged the total neglect of the physical condition
of the African population which had prevailed since the
prewar days.[57] The European settler community and the
British authorities simply ignored the precautions of the
Labour Bureau Commission of 1921:

> The Commissioners are of the opinion that it is the
> right policy to maintain a medical standard graduated
> to the work for which the Native is required, since a

labourer who is physically unfit for his work is a source
of expense to his employer, and, after he returns to
the Reserve is apt, by his stories of the hard work and
long work to which he attributes his illness, to act as
a deterrent to others.[58]

Kenya's labor policy fostered and maintained an extremely
high rate of worker mortality and physical exhaustion. In
1922 Kenya medical administrators calculated general infant
mortality rates of 400 per 1,000 among large sample populations. In 1932 medical authorities still concluded that "at
the present time therefore well over 90 percent of three million
people almost all of whom must be sick at one time or another
during the year, are never seen by a qualified medical man."[59]
Inadequate land, housing, and income combined with official unwillingness to spend government revenues for medical
facilities to cause these conditions to continue. "In a country
where men can be hired for from £5 to £18 a year it does
not pay employers to spend large sums in keeping them
alive."[60] To meet the most minimally adequate standard of
medical care, medical authorities in the early 1930s estimated
that a 5,000 percent increase in staff would be required.[61]

The few official exhortations heard about the need to
keep up the physical condition of African workers had little
or no effect.[62] The expenses of the tax system, pass system,
and other government measures led the British authorities
to economize on medical facilities.[63] The success of the
former seemed to them to obviate any need for the latter.

In the economic development of Kenya from 1900 to 1930,
British policies produced the land and the labor force needed
to complement immigrant European capital and "entre-
preneurship" in producing certain foods and raw materials
for export.

7 The Significance of British Colonialism in Kenya

The words and deeds of British policy makers from the 1890s to 1930 conform to a basic design. Great Britain had decided to take East Africa and to make it as low cost—in other words, as profitable—a part of the empire as possible. Under the pressure of changing events during this period, Britain altered and adjusted the methods appropriate to furthering the design. But the design itself endured as the unifying theme of British policy.

Shaped by this design, Britain's economic development plan for the territory involved a bold reorganization of land, labor, and capital resources. This reorganization brought drastic changes to the daily lives of all the people in Kenya and to the colony's economic history.

What were the consequences of the colonial process for both the majority African and the minority European population? And what were the costs and benefits, the interests served and the interests ignored, during British colonial rule in Kenya before 1930?

THE DESIGN OF COLONIALISM

However complex the motivations lying behind Great Britain's destruction of the Arab-Indian slave trade in East Africa, the success of that policy forced British officials and private business interests to confront the issue of how to develop this new appendage of the empire. Professor Knowles, preeminent as an analyst of the economics of the British Empire, discussed and revealed in her writings the development plan which—sometimes explicitly, more often implicitly —gradually came to predominate in the views of Englishmen concerned with East Africa.[1] British assumptions and ideas about economic development in East Africa, Knowles argued, were derived from broader conceptions of the role of tropical dependencies within the empire. By the end of the nineteenth century it was generally understood that if, as

132

expected, the dominions followed the experience of the United States and consumed much of the food and raw materials they produced, "the tropics and sub-tropics are destined to bulk larger and larger in imperial economics."[2]

Between 1899 and 1920 British officials and private businessmen established a wide variety of special institutions to assist in developing the tropical dependencies to fulfill their assigned roles in the empire. The following is a partial list:

1899   Schools of Tropical Medicine established in Liverpool and London
        Tropical Diseases Bureau established in London
1909   Medical and Sanitary Committees established with a special orientation to African problems
1913   Imperial Bureau of Entomology established
1918   Imperial Bureau of Mycology established
1920   Empire Forestry Conference held
        Imperial Shipping Board established[3]

Such institutions supplemented the crucial services of the Botanical Gardens at Kew and the testing laboratories of private merchants, which carried on experiments with samples sent from the tropical areas. The efforts of these institutions guided the choice of crops and livestock to be developed in these areas, and their work in finding suitable hybrids was of vital importance. Private research groups were founded—by the Federation of British Industries, among others—to survey and assess the actual and potential resources of the empire.[4]

The proper basis of life in the tropics was universally assumed to be agricultural production.[5] In the context of colonialism, this meant agriculture for export. The objectives of Livingstone's trips to Africa included testing the possibility of growing cotton in order to relieve British dependence on U.S. sources.[6] British experiences with raw rubber, coffee, sisal, and other similar agricultural commodities in the late nineteenth century led to literally hundreds of comparable missions by other Britons throughout Africa based on the Livingstone prototype.

In the East Africa Protectorate the British confronted a

difficult economic problem when they established formal control in 1895. First, their commitment to the Uganda Railway completed the destruction of the slave trade, slavery, and the complex economic system based on slavery. Some other mode of economic activity had to be established. Second, the British objective was a thriving agricultural export economy which would pay for the import of manufactures from Britain while supplying it with needed food and raw materials. Third, British decision makers, as they pursued their objective, were subject to some constraints. They sought to encourage the particular agricultural export commodities that would lessen British reliance on non-empire sources. They were also under great pressure to devise means to offset the costs of the Uganda Railway and the protectorate's administration without recourse to London, that is, from within the protectorate. In more ideological terms, the British defined their task in the protectorate as follows: "Some alternative employment and the creation of a free labour market were the two necessities if personal freedom was to become a reality."[7]

Prime Minister Salisbury described British interests and intentions in East Africa to Parliament in 1895 in these terms:

> It is our business in all these new countries to make smooth the paths for British commerce, British enterprise, the application of British capital, at a time when other paths, other outlets for the commercial energies of our race are being gradually closed by the commercial principles which are gaining more and more adhesion. . . .
>
> We have so many interests in so many parts of the world, we are so much exposed, that it may be doubtful whether we shall be willing to run anything approaching risk for the sake of the African possession, but we have another means of making ourselves secure—a means which it may be said belongs to us alone—and that is not the power of our Government or the negotiation which they may carry on, but the energy, the initiative, the force, the individual force which our people carry with them into any new country which they inhabit. . . .
>
> I do not think that our Government is of much ad-

vantage to Englishmen who go into a new country. I
think it is rather a disadvantage. Almost everything that
is done at home is apt to hinder them . . . the spirit
of the Treasury like Care behind the horseman, which
paralyses every effort and casts a shadow on every en-
thusiasm they may feel. . . .

In a few years it will be our people that will be
masters, it will be our commerce that will prevail, it
will be our capital that will rule. . . .

My Lords, this is a tremendous power, but it requires
one condition. You must enable it to get to the country
where its work is to be done. You must open the path.[8]

As discussed earlier, the destruction of slavery as well as
the nineteenth-century impact of slave trading on East Africa
had dislocated earlier patterns of economic behavior among
the Africans and Asians there. British officials and private
businessmen well understood the dislocation and maneuvered
within it to advance their interests at every possible point
while they were reviving a functioning economy. After many
trials and errors, British officials in the East Africa Protectorate evidently came to conclude that there were only two
real alternatives available in the depressed economic conditions facing them, either to revert to an "earlier, primitive"
form of tribal, more or less subsistence economy or to implant
non-African settlers in order to organize, invest in, and manage agricultural production of cash crops.[9] The first alternative appears to have been totally unacceptable to British officials, committed as they were to the spread of European
civilization, not to mention British prosperity and hegemony.
They chose the second alternative, and in particular they
chose Europeans as the key non-African group. Private
British businessmen moved to replace Indians as the dominant
merchant group and to purchase large tracts of land either
for speculative purposes or for plantation farming patterned
on British tropical dependencies in Asia.

The basic economic interests of British officials, merchants,
and landholders merged in the pressure for European settlement. Landholders envisioned speculative gains, merchants
saw expanded trade, and officials found in European immi-

grant settlers the best possible agents to build up and manage production of agricultural exports.[10] From 1895 to 1914 British officials in the protectorate experimented with crops and livestock that London wished to encourage within the empire. During these years the settlers brought in by the officials also experimented to find profitable crops and/or livestock. The high cost and risk of experimenting with crops and livestock meant that only a very few of the richest private settlers could afford it. Occasionally missionaries also experimented. In general, however, experimentation and the expertise in matters of choosing crops and livestock for development which resulted rested with protectorate officials. Their biases, in particular those favoring crops needed *within* the empire, had a determining influence on the mix of agricultural crops produced in the territory. By the end of the first twenty years of British rule, the consequence was a basic emphasis on a very few crops, chiefly coffee, sisal, and maize.

The dual commitment of British officials to European settlement and to a few specific crops essentially fixed the structure and direction of development of the protectorate's economy. Settlers had to have land and labor to produce the export crops encouraged by the administration. The period 1895–1920 encompasses the trials and errors of British officials as they systematically provided European settlers with land and labor through the military, legislative, judicial, and fiscal actions that came to define the colonial economy of the protectorate. The 1920s then saw the fruition of these efforts.

The actual course of development charted by the British officials is perhaps most succinctly shown in tables 7.1, 7.2, and 7.3. Table 7.1 depicts the changing pattern of exports according to their origin within the protectorate. The final phase of the concentration of exports is demonstrated in table 7.2. Lastly, table 7.3 shows the distribution of net national income resulting by 1930 from this pattern of production.

The British in Kenya conceived of and implemented an economic development model. They created a modern labor force by withdrawing from the African population the possibility of earning sufficient income in any way other than

TABLE 7.1: Export Commodities as Percentages of Value of
Total Domestic Exports

	1913	1923	1932
From European settler areas			
Coffee	3	32	53
Sisal	0	15	8
Sodium carbonate	0	9	8
Tea	0	0	1
Gold bullion	0	0	3
Dairy products	2	0	2
Sugar	0	0	1
Subtotal	5	56	76
From African areas			
Hides and skins	21	8	5
Wattle, bark, etc.	0	0	4
Raw cotton	3	0	0
Subtotal	24	8	9
From both areas			
Maize	13	16	5
Miscellaneous	58	20	10
Subtotal	71	36	15
Total exports	100	100	100

SOURCE: GB *CP* CO, "Report of the Commission Appointed to Enquire into and Report on the Financial Position and System of Taxation of Kenya," Colonial Office Paper no. 116, 1936, p. 8, and app. 2, pp. 254–55.

TABLE 7.2: Export Concentration

Export Commodity	Percentage of Value of Total Domestic Exports		
	1920	1925	1930
1. Coffee	33	30	42
2. Sisal	10	20	13
3. Maize	4	15	17
Subtotal: items 1–3	47	65	72
4. Hides and skins	12	12	5
5. Sodium carbonate	12	8	7
Subtotal: items 1–5	71	85	84
6. Miscellaneous	27	14	12

SOURCE: Same as for table 7.1.

NOTE: The category "Miscellaneous" is not a simple residual; it includes only some of the commodities not included in the above categories; see the source document.

TABLE 7.3: Distribution of Net National Income, 1930

Recipient Group	Total Income (In million £)	£ per capita
Africans	3.20	1.1
Indians	0.75	18.8
Europeans	3.54	208.2
Companies[a]	0.75	
Government	0.50	

SOURCE: S. and K. Aaronovitch, *Crisis in Kenya*, table 24, p. 151.

[a] Company data are based on an extrapolation to 1930 of company income figures first collected in 1937.

providing wage labor for Europeans. The chief means used to create this labor force were the transfer of prime agricultural land from African to European ownership and the severe restrictions that were placed on African peasant agriculture. When they confronted the problem of obtaining the capital needed for production, British officials secured it initially through grants of cash from the imperial treasury, through free grants of large tracts of land that were intended to induce investment, and through the immigration of European settlers who brought with them their own capital resources, as well as access to more from friends and relatives left in Great Britain. The immigrants also played a crucial role as managers (entrepreneurs, in part) of the production encouraged in the economic development model.

With World War I, treasury grants ceased; free land grants had stopped even earlier. After 1915 British officials "raised" capital for investment in European production of agricultural exports by stimulating continued European immigration and by directly investing large proportions of tax revenues—drawn mainly from African wage earners—in European agriculture. This investment took the form of supporting scientific personnel and experiment stations that were specifically designed to improve European farming. They paid little or no attention to problems of African farming.[11] The administration's expenditure of tax revenues on public works in the 1920s similarly favored European over African areas in the key item of road building and maintenance, and, by the end of the 1920s, the combined expenditure on the Departments of Agriculture and Public Works exceeded any other single category of expenditure, including overall administration.[12]

Of course, broadly defined, all tax revenues contributed, if only indirectly, to the maintenance of the infrastructure and the coercive apparatus essential to any successful European plantation system. In this sense, expenditures on administration, the military, the police, and so on, represented unavoidable capital expenditures that would otherwise have been charged against the accounts of private European settlers.

To sum up, colonial officials in Kenya dealt broadly and freely with the problems of allocating land, labor, and capital to achieve the development desired. As Churchill observed about East Africa in 1908: "The British government has it in its hands to shape the development and destiny of these new countries and their varied peoples with an authority and from an elevation far superior to that with which Cabinets can cope with the giant tangles at home."[13] Of the Kenyan experience it is certainly unwarranted to argue, as some have concerning Britain's tropical empire, that "it had absolutely no unity of character and no necessary imperial function."[14]

THE EFFECT ON AFRICANS

The economic development charted by British officials in the East Africa Protectorate had far-reaching consequences for the majority African population. There was, above all, the rapid transformation of the African population into a wage labor force as analyzed above. The counterpart of that process was the systematic suppression of an African peasant agriculture.

African peasants in the protectorate around 1900 regularly harvested maize, millet, peas, beans, sweet potatoes, yams, cauliflowers, potatoes, bananas, sugar, and tobacco.[15] The first coffee shipments carried on the Uganda Railway came entirely from African cultivators in Uganda.[16] Missionaries had good results when they gave improved maize seeds to Kamba and Teita cultivators in 1904.[17] Similarly, African peasants harvested promising cotton crops with seeds supplied by government experimental farms in 1904.[18]

These few among many comparable bits of evidence indi-

cate that African cultivators in general possessed a wide
variety of agricultural skills and experiences albeit at primitive levels of technology. Moreover, it seems quite clear that,
given adequate assistance, Africans were willing and able
to benefit from expert advice and aid. By 1905, however,
such help from official sources all but ceased. The direction
of economic change planned for the protectorate required
that scarce resources of money and knowledge be made available exclusively to European immigrant settlers. By 1910 the
only consideration of systematic aid to African cultivators
focused on Africans in the coastal areas. There, one authority argued, returns from farming were so low and rainfall so unsure that no European would consider settling
there.[19] By the beginning of World War I, the demands of
European farmers for government services and for an African labor force reduced official interest in and support for
African peasant agriculture to totally insignificant levels.

European demand for African plantation wage earners
mitigated against any efforts to develop African agriculture.
Sometimes European sentiment on this point was expressed
in abstract, lofty terms:

> The theory that provision must be made by the State not
> merely for the eldest but for every son in a family
> becoming a land owner would be regarded as absurd
> in Europe. We see no reason for imposing it on East
> Africa, the natives of which can only stagnate under
> a regime of universal peasant proprietorship.[20]

On other occasions, European planters enunciated their fears
regarding their labor supply more concretely. At the Tukuyu
conference of European farmers from throughout East Africa,
it was agreed to oppose all government aid to African cultivation of "economic crops" such as arabica coffee, tobacco,
and cotton. A main reason given was the "slothfulness" of
male Africans if and when their women and children could
successfully harvest cash crops.[21] Only rarely was the full
meaning of the settlers' position explicitly stated. For example, in 1925 the East Africa Commission concluded that
the Kenya authorities were justified in prohibiting all Afri-

can cultivators from growing arabica coffee, by far the most lucrative cash crop in Kenya. The commission's reason: "There is no doubt that the present difficulty in obtaining labour in Uganda . . . is due to the high prices which the Uganda native is at present obtaining for his cotton crop."[22] Some Europeans in Kenya also pondered, evidently with a degree of approval, the remarks of Europeans in Northern Rhodesia who considered the ubiquitous tsetse fly an asset because it sharply reduced African herds, thereby forcing the African tribesmen to turn to wage labor for Europeans.[23]

The complex of measures that created an African labor force also operated in a general way to inhibit African peasant agriculture. Perhaps the best summary of this process is the commentary of an official British specialist on African agriculture:

> It has been said with some force that a tribe possessing such valuable agricultural land as Kikuyu cannot expect to develop it under stock, but should rather aim at greater agricultural production, so as to be able to supplement their meat supply by purchase. *This postulates an amount of free money and market facilities greater than they yet possess.*[24]

This remark in effect points to the consequences of British policy on the land, labor, and taxation of Africans; it prevented the accumulation of the capital needed to achieve even a minimally efficient agriculture within the reserves. The matter of reserve size and its corollary, overcrowding, is demonstrated in table 7.4. One close observer of such reserve conditions remarked: "There is certainly no district in any European country where people engaged in agriculture, except as market gardeners, have so few acres per head as in the parts of the Reserves in Kenya where soil and rainfall are good."[25]

A particular factor which consistently blocked development of African peasant agriculture was the nearly total absence of any governmental assistance to African farmers.[26]

> Lack of flexibility in the agrarian system with consequent lack of fluidity in distribution, lack of skill, lack

of marketing facilities and perhaps also lack of direction, are more responsible for the defects which have been revealed than lack of land.[27]

Neither British officials nor anyone else acted to remedy this situation prior to 1930. Uganda and Tanganyika had state aided schemes for marketing African products. Before 1930 Kenya lacked any comparable program. Moreover, various European regulations and biases effectively blocked Kenya Africans from selling their stock: their animals were deemed too heavily infected with diseases and/or pests. "Yet nearly all the State-paid veterinary officers and other experts of the Agriculture Department are employed in the European areas."[28] In 1934 the Kenya Land Commission reported on what it called the "preposterous situation" of African livestock holdings: "In the midst of plenty the natives in pastoral and semi-pastoral areas are, in fact, living under conditions of extreme poverty," although "the native reserves . . . should be capable not only of providing ample supplies of meat and milk for their inhabitants, but also of exporting large quantities of dairy produce."[29]

TABLE 7.4: Reserve Population Densities

African Area	Population (In thousands)	Acres per Head
Kavirondo		
North	333	4.6
Central	370	3.1
South	321	5.9
Kikuyu		
Meru	162	3.9
Embu	92	4.5
Nyeri	191	2.5
Fort Hall	173	2.2
Kiambu	60	2.4

SOURCE: "Report on Kikuyu Land Tenure, 1929," quoted in N. Leys, *A Last Chance in Kenya*, app., p. 171.

But there was one apparent exception to this general picture. Government spokesmen and brochures in the 1920s spoke glowingly of the success of agricultural training schools established by the administration for Africans. Presumably, African trainees would provide the service that European and Asian officers rendered almost exclusively to the European settlers. Given the poor and deteriorating condition of reserve agriculture, the following findings of the Kenya Land Commission illuminate the significance of these training schools in improving African agriculture. As of 1930, a total of 117 Africans had been trained as agricultural instructors, but it had "proven impossible" to provide employment for all.[30]

In his exhaustive study of economic development in the Nyanza Province of Kenya between 1903 and 1953, Fearn reached a similar conclusion regarding African agriculture. Traditional land tenure systems and customary methods of cultivation, he argued, kept African peasant agriculture in a low productivity trap. However, the confinement of African producers within limited reserve areas seriously aggravated their difficulties. In this situation, the refusal of British officials to encourage and facilitate more efficient methods was tantamount to systematically eroding the possibilities for the future of African peasant agriculture. Fearn also specifically denies any significance to the "beneficial example" of European farming for Africans. He reasons that the size of settler land units precluded the transfer of European technology to the typically much smaller African plots.[31] Nor had African peasants access to credit from Europeans or Asians. And the taxes imposed on them precluded their accumulating their own funds from which loans could be made. Finally, British policies on licensing merchants effectively denied Africans opportunities to become merchants. This policy further limited potential marketing opportunities for African produce.[32]

The objective reality of insuperable obstacles to successful African peasant agriculture created by the British had, as one consequence, the result that *subjectively* Africans came to prefer wage labor as an alternative source of income, which militated against their making any strenuous efforts to overcome low peasant productivity.[33]

Noting the dramatic change in fortune of African peasants in Nyanza *after* 1930, Fearn found confirmation of his analysis of the pre-1930 Nyanza economy. After 1930 the Great Depression so affected Kenya's international economic posi-

tion that officials were forced to search in desperation for
any possible source of badly needed exports. Suddenly African cash cropping appeared attractive to official minds—a
possible solution to their economic dilemma. Such a solution
took on added attractiveness since the depression had hurt
European farmers, who therefore laid off large numbers of
African workers. Officials turned their attention to cotton
production by Africans in Nyanza. African cotton output in
1930–31 measured 918,967 pounds of seed cotton. By 1935–36,
after intensive governmental assistance, output stood at 15,-
701,756 pounds of seed cotton—a sixteen-fold increase.[34]

Ironically, if not unpredictably, the hurry to promote African cash cropping at all costs resulted, by the later 1930s, in
extremely serious problems of soil erosion.[35] In any case,
Fearn found that, when European agricultural experts finally
tried seriously to develop African agriculture, significant gains
proved to be within relatively fast and easy reach.[36]

In sum, the British development program for Kenya initially
created new and different constraints upon the African population—chiefly limitation of their land in the reserves, with
labor forcibly diverted from peasant agriculture to wage labor for Europeans. Then, the nearly total absence of agricultural assistance from the administration guaranteed the
steady disintegration of the traditional African peasant economy, already shaken under the impact of both the slave
trade and its abolition. The root cause of this destruction
of the African economy was the official commitment to European settler plantations as the chief economic agents of development, and the consequent pressure from the settlers
for provision of an African labor force. Within a few years
after the arrival of the first settlers, the very question of
possibly allocating land, labor, and capital in different, possibly more efficient ways had lost all relevance in the reality
of Kenya Colony as it had developed.[37]

The Effect on Britons

Economic development in Kenya after 1895 brought some
direct benefits to Britain. By gaining certain access to Uganda
via a secure railway, the headwaters of the Nile were made
safe. Such safety was then considered absolutely vital for con-

trol of Egypt and thus for an open canal at Suez. This in turn was the essential precondition for safe passage to India for British trade. Control of Kenya also brought added influence and power for the imperial navy in the Indian Ocean. The protectorate succeeded in removing any need for imperial grants from the London treasury within two decades of its formal establishment. Great Britain could make explorations for, and experiments with, a variety of raw materials and foods she sought to develop—as a vital national interest—inside the boundaries of the British Empire. Eventually sizable exports of cotton, coffee, sisal, maize, and so on, did flow out of Kenya, and from Uganda through Kenya. Preference for British goods early made Kenya a special, although not exclusive, outlet for British manufactures. Altogether, the colony paid for its administration and its railway by exporting agricultural produce and, to a lesser degree, by importing British manufactures: just as the colonial authorities intended.

The process of development at every point was strongly influenced by policy decisions made earlier. The choice of settlement by Europeans powerfully influenced virtually every subsequent development decision, including the disposition of African land, labor, and income.

The European immigrant settlers continuously reinforced their predominant economic and political position: "East African colonists stand on principle that the white race is the only people which has proved its capacity to govern mixed races."[38] The colonists' dominance ensured them a monopoly of official expertise and legislative and executive assistance of all possible sorts. Their position as the captains of agricultural export production forced an administration that was rarely reluctant to adjust any differences over policy in the direction of the colonists' preferences, in practice, if not always in public rhetoric.[39]

The European settlers, as a class, more resembled a landed aristocracy than a capitalist entrepreneur group.[40] Their concern with secure leisure, conspicuous display, and a generally gentlemanly status outweighed any tendencies toward maximum reinvestment of surpluses whenever such reinvestment was not essential to the very continuity of the plantation.

The 1920s were years of rapidly increasing indebtedness among settlers.

The settlers' monopoly of official aid, as well as the consequent cheapness of African land and labor, permitted many of them to live in styles at least roughly approximating what they came to Kenya to enjoy. However, the evidence indicates that European settler farming could only barely survive, even when land, labor, and capital were furnished as cheaply and lavishly as was "normal" in the 1920s. Throughout its history, many Europeans quit the protectorate when their farming ventures failed. The underlying economic precariousness of the settlers' condition in the 1920s became obvious retrospectively, in the aftermath of the 1929 depression. By 1938, reviewing the entire evolution of economic development in Kenya, Professor Frankel concluded: "The real task which now faces Kenya is that of considering objectively whether the types of production it has fostered are best suited to the advancement of the country, and therefore of both the European and the non-European population."[41]

As of 1930, Europeans cultivated less than 10 percent of the White Highlands allotted exclusively to them.[42] Two recent studies of European agriculture have had to conclude that, as of the late 1920s, European agriculture was an inefficient, artificially protected, and, in strict accounting terms, even privately unprofitable use of resources.[43]

KENYA AND THE EMPIRE

Given Britain's evolving international economic position in the 1870–1914 period, her officials' decisions in Kenya conformed to a policy of acquiring and managing new overseas possessions so as at least to safeguard, and at best to advance, imperial economic objectives. These objectives included chiefly the protection of existing international economic relations, mainly those with India, and the speediest possible lessening of British dependence on extra-empire markets and sources of food and raw materials.

Acquired originally partly to achieve the first objective, Kenya was transformed by colonial officials to fulfill the second. In the process, African land, labor, and capital were

allocated to European settlers. British officials differed occasionally with settlers as to details of the procedure of allocation. However, the ultimate dependence of officials on the
private settlers to provide exports outweighed the reverse
dependence. The result was a fairly clear, fairly consistent
development program, which achieved some short-term successes in meeting immediate objectives.

The development program was not the only conceivable
course of action the British might have taken. It was, we
have tried to show, a rational process, given the level of
information, the dominant imperial class and race biases,
and the market conditions prevailing in the late nineteenth
and early twentieth centuries. The British officials in Kenya
were neither remarkably selfish nor unusually short-sighted.
While they may perhaps have underestimated the full consequences of importing European settlers, their decision to
allow European immigration was a careful, reasoned decision responding to the Imperial needs and circumstances
of the time. British policy in Kenya to 1930 grew from a
continued commitment to that decision.

The only real alternative might have been the development of peasant agriculture, possibly along the lines followed
in Uganda. This might have resulted, although not necessarily so, in economic conditions similar to those which came
to characterize Uganda. It is possible to argue that, had
Britain in, say, 1910, changed her basic policies in Kenya,
the African population might, in some ways, be better off
today.

However, it has not been the purpose of this study to cas-
tigate any policy makers for decisions they did not make.
Rather, it has been my purpose to investigate both the reasons for the decisions they did make and some of the major
consequences of those decisions. The British administrators
acted in a generally consistent way to further what they
deemed to be the economic interests of the British economy
and the European settlers. In this connection it is perhaps
useful to note that French economic policies in equatorial
Africa showed very similar patterns.[44]

At least until 1930, the economic interests of the African

population, we may conclude, were not advanced. But then, they never really entered into the decision-making process that determined Kenya's economic development.

In Kenya, the long-term economic costs of Britain's development policies became drastically evident later—in the depression of the 1930s, during World War II, and during the Mau Mau revolt.[45] Currently, they have much to do with the prospects for the future of the political economy of Kenya.

Reference Matter

Abbreviations

The following abbreviations are used in citing documents. See the Bibliography for full listings.

GB   Great Britain
GB *CP* CO   Great Britain, *Cabinet Papers,* Colonial Office
GB *CP* FO   Great Britain, *Cabinet Papers,* Foreign Office
GB CPK   Great Britain, Colony and Protectorate of Kenya Publications
GB EA   Great Britain, East Africa Protectorate Publications
GB *PP*   Great Britain, *Parliamentary Papers*

Notes

INTRODUCTION

1. J. B. Carson, *The Life-Story of a Kenya Chief, Kasina Ndoo* (London: Evans Brothers, 1958), p. 13.
2. O. Odinga, *Not Yet Uhuru*, p. xiv.
3. See Karl Marx, *Capital* (Moscow: Foreign Language Publishing House, 1959) 1: 765–74, and the collections of his works on colonialism in S. Avineri, ed., *Karl Marx on Colonialism and Modernisation* (Garden City, N.Y.: Doubleday, 1968); and Karl Marx and Friedrich Engels, *On Colonialism* (Moscow: Foreign Language Publishing House, n.d.). Following Marx, some key figures and some of their contributions to the evolving theory are: R. Hilferding, *Das Finanzkapital;* R. Luxemburg, *The Accumulation of Capital;* V. I. Lenin, *Imperialism, the Latest Stage of Capitalism;* M. Dobb, *Political Economy and Capitalism;* P. M. Sweezy, *The Theory of Capitalist Development;* and P. A. Baran, *The Political Economy of Growth.*
4. Marx, *Capital*, 1: 451.
5. This statement is consistent with the conclusions reached by the political historian who wrote the classic and definitive study of settler-official relations up to 1930: M. R. Dilley, *British Policy in Kenya Colony*, esp. pp. 275–79.

CHAPTER 1

1. J. A. Hobson, *Imperialism: A Study*, p. 18. Hobson presents a complete list of "new" empire territories on p. 17.
2. See A. P. Thornton, *The Imperial Idea and Its Enemies* (New York: St. Martin's, 1959), esp. pp. 57–122. For detailed studies of this subject, see also C. A. Bodelsen, *Studies in Mid-Victorian Imperialism;* B. Semmel, *Imperialism and Social Reform, 1895–1914;* and J. E. Tyler, *The Struggle for Imperial Unity, 1868–1895* (London: Green, 1938).
3. J. A. Hobson, *Imperialism*, pp. 38 ff. Hobson's theory concluded with an explanation of the new imperialism as a policy pushed on the government by a few private business interests who would benefit while the British economy as a whole suffered.
4. Cf. D. K. Fieldhouse, "Imperialism: An Historiographical Revision," *Economic History Review*, 2d ser., 14, no. 2 (1961): 187–209, and *The Colonial Empires*, p. 288. See also W. W. Rostow, *The Stages of Economic Growth* (Cambridge University Press, 1960), p. 110; R. E. Robinson and J. Gallagher, with A. Denny, *Africa and the Victorians*, p. 472; and M. B. Brown, *After Imperialism*, p. 94.
5. See the comprehensive discussion of this and related points in D. C. M. Platt, "Economic Factors in British Policy During the 'New

Imperialism,'" *Past and Present* 39 (April 1968): 120–38. The reality of the protectionist threat to Britain's international economic position as well as the increasingly damaging competition from Germany, the United States, and other countries has been adequately demonstrated elsewhere. See, for example, R. J. S. Hoffman, *Great Britain and the German Trade Rivalry, 1875–1914*, and D. H. Aldcroft, ed., *The Development of British Industry and Foreign Competition, 1875–1914*.

6. Certainly it would be an extremely difficult task–if at all possible–to estimate the parameters of the relevant cost curves of important industries affected directly and indirectly by imports from or exports to the new colonies. Yet final, formal proof of the smallness or insignificance of economic relations with these colonies is possible only in reference to these curves. By simply comparing aggregated trade data and not specifying any real or hypothesized underlying economic structure, or economic trends, for Britain after 1870, Fieldhouse does not solve the problem; he just ignores it.

7. See W. H. B. Court, *British Economic History: Documents, 1870–1914*, p. 83. Besides the industries here under consideration, Court includes only coal mining in the above description.

8. P. Deane and W. A. Cole, *British Economic Growth, 1688–1959*, p. 196.

9. J. H. Clapham, *An Economic History of Modern Britain* (Cambridge University Press, 1951), 3: 145, 169.

10. W. G. Hoffmann, *British Industry, 1700–1950*, p. 105.

11. Brown, *After Imperialism*, p. 94.

12. R. Nurkse, *Patterns of Trade and Development* (London: Oxford, 1961), pp. 18–19; see also J. A. Hobson, *Imperialism*, pp. 36–40.

13. W. Schlote, *British Overseas Trade from 1700 to the 1930's*, p. 162.

14. Ibid., pp. 164–65.

15. GB *PP*, "Memorandum on Government Action in Encouragement of Cotton-Growing in Crown Colonies," Cd. 5215, 1910, p. 3.

16. Schlote, *British Overseas Trade*, pp. 164–65.

17. Ibid.

18. GB, *Statistical Abstract for the Several British Overseas Dominions and Protectorates*, no. 54, pp. 406–07.

19. Deane and Cole, *British Economic Growth*, pp. 205–06.

20. Cf. John R. Meyer, "An Input-Output Approach to Evaluating the Influence of Exports on British Industrial Production in the Late Nineteenth Century," *Explorations in Entrepreneurial History* 8, no. 1 (October 1955). Meyer's input-output matrix is extremely crude and highly aggregated. However, his conclusion–that declining rates of growth in British exports helped cause the slowdown in British growth–only reinforces the point at issue: the importance of the empire as a commodity market.

21. Cf. J. Stamp, *The National Capital*, p. 236; Deane and Cole, *British Economic Growth*, p. 274.

22. Cf. R. J. S. Hoffman, *Great Britain and the German Trade Rivalry*, p. 119.

23. A useful summary of Britain's world trade position, which emphasizes the points at issue here, is given in D. H. Aldcroft, *British Industry and Foreign Competition*, pp. 11–36.

24. Given Britain's presumed preponderance in the financing, shipping, insurance, etc., of all aspects of the re-export trade, it is clear that the value of the commodities purchased for import (the debit item on current account) was less than the value of those same commodities when re-exported (the credit item). In addition, British citizens usually *owned* the colonial sources of the re-exportables. Thus, they in all likelihood repatriated considerable profits (a credit item) which offset, or exceeded, the capital exports needed to develop re-export production (the debit item on capital account).

25. GB, *Statistical Abstract for the United Kingdom*, nos. 32, 52, 64.

26. G. L. Wallace, "Statistical and Economic Outline," in P. Schidrowitz and T. R. Dawson, eds., *History of the Rubber Industry* (Cambridge: W. Heffer, 1952), pp. 328–29.

27. J. C. Lawrence, *The World's Struggle with Rubber, 1905–1931* (New York: Harper, 1931), p. 12.

28. R. Fyffe, "Rubber in Uganda: Retrospective and Prospective," in J. Torrey and A. S. Manders, eds., *The Rubber Industry*, pp. 46–50.

29. Investments were usually promoted by and made through the trading companies who had experience in that area and in the selling of such commodities in London. Average crude rubber prices, per pound, of imports into New York were:

1899–1900	64.9¢
1901–1902	49.4¢
1903–1904	68.2¢
1905–1906	61¢ to $1.50
1909–1910	72¢ to $3.06

See Lawrence, *World's Struggle with Rubber*, p. 12; also Audrey Donnithorne, *British Rubber Manufacturing: An Economic Study of Innovations* (London: G. Duckworth, 1958), p. 27.

30. GB, *Statistical Abstract for the Several British Overseas Dominions and Protectorates*, no. 54, pp. 83, 89.

31. The fact that concern for such security affected policy makers is clearly shown in GB *PP*, "Report of the Royal Commission on Supply of Food and Raw Material in Time of War," Cd. 2643, 1905, quoted in Court, *British Economic History*, pp. 188–94.

32. See corroborating conclusions drawn in GB *PP*, "Report of the Tariff Commission," vol. 1, "The Iron and Steel Trades," 1904, para. 46, in Court, *British Economic History*, p. 104. R. J. S. Hoffman also finds that colonial markets withstood foreign competition better than other markets and that British industrial leaders were very well aware of their special position in colonial trade (*Great Britain and the German Trade Rivalry*, pp. 198 ff.).

33. See the collection of essays in Aldcroft, *British Industry and Foreign Competition*, as follows: cotton, p. 127; woolens, p. 156; chemicals, pp. 295–98; shipping, pp. 328–29; engineering, p. 228; electrical machinery, pp. 258–68; and locomotives, pp. 199–200.

34. GB *CP* CO 273/304/23875, cited in R. V. Kubicek, *The Administration of Imperialism* (Durham, N.C.: Duke University Press, 1969), p. 123.

35. See V. Ponko, Jr., "Economic Management in a Free-Trade Empire," *Journal of Economic History* 26, no. 3 (September 1966): 363–77.

36. Cf. the statement of a French undersecretary of state for the colonies in 1891: "Since France must incur the obligations involved in a colonial domaine, it is just and proper that this domaine be reserved as a market for French products," quoted in Platt, "Economic Factors in British Policy," pp. 125–26. Or note the dramatic rise of Germany's exports to her East African territory as a proportion of the territory's total imports: from 27 percent in 1895 to 47 percent in 1909. See the elaboration of this point with further data in W. O. Henderson, "Germany's Trade with her Colonies, 1884–1914," *Economic History Review* 9, no. 1 (November 1938): 1–16. For further remarks on protectionism in non-British empires, see also Fieldhouse, *The Colonial Empires*, pp. 307, 345–46, 358, 371. For a clear statement by a high British official of the need to annex colonies to gain commercial advantages, see GB *PP*, Sir Gerald Portal, "Reports Relating to Uganda," C. 7303, 1894, pp. 31–32.

37. Cf. C. K. Hobson, *The Export of Capital*; A. K. Cairncross, *Home and Foreign Investment, 1870–1913*; A. H. Imlah, *Economic Elements in the Pax Britannica*; and Deane and Cole, *British Economic Growth*. An excellent summary statement is provided in L. H. Jenks, "British Experience with Foreign Investments," *Journal of Economic History*, supplement, December 1944, pp. 68–79.

38. H. Feis, *Europe, the World's Banker, 1870–1914*, p. 23. A higher estimate, 5 percent, is contained in Brown, *After Imperialism*, p. 110.

39. Fieldhouse, "Imperialism," pp. 197–99. For a similar argument, see W. L. Langer, "A Critique of Imperialism," *Foreign Affairs* 24 (1935): 103–07.

40. For a masterful survey of this topic, from which several points are here taken, see L. H. Jenks, *The Migration of British Capital to 1875*.

41. This is demonstrated in Jenks, *The Migration*, and, for the post-1875 period, in Feis, *Europe*. Feis summarized his research as follows: "In the lending countries international financial transactions were supervised in accord with calculations of national advantages, which were often unrelated to the direct financial inducement offered the owners of capital. People and governments exerted themselves to direct the capital to those purposes which were judged likely to strengthen the national state . . . or increase the chance of extended dominion. Capital was called upon to abstain from investment in the lands of potential enemies. It was urged or commanded into the service of allies" (p. 465). Of course, "calculations of national advantages" were significantly de-

termined by the nature of already implanted foreign investments made
by British citizens. At issue here is the linkage between capital movements and government policies, not the lines of causation.

42. Feis, *Europe*, p. 27. See also D. R. Adler, *British Investment in
American Railways* (Charlottesville: University Press of Virginia, 1970).

43. C. K. Hobson, *Export of Capital*, pp. 119 ff., 152 ff.

44. The construction was both rapid and unusually expensive. It
provided a very large amount of railway lines, which used almost exclusively British materials and capital and which had their earnings
guaranteed by the British government. See D. H. Buchanan, *The Development of Enterprise in India* (New York: Macmillan, 1934), pp.
152, 183.

45. Cf. Peter Temin, "The Relative Decline of the British Steel
Industry, 1880–1913," in H. Rosovsky, ed., *Industrialization in Two
Systems: Essays in Honor of Alexander Gerschenkron* (New York: Wiley,
1966), p. 142.

46. See, for example, P. Head, "Boots and Shoes," in Aldcroft, *British
Industry and Foreign Competition*, pp. 170–71.

47. The immense literature on why British businessmen responded
as they did is summarized in A. L. Levine, *Industrial Retardation in
Britain, 1880–1914*.

CHAPTER 2

1. K. Ingham, *A History of East Africa*, pp. 24–60.

2. Cf. J. M. Gray, "Zanzibar and the Coastal Belt, 1840–1884," in R.
Oliver and G. Mathew, eds., *History of East Africa*, 1: 219 ff. Investi-
gating the slave trade, a select committee of Parliament, active at the
time in East Africa, found that from one mainland port (Kilwa) alone,
nearly 100,000 slaves were exported between 1862 and 1867, according
to customs house records. See quotations from and discussion of report
of this select committee in E. Hutchinson, *The Slave Trade of East
Africa*, pp. 38, 50.

3. Besides slaves and ivory, exports of lesser importance from East
Africa included large quantities of cloves and sizable amounts of gum
copal, sesame and cowrie shells. Imports, until late in the century, comprised mainly cheap cotton cloth, chiefly cotton sheeting. An excellent
sourcebook on this trade is N. R. Bennett and G. E. Brooks, Jr., eds.,
New England Merchants in Africa. See also Z. Marsh and G. W. Kingsnorth, *An Introduction to the History of East Africa*, 3d ed., p. 33;
C. T. Brady, Jr., *Commerce and Conquest in East Africa*, pp. 115–26;
Gray, "Zanzibar," in Oliver and Mathew, *History*, 1: 219; and R. Coupland, *The Exploitation of East Africa, 1856–1890*, pp. 322 ff. In general,
the Arab trade made for a rich empire: cf. C. T. Wilson and R. W. Felkin,
Uganda and the Egyptian Sudan, 1: 189 ff.

4. Hutchinson, *Slave Trade*, p. 14.

5. The United States was the first to sign a commercial treaty with
the sultan in 1833, sending a consul in 1837. The British followed with

a treaty and consul in 1839 and 1840; the French in 1844; and the three Hanseatic Republics (Lübeck, Bremen and Hamburg) in 1859. The Portuguese had been dominant in East Africa during the sixteenth century until displaced by the Arabs.

6. The sultan levied a tax of $2.50 on each slave exported from the mainland plus another $2 for each slave landed in Zanzibar.

7. Coupland, *Exploitation*, p. 391; Gray, "Zanzibar," in Oliver and Mathew, *History*, 1: 218; and F. D. Lugard, *The Rise of Our East African Empire*, 1: 446.

8. Indian commercial development both stimulated and was stimulated by British policy in Zanzibar. See J. S. Mangat, "Aspects of 19th Century Indian Commerce in Zanzibar," *Journal of African and Asian Studies* 2, no. 1 (Autumn 1968): 17–27. For a broader discussion, see J. S. Mangat's *History of the Asians in East Africa, 1886–1945*, pp. 6–24.

9. See F. F. Müller, *Deutschland-Zanzibar-Ostafrika*, p. 85.

10. Cf. G. E. Hieke, *Zur Geschichte des deutschen Handels mit Ostafrika*, pt. 1, and also Brady, *Commerce*, pp. 117–26. British officials did, however, use their influence to try to stimulate the sale of British cloth, often with a "notable lack of success"; see the memoirs of an official, F. Jackson, *Early Days in East Africa*, pp. 177–79, and the discussion in Coupland, *Exploitation*, pp. 77 ff.

11. Cf. Müller, *Deutschland*, p. 77. Also, see D. and C. Livingstone, *Narrative of an Expedition to the Zambezi and its Tributaries;* D. Livingstone, *The Last Journals of David Livingstone in Central Africa,* comp. H. Waller; H. M. Stanley, *Through the Dark Continent;* J. H. Speke, *Journal of the Discovery of the Source of the Nile;* J. L. Krapf, *Travels, Researches and Missionary Labour in East Africa;* R. F. Burton, *The Lake Regions of Central Africa;* and J. Thomson, *To the Central African Lakes and Back.*

12. Hutchinson, *Slave Trade*, pp. 9 ff.

13. For early British economic interests, see J. Flint, "The Wider Background to Partition and Colonial Settlement," in Oliver and Mathew, *History*, 1: 355 ff. For descriptions of internal resources see Stanley, *Through the Dark Continent*, 1: 209 ff.; Burton, *The Lake Regions*, 1: 7; and the discussion in Coupland, *Exploitation*, pp. 129 ff. By 1870, Britons had £1.5 million sterling invested in the Zanzibar trade: see GB *CP*, History Section of the Foreign Office, "Peace Handbook no. 96: Kenya, Uganda, and Zanzibar," pp. 43–44.

14. In the 1840s and 1850s, however, the British had acted to constrain French activity. Cf. Ingham, *A History*, pp. 47–84.

15. The discussion following draws heavily on Kirk's private papers, as presented and analyzed by Coupland, *Exploitation*, passim.

16. Cf. N. Ascherson, *The King Incorporated: Leopold II in the Age of Trusts* (London: G. Allen & Unwin, 1963), pp. 105, 113 ff.

17. H. Brunschwig, *French Colonialism, 1871–1914*, trans. W. G. Brown, rev. ed. (London: Pall Mall Press, 1966), pp. 31–49. See also G. Revoil, *Voyage au Cap des Aromates* (Paris: 1880).

18. In fact, the original surge of interest in East Africa from British

businessmen and their government took place during the Napoleonic Wars, when it emerged as the result of a combination of urgent commercial interests and the anti–slave trade agitation. See M. V. Jackson, *European Powers and South-east Africa,* pp. 64–83.

19. See the excellent discussion in Müller, *Deutschland,* pp. 70–71; also, R. E. Robinson, J. Gallagher, with A. Denny, *Africa and the Victorians,* chap. 2. For specific references to British policy by region, see G. S. Graham, *Great Britain in the Indian Ocean,* esp. chap. 2, 4, 5, and 6. Graham well documents the steady development of the British economic position in the area alongside the very mixed impact of that position on the slave trade. However, he avoids comment on the degree to which British anti–slave trade efforts disguised British economic expansion. He prefers to touch lightly on the point in terms of French attitudes toward Britain: "Deeply suspicious of British humanitarian aims that appeared to cloak a voracious imperialism" (p. 95).

20. See M. J. de Kiewiet (Hemphill), "History of the Imperial British East Africa Company, 1876–1895" (Ph.D. diss., University of London, 1955), p. 11. There is also clear evidence that a major reason for the ineffectiveness of much earlier activity against the slave trade was Palmerston's fear that such measures might well undermine the sultan and open the way to French influence in Zanzibar. In fact, during the 1850s the sultan's power was threatened—until rescued by British military power—by a short-lived, overzealous antislavery campaign: see M. V. Jackson, *European Powers,* pp. 167–68.

21. See J. E. Flint, "Zanzibar, 1890–1950," in V. Harlow, E. M. Chilver, and A. Smith, eds., *History of East Africa,* 2: 647–49.

22. Dispatch from Kirk to Lord Salisbury at the Foreign Office, March 1880, quoted in Coupland, *Exploitation,* p. 373.

23. Cf. E. R. Turton, "Kirk and the Egyptian Invasion of East Africa in 1875: A Reassessment," *Journal of African History* 11, no. 3 (1970): 355–70. The author notes the coastal Arabs' view that British policy sought reduction in slave trading *and* establishment of a British occupation (p. 368).

24. Cf. de Kiewiet, "History," pp. 9 ff.

25. See evidence in H. von Wissmann, *My Second Journey Through Equatorial Africa,* pp. 184, 200–10. Also, A. Smith, "The Southern Section of the Interior, 1840–1884," in Oliver and Mathew, *History,* 1: 294–95; J. Lamphear, "The Kamba and the Northern Mrima Coast," in R. Gray and D. Birmingham, eds., *Pre-Colonial African Trade,* p. 91; A. Roberts, "Nyamwezi Trade," in R. Gray and D. Birmingham, eds., *Pre-Colonial Trade,* pp. 58–73; and K. M. Stahl, *History of the Chagga People,* p. 50.

26. Müller, *Deutschland,* p. 91.

27. Smith, "The Southern Section," in Oliver and Mathew, *History,* 1: 295.

28. Cf. de Kiewiet, "History," chap. 1.

29. Flint, "The Wider Background," in Oliver and Mathew, *History,* 1: 354. Flint notes that a key missionary group, the Church Missionary

Society, was controlled by influential laymen, not ecclesiastical authorities. Lugard observed, "it is quite possible that here . . . advantage may run parallel with duty" (*Rise of Our East African Empire*, 1: 381–82).

30. J. Thomson, "East Africa as It Was and Is," *Contemporary Review* 55 (January 1889): 43.

31. See N. R. Bennett's essays, "Mirambo of the Nyamwezi" and "Mwinye Mtwama and the Sultan of Zanzibar," in his *Studies in East African History*, pp. 1–30, 76–80; also his later *Mirambo of Tanzania, 1840–1884* (New York: Oxford University Press, 1971).

32. See Thomson, "East Africa," p. 44; and Gray, "Zanzibar," in Oliver and Mathew, *History*, 1: 241.

33. Thomson, "East Africa," p. 42. Kirk's objective had analogues in Britain's policy of developing strong states in West Africa likely to permit British commercial expansion: cf. Flint, "The Wider Background," in Oliver and Mathew, *History*, 1: 356.

34. See Mathew's biography: R. N. Lyne, *An Apostle of Empire*. For further evidence of Mathew's role as an agent of British policy, note the following remark by an official who knew him well: "He more than once paid all his men and kept them going when the Sultan would not, or could not do so" (F. Jackson, *Early Days*, p. 65).

35. Coupland, *Exploitation*, p. 372.

36. One group of officials argued against "implicating ourselves in matters over which we could exercise no real influence without an expenditure of money . . . out of all proportion to the advantages to be gained" (Coupland, *Exploitation*, p. 380).

37. Gladstone to Granville, 12 December 1884, in A. Ramm, ed., *The Political Correspondence of Mr. Gladstone and Lord Granville, 1876–1886* (Oxford: Clarendon Press, 1962), 2: 244–45.

38. Cf. Ingham, *A History*, pp. 134–35. A good summary of this episode emphasizing the view from London is in C. J. Lowe, *The Reluctant Imperialists*, 1: 121–46. On German colonialism in East Africa, see Müller, *Deutschland;* M. E. Townsend, *The Origins of Modern German Colonialism, 1871–1885* (New York: Columbia University Press, 1921); and W. O. Henderson, "German East Africa, 1884–1918," in Oliver and Mathew, *History*, 1: 122–62.

39. Cf. Coupland, *Exploitation*, p. 397, and Flint, "The Wider Background," in Oliver and Mathew, *History*, 1: 369.

40. "The establishment of the German protectorate brought to an abrupt end the British policy of controlling East Africa through Zanzibar" (Flint, "The Wider Background," in Oliver and Mathew, *History*, 1: 369).

41. Kirk was also worried lest Germany utilize "the trading capacities of our Indian subjects to advance and develop her commerce" (Kirk to Salisbury, 4 and 5 June 1886, quoted in Mangat, *A History*, pp. 25–26).

42. Cabinet note, Kimberley to Granville, 24 November 1884, quoted in A. J. P. Taylor, *Germany's First Bid for Colonies, 1884–1885* (London: Macmillan, 1938), p. 86.

43. For a full discussion, see A. Holmberg, *African Tribes and European Agencies*, pp. 324–70.

44. C. E. Foot, "Transport and Trading Centers for Eastern Equatorial Africa," *Journal of the Society of Arts* 28 (19 March 1880): 362. German documents offer parallel evidence of the inability of Europeans to compete with Arabs and Indians: cf. Müller, *Deutschland*, pp. 540–41.

45. Cf. the *Times* (London), 23 February 1893; Lugard, *Rise of Our East African Empire*, 1: 273 ff., 444, and 476.

46. This point is firmly established in R. Oliver, "Some Factors in the British Occupation of East Africa, 1884–1894," *Uganda Journal* 15, no. 1 (1951): 49–64; and R. Oliver, *The Missionary Factor in East Africa*, pp. 94–116. Modifying considerations are introduced in N. R. Bennett's introduction to A. J. Swann, *Fighting the Slave Hunters in Central Africa*, 2d ed. (London: Cass, 1969), pp. xxvi ff.

47. Cf. D. A. Low, "British East Africa: The Establishment of British Rule, 1895–1912," in Harlow, Chilver and Smith, pp. 7–8. See also Müller, *Deutschland*, pp. 371 ff.

48. Flint, "Zanzibar," in Harlow, Chilver, and Smith, *History*, 2: 642–43.

49. See P. L. McDermott, *British East Africa or IBEA*, and M. F. Hill, *Permanent Way*, p. 48.

50. A related point: in the late 1880s and 1890s, because human porterage had become too expensive for any sizable trade in the British sphere and, moreover, porters in the German sphere (the famous Wanyamwezi tribesmen) were relatively cheaper, only a railway offered IBEA and Britain the means to direct trade with the far interior through British-controlled territory. See Hill, *Permanent Way*, pp. 115–32; and also M. Perham and M. Bull, eds., *The Diaries of Lord Lugard*, 1: 30 ff.

51. Lugard, *Rise of Our East African Empire*, p. 445.

52. See C. E. B. Russell, ed., *General Rigby, Zanzibar and the Slave Trade*, esp. pp. 200–19. This was also true of British official behavior even after the formal abolition of slavery as a legal status in Zanzibar in 1887 (Flint, "Zanzibar," in Harlow, Chilver, and Smith, *History*, 2: 647–51). See also the similar observations and official attitudes expressed in C. W. Hobley, *Kenya*, pp. 35 ff. Hobley was an early British Protectorate official.

53. Flint, "Zanzibar," in Harlow, Chilver, and Smith, *History*, 2: 647.

54. Reverend H. Waller, "The Two Ends of the Slave Stick," *Contemporary Review* 55 (April 1889): 533.

55. Sir A. Hardinge to Salisbury, 12 April 1896, in GB *CP* FO 107/51. See also G. H. Mungeam, *British Rule in Kenya, 1895–1912*, pp. 25 ff.

56. See citations in footnote 11 above. See also Hutchinson, *Slave Trade*, passim and pp. 13–14, where the point is made that slave trading caused intertribal warfare and was not a matter of Arab merchants passively purchasing prisoners of intertribal warfare.

57. Cf. P. Collister, *The Last Days of Slavery*, pp. 1–11.

58. Lugard, *Rise of Our East African Empire*, p. 328, indicates the impressive sizes of agricultural sales by African tribes to caravans. See Roberts, "Nyamwezi Trade," in Gray and Birmingham, *Pre-Colonial Trade*, pp. 72 ff.; Stahl, *History of the Chagga*, pp. 50, 132. For evidence of general intertribal trading in the nineteenth century, see D. A. Low, "The Northern Interior, 1840–1894," in Oliver and Mathew, *History*, 1: 314–20.

59. Cf. B. Davidson, *The African Slave Trade*, p. 194.

60. Ibid., pp. 193–95; Müller, *Deutschland*, pp. 93–94; Smith, "The Southern Section," in Oliver and Mathew, *History*, 1: 294; and Coupland, *Exploitation*, p. 140.

61. Cf. Hobley, *Kenya*, p. 67.

CHAPTER 3

1. Commissioner Charles Eliot was the protectorate's second chief officer (1900–04). See his "Report on the Native Tribes in East Africa, 9 April 1902," GB *CP* FO 2/570.

2. GB *PP*, C. Eliot, "Report on the East African Protectorate for the Year 1902–03," Cd. 1626, 1903; and GB *PP*, C. Eliot, "Report on the East African Protectorate for the Year 1903–04," Cd. 2331, 1904.

3. GB *PP*, C. Eliot, "Report for 1902–03." See also Eliot's book, *The East Africa Protectorate*, pp. 309–10.

4. GB *PP*, "Report on the Uganda Protectorate for 1904," Cd. 2250, 1905.

5. Winston Churchill, *My African Journey*, pp. 209 ff.

6. GB *PP*, C. Eliot, "Report by H. M. Commissioner on the East Africa Protectorate," Cd. 769, 1901, p. 4.

7. GB, *Hansard Parliamentary Debates*, 4th ser., 118 (1903): 1199. See table 3.1.

8. See, for example, GB *PP*, "Correspondence relating to the Murder of Mr. Jenner, and the Ogaden Punitive Expedition," Cd. 591, 1901; GB *CP* CO, "Returns of Military Operations in the British East Africa Protectorate, 1902–1906," CO 534/5, 17 April 1907. See also G. H. Mungeam, *British Rule in Kenya, 1895–1912*, pp. 132–33. "Military" expenditures here do not include the sizable sums spent on police and prisons, which served closely allied functions.

9. Lansdowne to Eliot, 27 August 1901 (GB *CP* FO 2/443).

10. Sir Arthur Hardinge, commissioner from 1895 to 1900; Sir Donald Stewart, commissioner from 1904 to 1905; and Sir James Hayes Sadler, commissioner from 1905 to 1906. Then, as jurisdiction over the protectorate shifted from the Foreign Office to the Colonial Office in 1905, Sadler's title became governor from 1906 to 1909.

11. P. L. McDermott, *The British East Africa Company or IBEA*, p. 477.

12. See the remarks of the first commissioners of both the East Africa (Hardinge) and Uganda (H. H. Johnston) Protectorates: GB *PP*, "Report by Sir A. Hardinge on the Condition and Progress of the East Africa

Protectorate," C. 8683, 1897; and GB *PP*, "Report on the Uganda Protectorate," Cd. 671, 1901, p. 7. See also the general discussion in J. S.
Mangat, *A History of the Asians in East Africa, 1886–1945*, pp. 63 ff.

13. Eliot to Lansdowne, 6 September 1901 (GB *CP* FO 2/450).

14. Sir Clement Hill, marginal comments on Eliot letter of 25 February 1902 (GB *CP* FO 2/569).

15. *East African Standard*, 7 April 1906 and 12 May 1906. After
1901 Eliot began to change his mind, favoring European over Indian
settlement. This is seen in the proviso he added to his approval of
Indian settlers: their settlements, he wrote, should be kept "small."

16. GB *PP*, "Report of the Committee on Emigration from India to
the Crown Colonies and Protectorates," Cd. 5192, 1910, pt. 3, pp. 44–45.

17. See Eliot to Lansdowne, 5 January 1902 with enclosures (GB
CP FO 2/569).

18. Cf. Mangat, *A History*, p. 70. The earliest statement of Eliot's
favoring European colonization appears in his letter to the Foreign
Office of 15 May 1901 (GB *CP* FO 2/447).

19. M. P. K. Sorrenson, *Origins of European Settlement in Kenya*,
p. 67.

20. E. Huxley, *White Man's Country*, 1: 117. This is the definitive
two-volume biography of Lord Delamere, one of the earliest and the
richest British settlers in the protectorate.

21. J. Amery, *The Life of Joseph Chamberlain* (London: Macmillan,
1951), 4: 87; also see R. G. Weisbord, *African Zion*.

22. GB *PP*, "Correspondence Relating to the Resignation of Sir Charles
Eliot and to the concession of the East Africa Syndicate," Cd. 2099, 1904.

23. Sorrenson, *Origins*, pp. 86 ff.; and Huxley, *White Man's Country*,
1: 287.

24. J. Ainsworth, "The East Africa Protectorate and Development,"
East Africa Quarterly 4 (October-December 1906): 840. Ainsworth founded
the East Africa Agricultural and Horticulture Society, which published
this quarterly. See also, F. H. Goldsmith, *John Ainsworth, Pioneer Kenya
Administrator, 1864–1946*.

25. "Address of the Pastoralists Association," an enclosure in Sadler
to Lord Elgin [Colonial Secretary], 9 December 1907 (GB *CP* CO 533/33).
Sorrenson, *Origins*, presents a full and excellent discussion of this topic.

26. Stewart to Lansdowne, correspondence, October 1904 (GB *CP* CO
519/1).

27. Sir Clement Hill, minute of January 1904 on dispatch, Eliot to
Lansdowne, 19 December 1903 (GB *CP* FO 2/807).

28. W. D. Ellis [an official of the East Africa Department within
the Colonial Office], minute of 1 May 1908 on confidential dispatch,
Sadler to Elgin, 8 April 1908 (GB *CP* CO 533/43).

29. Sadler to Crewe [Colonial Office Secretary], confidential, 31 May
1908 (GB *CP* CO 533/44).

30. GB *PP* (Lords), "Papers relating to British East Africa," House
of Lords no. 158, 1907. This Committee was an unofficial body chaired
by Lord Delamere.

31. Churchill, *My African Journey,* p. 78.

32. GB *CP* CO, Kenya Land Commission, "Evidence and Memoranda," Colonial Office Paper no. 91, 1934, 2: 1595. "Alienation" was the term used to denote transferring ownership of land to Europeans through leasehold or freehold.

33. The misgivings (discussed further below) stemmed from the suspicions of several officials, e.g., W. M. Ross, C. W. Hobley, and N. Leys, that the settlers were clothing demands for official aid for their private efforts in the rhetoric of aid for the overall development of the protectorate. They feared the two objectives might be opposed.

The political aspects of the settlers' procurement of control over administration policy is not the focus here. This issue receives excellent treatment in M. R. Dilley, *British Policy in Kenya Colony,* 2d ed., esp. pt. 2, pp. 36–140.

34. Lord Hailey, *An African Survey,* 1st ed., p. 751.

35. GB *PP,* "Annual Report for the Colony and Protectorate of Kenya, 1919–1920." At first the majority of plots were designated for purchase. However, by local Ordinance no. 29 of 1922, these plots were redesignated as costless to the grantees (GB CPK, *Official Gazette,* 1922, p. 790).

36. GB Parliamentary *Debates* (Commons), 5th ser., 27 July 1925. One group of such settlers founded the British East Africa Disabled Officers Colony (BEADOC). Their specific project was to make rapid profits by growing flax in East Africa. London prices for the fiber were at extremely high levels right after World War I. Unfortunately, the recession of 1921–22 collapsed the flax market and also, therefore, the farms of most BEADOC members, despite financial assistance from protectorate authorities in addition to the grants of free lands (GB *PP,* "Report of the East Africa Commission," Cmd. 2387, p. 150).

37. GB EA, Department of Agriculture for British East Africa, "Annual Report for 1912–1913," pp. 1–2.

38. The five owners were: Lord Delamere, his brothers-in-law (the Coles), E. S. Grogan, the East Africa Syndicate, and the East Africa Estates, Ltd. The figures are compiled from local land office records (Sorrenson, *Origins,* pp. 130, 146).

39. See M. P. K. Sorrenson, "Kenya Land Policy," app. 1 in V. Harlow, E. M. Chilver, and A. Smith, eds., *History of East Africa,* 2: 672–89, and also Dilley, *British Policy,* pp. 36–140, and Sorrenson, *Origins,* passim.

40. The IBEA Company could appreciate these subtleties in view of the difficulties it had encountered during and after having negotiated the 87 treaties by which it had taken possession of land in East Africa.

41. Colonial Office to Foreign Office, 4 Sept. 1896, GB *CP* Foreign Office Confidential Print 6861, p. 212, quoted in Sorrenson, "Kenya Land Policy," in Harlow, Chilver and Smith, *History,* 2: 673 (italics added). At this time it was still an open question whether it would be Indians or Europeans who would be the main beneficiaries of land alienation by the authorities.

42. Foreign Office to Law Officers of the Crown, 18 Nov. 1899, in GB *CP* Foreign Office Confidential Print 7403, pp. 78–82, quoted in Sorrenson, "Kenya Land Policy," in Harlow, Chilver and Smith, *History,* 2: p. 675.

43. According to Lord Hindlip, a settler with extensive holdings, the dissatisfaction of Europeans with the land laws before 1902 was only partly assuaged by the acts of Commissioner Eliot in 1903. Hindlip's views are representative of the constant theme of the settlers' wishes and efforts regarding land policy (Lord Hindlip, *British East Africa,* pp. 80–90, and passim).

44. GB *PP,* "Report on the East Africa Protectorate for 1902–1903," Cd. 1626, 1903, pp. 29–30.

45. Cf. C. G. Rosberg, Jr. and J. Nottingham, *The Myth of "Mau Mau": Nationalism in Kenya,* passim. This has also been true in many other parts of Africa as well: cf. Lord Hailey, *An African Survey,* rev. ed., p. 686.

46. Cf. GB *CP* CO, Kenya Land Commission, "Evidence and Memoranda," passim. See also Dilley, *British Policy,* pp. 248–74; W. M. Ross, *Kenya from Within,* esp. pp. 41–68, 238–57.

47. See GB *CP* CO, G. W. B. Huntingford, "Nandi: Work and Culture," Colonial Office doc. DS 56987/1, mimeographed, 1950, pp. 13, 20–21. See also C. W. Hobley, *Kenya,* pp. 109 ff., 123 ff.

48. Huxley, *White Man's Country,* 1: 157; GB *PP,* "Report of the Kenya Land Commission," Cmd. 4556, 1934, pp. 271 ff.

49. Ross, *Kenya,* p. 81. The fate of a related tribe, the Kipsigis, reads like a variation on the Nandi theme. European settlements on their land occurred in 1906–07 and again in 1935–36. See R. A. Manners, "The Kipsigis: Change with Alacrity," in P. Bohanan, ed., *Markets in Africa* (New York: Doubleday, 1965), pp. 222–25.

50. GB *PP,* "Report of the Kenya Land Commission," pp. 101, 1929–31; and Sorrenson, *Origins,* pp. 176–80. Prior to British reorganization of their lands and people, the Kikuyu group comprised four major tribal units: the "Kikuyu proper," the Meru, the Chuka, and the Embu. Unless otherwise specified, references here to "the Kikuyu" are to the entire group.

51. Huxley, *White Man's Country,* 1: 111.

52. GB CPK, Department of Native Affairs, "Annual Report for 1925," pp. 30 ff.

53. Civil Case no. 626 of 1922 in GB CPK, "Kenya Law Reports," vol. 9, pt. 2, 1923. The 1915 Crown Lands Ordinance was tested and affirmed in this case.

54. See chiefly the work commissioned by the protectorate government (G. R. Sandford, *An Administrative and Political History of the Masai Reserve*). For the accounts of dissenting officials, see Ross, *Kenya,* pp. 130–44; Hobley, *Kenya,* pp. 45–86, 125 ff.

55. Sandford, *Administrative and Political History,* pp. 20, 24–26.

56. Sorrenson, *Origins,* pp. 197 ff., esp. 203–04.

57. GB *PP*, "Correspondence Relating to the Resignation of Sir Charles Eliot and to the Concession to the East Africa Syndicate," Cd. 2099, 1904, p. 26.

58. Despite the fact that these Africans paid head tax, their "villages" were not supplied with any sanitary equipment or facilities.

59. See GB CPK, "Annual Medical Report, 1927," p. 31, and *East African Standard*, 1 May 1915—both quoted in GB *CP* CO, Mary Parker, "Political and Social Aspects of the Development of Municipal Government in Kenya with Special Reference to Nairobi," Colonial Office doc. DH 65550/1, mimeographed, n.d., pp. 77–81.

CHAPTER 4

1. Federation of British Industries, *The Resources of the Empire*, ed. W. A. Maclaren, vol. 5, *Rubber, Tea and Cacao*, p. 17.

2. F. Parry, "The Capabilities of Eastern IBEA," *The Imperial and Asiatic Quarterly Review*, July 1893, pp. 1–16, reprinted as East Africa Pamphlet, no. 1 (see bibliography, primary sources).

3. *Report of the Sixth International Geographical Congress Held in London, 1895*, pp. 523–82.

4. G. S. Elliot, "Commercial Prospects of British Central and East Africa," *Journal of the Society of Arts* 44 (27 March 1896): 423–31.

5. Ibid., pp. 430–31. Elliot's commentators agreed explicitly on the fine prospects for Africa as an outlet for capital, population, and British exports, and as a new source for food and raw materials.

6. GB *PP*, "Report by Mr. A. Whyte on his Recent Travels Along the Sea-Coast Belt of the British East Africa Protectorate," Cd. 1534, 1903.

7. Ibid., p. 18.

8. GB *PP*, "Report on the Agricultural Prospects of the Plateaux of the Uganda Railway," Diplomatic and Consular Reports, Miscellaneous Series no. 577, Cd. 1787–13, 1902.

9. R. B. Buckley, "Colonization and Irrigation in the East Africa Protectorate," *Geographical Journal* 21 (April 1903): 349–75.

10. GB *PP*, C. Eliot, "Report on the East Africa Protectorate for 1902–1903," Cd. 1626, 1903.

11. F. D. Lugard, *The Rise of Our East African Empire*, 1: viii. Cf. Commissioner Eliot's remark: "there seems to be no reason why East Africa should not offer as favorable a ground for colonization as Australia or New Zealand" (GB *PP*, Eliot, "Report . . . 1902–03," p. 9.

12. In reality, the very richest immigrant settlers, possessed of "venture capital" and carrying on systematic experiments, had a disproportionate influence on agricultural activities in the protectorate. See E. Huxley, *White Man's Country*, vol. 1, passim, and esp. chaps. 7–9, pp. 135–209, for the experiences of the wealthiest planter, Lord Delamere. In another way, missionaries exerted some early influence on the choice of crops through their efforts to supply their own needs. The Scottish Mission in 1893 and the French Catholic Mission in 1895 experimented with coffee seeds supplied by the British India Company. No regular exports developed, but early coffee samples sent to London received very fa-

vorable appraisals by specialists: see W. J. Dawson, "The Importance
of Plant Introduction with Special Reference to the Highlands," *British
East Africa Agricultural Journal* 4, pt. 2 (January 1912): 106–09.

13. G. W. Evans, "Report," *East Africa Quarterly* 1, no. 2 (April–
June 1904): 64.

14. *East Africa Quarterly* 3, no. 9 (January–March 1906): 615.

15. J. Ainsworth, "Staple Products for East Africa," *East Africa
Quarterly* 3, no. 10 (April–June 1906): 685–89.

16. For example, according to the Land Regulations of 1897, certificates of occupation issued to settlers were subject to the provision
that at least 25 percent of the lands owned had to be planted within
the first five years to coffee, cocoa, cotton, indigo, rubber, or other
plants approved by the commissioner: see M. F. Hill, *Planters' Progress,*
p. 10. The settlers could safely ignore such provisions because the protectorate's facilities for inspection were simply too crude and too easy
to evade. In these early days, the scarcity of competent inspectors forced
the police to assume this responsibility. However, the policemen, "being
ignorant of farming . . . usually accepted what the farmer claimed to
have done and reported accordingly. It was often all rather farcical"
(W. R. Foran, *The Kenya Police, 1887–1960,* pp. 31–32).

17. Prices over the period 1892 to 1896 were the highest to date in
coffee history. They were not to be equalled again until the special circumstances of World War I: see W. H. Ukers, *All About Coffee,* p. 500.

18. The most notorious of the speculative maneuvers were those of
B. G. Arnold in New York during the 1870s and of D. J. Sully in New
York from 1901 to 1904. By its physical nature, coffee is relatively easy
to store for indefinite lengths of time. Indeed, the quality of coffee
is said to improve with aging. See Ukers, *Coffee,* pp. 404, 447.

19. U. S. Congress, Senate, *Production and Consumption of Coffee,*
57th Cong., 2d Sess., 1903, Doc. no. 35, esp. p. 62. This document
contains the complete reports and minutes of the entire series of
meetings.

20. Ibid., pp. 68–73.

21. See Ukers, *Coffee,* p. 404.

22. See L. E. Springett, *Quality Coffee* (New York: Van Rees, 1935),
esp. chap. 4, "Results from Artificial Price Raising," pp. 52–74.

23. GB *PP,* vol. 19 (1900), Board of Trade, "Statement on Tea and
Coffee," Trade Paper no. 351, 6 August 1900. British merchants and
officials frequently compared the deteriorating situation in coffee with
the bright story of tea. Indeed, the memorandum on which tables 4.4
and 4.5 (see pp. 74–75, above) are based offers a very telling comparison
of the two differing positions. United Kingdom tea imports, by geographic origin, were as follows:

Year	India, Ceylon, Hong Kong	Other	Total
1884	£4,400,000	£6,100,000	£10,500,000
1894	8,200,000	1,600,000	9,800,000
1904	8,200,000	1,200,000	9,400,000

United Kingdom tea re-exports, by geographic origin, were as follows:

Year	India	Ceylon	China	Other	Total
1894	£ 3,600,000	£ 5,200,000	£22,100,000	£1,100,000	£31,900,000
1904	13,200,000	14,100,000	12,100,000	2,700,000	42,100,000

24. Parry, "Eastern IBEA," pp. 1–16, esp. p. 10.

25. Hill, *Planters' Progress*, p. 6.

26. GB EA, Department of Agriculture for British East Africa, "Annual Report for 1909–1910," p. 15.

27. GB EA, Department of Agriculture for British East Africa, "Annual Report[s] for 1910–1911, 1912–1913 and 1914–1915."

28. GB CPK, "Report of the Proceedings of the Coffee Conference," 1922, esp. p. 4 (italics added).

29. Hill, *Planters' Progress*, pp. 68, 69. Coffee exports in the early 1920s were shipped mainly to the United Kingdom (70 percent), but the Coffee Planters Union was already searching for outlets in other markets.

30. F. C. Linfield, "Supplementary Memorandum," in GB *PP*, "Report of the East Africa Commission," Cmd. 2387, 1925, p. 192.

31. GB *PP*, "Report of the East Africa Commission," Cmd. 2387, 1925, pp. 20–21.

32. Colonial Office to Treasury, "Memorandum on the Relation between the British Cotton-Growing Association and Colonial Governments," Colonial Office Confidential Print, item no. 36466, 3 December 1909, in GB *CP* CO 879/105.

33. Elliot, "Commercial Prospects," passim. Elliot undertook his research in 1895–96.

34. J. Ainsworth, "East Africa and Agriculture," *East Africa Quarterly* 1, no. 1 (January–March 1904): 14–16. In 1905 the *East Africa Quarterly* reprinted an article entitled "Opportunities for Colonial Enterprise," from the *British Trade Review*, which said: "Time after time speculators in the United States have wrought untold havoc upon one of the greatest staple industries of this country . . . within a few years we may be able to do a great deal towards breaking the power of those who delight to 'corner' cotton and to spread dismay among the thousands of our Lancashire operatives" (*British Trade Review* 2, no. 6 [April–June 1905]: 359–60).

35. GB *PP*, "Agricultural Report on the District Between Voi and Kui in the East Africa Protectorate," Cd. 1953, 1904.

36. See the *East Africa Quarterly* 1, no. 2 (April–June 1904): 93.

37. Cotton exports from Uganda rose as follows:

Year	Value in £
1902–03	2
1903–04	6
1904–05	235
1905–06	1,089
1906–07	11,411
1907–08	49,696

See J. H. von Langnau, *Kolonization des britschen Protektorates Uganda* (Bern, 1921), pp. 20–22 and passim.

38. GB *PP*, "Report on the Possibilities of Cotton-growing in the East Africa Protectorate for 1904," Cd. 2406, 1906.

39. For example, government experimental farms distributed more cotton seed than any other kind of seed to European farms in 1905. See *East Africa Quarterly* 3, no. 9 (January–March 1906): 606–08.

40. J. E. Jones, "Native Cotton and Native Cultivation," *Agricultural Journal of British East Africa* 3, pt. 2 (July 1910): 146–50.

41. See, for example, the sentiments expressed by an elected representative of the settlers: he opposed allowing "the natives to be exploited in the interests of Lancashire" (*East African Standard*, 29 March 1924, quoted in N. Leys, *Kenya*, 2d ed., p. 380).

42. See H. Fearn, *An African Economy*, pp. 70–72, 102 ff.

43. In 1909 raw cotton exports from the East Africa Protectorate accounted for 4 percent of all domestic exports, their highest percentage in the period 1895–1935. In most years, cotton exports accounted for less than 1 percent of the protectorate's domestic exports.

44. Linfield, "Supplementary Memorandum," in GB *PP*, "Report of the East Africa Commission," Cmd. 2387, 1925, p. 192.

45. These were mainly Brazil and West Africa.

46. Elliot, "Commercial Prospects," p. 425.

47. GB *PP*, "Report by Mr. A. Whyte on his Recent Travels," Cd. 1534, 1903, pp. 18 ff. His remarks on Ceylon, quoted above, expressed his hopes for East Africa rubber.

48. Several purchases of land for rubber cultivation are noted in GB EA, Department of Agriculture for British East Africa, "Annual Report for 1909–1910," p. 18. See also J. Ainsworth, "Staple Products," p. 686.

49. GB EA, Department of Agriculture for British East Africa, "Annual Report for 1913–1914," pp. 20–21.

50. See, for example, the *East Africa Quarterly*, vol. 1, no. 2 (April–June 1904); vol. 1, no. 4 (October–December 1904).

51. *East Africa Quarterly* 3, no. 9 (January–March 1906): 615–16.

52. Ibid., table 4, p. 607.

53. J. Ainsworth, "Staple Products," p. 688.

54. G. Hewitt, "A Profitable Postwar Settlement Scheme," East Africa Pamphlet no. 43. Further fuel for London's fear of a United States "corner" was provided when a U.S. syndicate undertook experiments (ultimately unsuccessful) with wild sisal in the early years of the protectorate: see E. H. M. Leggett, "The Economic Development of British East Africa and Uganda," *Journal of the Royal Society of Arts* 63, no. 3246 (5 February 1915): 213 ff.

55. Planter (anonymous), "Importance of Kenya's Sisal Industry," *African World*, Supplement, 5 December 1925, p. vi, East Africa Pamphlet no. 96 (fol.).

56. Huxley, *White Man's Country*, 2: 32–33.

57. G. J. L. Burton, "Wheat Growing in Kenya Colony," in British

East Africa Department of Agriculture Bulletin no. 2, pp. 1–3. The same concerns stimulated stock raising in the protectorate. In this regard, flows of beef and mutton into the United Kingdom interrupted by the war were relevant.

58. Alex Holm, "Review of Agriculture in Kenya," in British East Africa Department of Agriculture Bulletin no. 9, p. 4. Of course, even in the case of maize, some concern was expressed regarding the ever necessary export trade: GB EA, Department of Agriculture for British East Africa, "Annual Report for 1913–1914," p. 19.

59. Edwin Wigglesworth and Co., "Notes on the Growing and Preparation of Flax for Fibre," pp. 2–3, East Africa Pamphlet no. 51.

60. Compare such rare comments to the contrary as, "The climate of the Coast stations may be summed up as on the whole not unhealthy for Europeans," in GB PP, "East Africa Protectorate Report for 1907–1908," Colonial Report no. 592, Cd. 4448–1, 1908, p. 24. See also the statement of the commissioner of lands: "Certainly the lowlands are by no means a white man's country, though, of course, *this class can reside there as planters*" (italics added) (GB PP, "Correspondence relating to the Tenure of Land in the East Africa Protectorate," Cd. 4117, 1908, p. 26).

61. Leggett, "Economic Development," p. 213.

62. See the "Minutes of the Executive Council," 17 March 1908 in GB CP CO 544/3. The Executive Council at this time included officials, the majority, and unofficials, who were appointed by and served the governor.

63. See GB PP, "Correspondence Relating to the Tenure of Land," pp. 6–7.

64. See, for example, GB PP, "Annual Report of the Veterinary Department for 1906–1907," Colonial Report, Miscellaneous no. 49, Cd. 3917, 1908.

65. See GB PP, E. H. Hills, "Report on the Survey Department, East Africa Protectorate," Colonial Report, Miscellaneous no. 44, Cd. 3794, 1907, pp. 4 ff.

66. These demands are listed in GB PP (Lords), "Papers relating to British East Africa," House of Lords Paper no. 158, 1907, pp. 30 ff. See also the similar kinds of demands in 1909 open letter to the *East African Standard*, 27 January 1909, "The Financial Position of the East Africa Protectorate," reprinted as East Africa Pamphlet no. 29.

67. GB CP Colonial Office Confidential Print, items no. 26817 and 32686, 18 August 1905, in CO 879/87. For special reasons, the company refused.

68. British East Africa Department of Agriculture, *Settler's Prospects*, 1905, app., p. 19, East Africa Pamphlet no. 22.

69. See the full discussion of early activities of these departments in R. A. Remole, "White Settlers" (Ph.D. diss., Harvard University, 1959), pp. 118 ff.

70. GB PP, "East Africa Protectorate, Report for 1907–1908," Colonial Report no. 592, Cd. 4448–1, 1908, p. 37.

71. The *East Africa Quarterly*, the *British East Africa Agriculture Journal*, and the Department of Agriculture Bulletins of the British East Africa Protectorate contain most of these—which are far too numerous to list separately.

72. Alex Holm [Director of Agriculture], "A Decade of Agricultural Progress in Kenya" Memorandum in GB *CP* CO, Kenya Land Commission, "Evidence and Memoranda," Colonial Office Paper no. 91, 1934, 3: 3064.

73. See the discussion of this precariousness by J. R. Schott in "The European Community of Kenya" (Ph.D. diss., 2 vols. Harvard University, 1964), pp. 68 ff.

CHAPTER 5

1. See, for example, J. Kenyatta, *Facing Mt. Kenya;* A. C. Hollis, *The Nandi;* G. W. B. Huntingford, *The Nandi of Kenya;* G. Lindblom, *The Akamba in British East Africa;* W. S. Routledge and K. Routledge, *With a Prehistoric People;* and G. Wagner, *The Bantu of North Kavirondo.*

2. Cf. F. D. Lugard, *The Rise of Our East African Empire,* 1: 471.

3. Kenyatta, *Facing Mt. Kenya,* pp. 53 ff.

4. See C. W. Hobley, *The Ethnology of A-Kamba and Other East African Tribes,* pp. 29 ff.; and also Kenyatta, *Facing Mt. Kenya,* pp. 70–90.

5. Cf. *East African Standard,* 10 March 1903. They comment on the excellent quality of Kikuyu stonemasons, noting their expert use of basic stonemasons' tools.

6. See H. Fearn, *An African Economy,* pp. 27–32; N. Leys, *Kenya,* p. 42; Kenyatta, *Facing Mt. Kenya,* p. 68; L. W. Hollingsworth, *The Asians of East Africa,* pp. 9–36; Huntingford, *Nandi of Kenya,* pp. 82–86; and F. Jackson, *Early Days in East Africa,* pp. 173–78, 328.

7. British officials concerned with the Railway noted repeatedly that the African population steadfastly refused to work for wages, even under the pressure of severe famine conditions in 1898–99. See GB *PP,* "Final Report of the Uganda Railway Committee," Cd. 2164, 1904, p. 11.

8. M. F. Hill, *Permanent Way,* p. 147.

9. Cf. the notion of "dual economy" in J. H. Boeke, *The Evolution of the Netherlands Indies Economy* (New York: Institute of Pacific Relations, 1946).

10. Speech in the House of Commons, 6 May 1898, quoted in L. C. A. Knowles, *The Economic Development of the British Overseas Empire,* 1: 178.

11. Response of R. Crawshay to R. B. Buckley, "Colonization and Irrigation in the East Africa Protectorate," *Geographical Journal,* April 1903, in East Africa Pamphlet no. 16, p. 31.

12. GB *PP,* "Report on Slavery and Free Labour in the British East Africa Protectorate," Cd. 1631, 1903, pp. 8–9.

13. J. Ainsworth, "The East Africa Protectorate and Development," *East Africa Quarterly* 4 (October–December 1906): 840.

14. S. Fichat to Sadler, 5 March 1908, printed in GB *PP*, "Correspondence Relating to Affairs in the East Africa Protectorate," Cd. 4122, 1908, p. 4 (hereafter cited as GB *PP*, "Correspondence").

15. See, for example, GB *PP*, "Report of the Commissioner of the East Africa Protectorate for the year 1903–04," Cd. 2331, 1904, p. 21; GB *PP*, "Reports Relating to the Administration of the East Africa Protectorate," no. 1, Cd. 2740, 1905, p. 20; GB EA, Department of Agriculture for British East Africa, "Annual Report[s]" for 1908–09, pp. 16–20, and for 1912–13, p. 3.

16. GB EA, Department of Agriculture for British East Africa, "Annual Report for 1908–1909," p. 20; Elgin to Sadler, March 1908, in "Correspondence Relating to the Tenure of Land in the East Africa Protectorate," Cd. 4117, 1908, p. 33.

17. W. D. Ellis, Minute of 1 May 1908, on Sadler to Elgin, Confidential Despatch, 8 April 1908, in GB *CP* CO 533/43. See chap. 3 above.

18. In April 1906, Indians at Mombasa held a mass rally to publicize their resolution demanding full rights for Indians to land in the Highlands. A deputation of Indians left to carry their case directly to the colonial secretary in London.

19. Lord Delamere, August 1907, letter quoted in E. Huxley, *White Man's Country*, 1: 206–07.

20. Ibid. Delamere also feared an Asian police force which, he asserted, would become so corrupt that irreparable damage would be done to the Africans' conceptions of authority—an extremely dangerous eventuality (p. 208).

21. East Africa Protectorate, "Minutes of the Executive Council," 13 February 1909, in GB *CP* CO 544/3.

22. Letter from "An Old Resident," *Agricultural Journal of British East Africa* 1, pt. 4 (January 1909): 369.

23. See the *East Africa Quarterly* 1, no. 4 (October–December 1904): 214 ff. Clear series of data on wage rates by region, age, skill level, and so on are unobtainable. It is necessary, rather, to compile partial and scattered references in the documents into "impressions" of levels and changes.

24. Ordinance no. 19 of 1903 made African adults other than hut-owners and their wives liable to poll tax. Ordinance no. 2 of 1910 exempted women from these taxes. See full discussion below.

25. Statement of Governor E. P. C. Girouard, *East African Standard*, 8 February 1913.

26. GB EA, Department of Agriculture for British East Africa, "Annual Report for 1907–1908," p. 13.

27. Ibid., p. 8.

28. GB EA, Department of Agriculture for British East Africa, "Annual Report for 1908–1909," pp. 19–20.

29. Article no. 45 of the East Africa Order in Council of 1897 allowed imposition of a hut tax on Africans of up to 2 rupees per year.

30. See the "Report of the Land Committee, 1905" in GB *PP* (Lords),

"Papers relating to British East Africa," House of Lords Paper no. 158, 1907.

31. See GB *PP*, "Correspondence," pp. 16, 20.

32. "Report of the Labour Inquiry Board," March 1908, quoted in W. M. Ross, *Kenya from Within*, p. 92.

33. C. W. Hobley, "Native Problems in Eastern Africa, Part One," *Journal of the African Society* 22, no. 87 (April 1923): 125.

34. *East African Standard*, 8 February 1913.

35. GB *PP*, "Correspondence," pp. 10–11.

36. See *East African Standard*, 25 March 1911.

37. An excellent summary of and quotations from the evidence presented appear in Ross, *Kenya*, pp. 92–98. A Scottish missionary, borrowing from experience in Nyasaland, offered a plan whereby an African who did not work would be taxed extra as a further incentive. See GB *PP*, "Correspondence," p. 13; and J. H. Harris, "Making the 'Lazy Nigger' Work," *Contemporary Review* 105 (June 1914): 819–25.

38. For an historical discussion of hut and poll taxes in the East Africa Protectorate, see the detailed study of G. Walsh and H. R. Montgomery, "Report on Native Taxation," 1936, pp. 4 ff. This was an officially commissioned and supported document.

39. Cf. "Report on the Pastoral and Agricultural Capabilities of the East Africa Protectorate," 1904, East Africa Pamphlet no. 21, p. 8; and GB *PP*, "Correspondence," passim.

40. Minute of Secretary Lobb, 17 July 1907, on Sadler to Elgin, 11 June 1907, quoted in G. Bennett, *Kenya*, p. 25. The Land Committee of 1905, a body of settlers, had strongly urged the government to direct its officers to press Africans to do wage work.

41. GB *PP*, "Report on the East Africa Protectorate for 1903–04," Cd. 2331, 1904, p. 21.

42. Minute by W. S. Churchill, n.d., on Elgin to Sadler, 5 March 1908, in GB *CP* CO 533/33.

43. See GB *PP*, "Correspondence," p. 10, and passim.

44. See GB *PP*, "Despatch to the Governor of the East Africa Protectorate Relating to Native Labour and Papers Connected Therewith," Cmd. 873, 1920, pp. 29–31.

45. Cf. Ross, *Kenya*, pp. 109–11; Huxley, *White Man's Country*, 2: 65; and G. G. Parker, "British Native Policy in Kenya and Uganda, 1885–1939" (Ph.D. diss., University of Wisconsin, 1948), pp. 390 ff.

46. Cf. Fearn, *African Economy*, pp. 51–52; and GB *PP*, "Correspondence," p. 31.

47. GB *PP*, Joint Parliamentary Committee on Closer Union in East Africa, "Minutes of Evidence," vol. 2, 1931, pp. 830–31 (House of Commons Paper no. 156, 1931).

48. C. W. Hobley and J. Ainsworth, Memorandum, October 1909, enclosed in Girouard to Colonial Office, "Confidential Interim Report," 13 November 1909, in GB *CP* CO 879/105.

49. Hobley, "Native Problems" p. 196.

50. Girouard to Colonial Secretary Crewe, "Confidential Enclosure," 26 May 1910, in GB *CP* CO 533/74.

51. H. R. Tate, "Native Tenants on European Farms," *Agricultural Journal of British East Africa* 1, pt. 4 (January 1909): 361.

52. GB *CP* CO, G. W. B. Huntingford, "Nandi: Work and Culture," Colonial Office doc. DS 56987/1, mimeographed, 1950, p. 73.

53. Account of a meeting between settlers and the governor, March 1908; see GB *PP*, "Correspondence," p. 9.

54. M. Parker, "Political and Social Aspects of the Development of Municipal Government in Kenya," in GB *CP* Colonial Office doc. DH 65550/1, mimeographed, n.d., p. 17.

55. R. R. Kuczynski, *Demographic Survey of the British Colonial Empire*, 2: 270. See also the general discussion in A. Beck, *A History of the British Medical Administration of East Africa, 1900–1950*, esp. pp. 107 ff.

56. GB EA, "Report of the Native Labour Commission," quoted in Kuczynski, *Demographic Survey*, 2: 195, 270. The Native Labour Commission concluded that the physical conditions of African wage laborers had deteriorated significantly compared with the previous conditions associated with slave labor.

57. GB EA, "Annual Report of the Principal Medical Officer, 1908–09," CO 544/1, 1909.

58. The figures on African population for this period are, of course, necessarily rough. Yet the best available information supports the fall in population up to 1924: cf. the data from medical authorities compiled in Beck, *British Medical Administration*, p. 219.

59. The general refusal of European employers to provide even the most minimal shelter, a blanket, to servants and laborers led finally to a legal requirement that employers provide at least one blanket to each: the Masters and Servants Ordinance of 1910 (see G. St. J. Orde-Browne, *The African Labourer*, pp. 149–53).

60. Leys, *Kenya*, p. 287.

61. For this and other information pertaining to mobilization in the years 1914 to 1918, I am indebted to the excellent and comprehensive research of D. C. Savage and J. F. Munro, "Carrier Corps Recruitment in the British East Africa Protectorate, 1914–1918," *Journal of African History* 7, no. 2 (1966): 313–42.

62. Cf. the testimony of a missionary that "all" men between 18 and 35 years of age were taken from Kikuyu villages for the Carrier Corps (GB EA, "Report of the Land Settlement Commission," 1919, p. 15).

63. Leys, *Kenya*, p. 287. He adds that official death figures exclude "many thousands who died after their return home, from diseases contracted in service."

64. Savage and Munro, "Carrier Corps Recruitment," esp. pp. 320 ff. Cases of over-supply of labor were often reported.

65. Ibid., pp. 330 ff.

CHAPTER 6

1. GB EA, "Report of the Land Settlement Commission," 1919, p. 8.

2. In June 1920 the East Africa Protectorate was raised by London to the full status of a colony, officially named the Colony and Protectorate of Kenya.

3. See the general discussion of this period in W. M. Ross, *Kenya from Within,* pp. 183–237.

4. Statement of Major Grogan, a leading political figure among the European settlers, quoted in Ross, *Kenya,* p. 198.

5. See GB CPK, "Report of the Native Labour Commission," 1921. The alternative would have been to leave most such activities in the hands of private recruiters.

6. The South African Native Affairs Commission of 1903–05 had decided on particular methods of estimation as a result of its research. The Kenya Native Labour Commission evidently agreed that conditions were sufficiently similar to warrant use of the South African methods with only minor modifications. The Commission's estimates relate to farm labor supplies only and exclude the other kinds of labor performed by Africans. Thus, for example, in 1920 roughly 57,000 Africans worked as agricultural laborers, 18,000 in government, 12,000 as domestic servants and nearly 5,000 in assorted other capacities. In table 6.3, estimates prepared by the Native Affairs Department present comparable statistics on the labor supply as a whole.

7. The Commission's reasons for taking this position are not altogether explicit or clear. Perhaps it felt that Africans *had* to be present in the reserves half of each year to do minimum chores for the survival of the family, village, or tribal unit. Perhaps the need to pay taxes and buy desired goods required only six months' wages on the average. There are also other possible explanations.

8. The Commission made specific recommendations of measures to effect this increase, which are discussed below.

9. See GB CPK, Department of Native Affairs, "Annual Report[s]" for 1926 and 1927.

10. Cf. M. R. Dilley, *British Policy in Kenya Colony,* p. 235: "It is doubtful that it is in the interests of general native welfare for so large a proportion of the adult males to be away from their villages."

11. For example, the GB CPK, Department of Agriculture, "Annual Report for 1932" indicates that the Kenya squatter population was nearly 111,000, including families of the workers. A figure of 112,000 squatter population in 1928 is quoted by Dilley (*British Policy,* p. 235). Daily labor arrangements frequently specified the coffee berry picking season on European farms. Many Africans, particularly women and children, did this picking. For the period January to July 1927, the "Agricultural Census Report for 1927" showed 20,230 women and juveniles doing regular agricultural wage labor. See GB CPK, Department of Native Affairs, "Annual Report for 1927," p. 91.

12. See G. Walsh and H. R. Montgomery, *Report on Native Taxation,* pp. 4–9. This was an officially commissioned report.

13. An effort by the administration to impose an income tax on "non-natives" in 1920–21 was defeated by the resolute opposition of the European settler community (see Ross, *Kenya,* pp. 154–58).

14. Taken from remarks made by the Under Secretary for the Colonies in the House of Commons, 12 June 1923, quoted in Ross, *Kenya,* p. 163.

15. Ibid., p. 150.

16. See the discussion of this and other relevant sources on proportionate sizes of taxes on Africans in M. Salvadori, *La Colonisation Europeene au Kenya,* pp. 200–03. See also the discussion of labor contracts and wages in GB CPK, Department of Lands, "Land and Land Conditions in the Colony and Protectorate of Kenya," p. 11. There are some higher estimates of both family earnings and taxes paid; poor statistics prevent any great precision.

17. An African working regularly throughout the year could pocket 200 s., but only a small minority of the African labor force fell into this pattern.

18. This is also a final conclusion of the work of G. G. Parker, "British Native Policy in Kenya and Uganda, 1885–1939" (Ph.D. diss., University of Wisconsin, 1948), p. 430.

19. Cf. O. Odinga, *Not Yet Uhuru,* p. 24; G. Bennett, *Kenya,* pp. 44–46; and C. G. Rosberg, Jr., and J. Nottingham, *The Myth of "Mau Mau,"* pp. 44 ff. The opposition movements among African workers at this time marked a crucial step in the gradual formation of a strong anti-colonialist force in Kenya. However, the impact of these movements on Kenya's economic development is best studied in the period after 1930. For this reason, and because there is considerable published material available on early African political stirrings, discussion of these movements is not included in this study.

20. Cf. GB *PP,* "Report of the East African Commission," Cmd. 2387, 1925, p. 174.

21. GB *PP,* Joint Parliamentary Committee on Closer Union in East Africa, "Minutes of Evidence," vol. 2, 1931, pp. 849–50 (House of Commons Paper no. 156, 1931).

22. Cf. the previously mentioned practice of protectorate statisticians in the early 1920s who deducted 2.5 percent from the total of potential adult males ready to work to account for those engaged in trading activities.

23. G. V. Maxwell, *Memorandum on Native Progress,* East Africa Pamphlet no. 13, pp. 2 ff.

24. See the documents published in GB *PP,* "Compulsory Labour for Government Purposes," Cmd. 2464, 1925, pp. 18 ff.

25. GB EA, "Report of the Land Settlement Commission," 1919, pp. 8–9.

26. See GB *PP,* "Despatch to the Governor of the East Africa Protectorate Relating to Native Labour and Papers Connected Therewith,"

Cmd. 873, 1920. This Parliamentary Paper published both circulars and other related documents (hereafter cited as GB *PP*, "Despatch").

27. See the Bishops' Memorandum in GB *PP*, "Despatch"; and J. H. Harris, "Back to Slavery," *Contemporary Review* 120 (July–December 1921): 190–97.

28. See GB *PP*, "Despatch."

29. Cf. G. G. Parker, "British Native Policy," pp. 383–428.

30. GB *PP*, "Despatch," p. 10.

31. Ibid.

32. Cf. S. and K. Aaronovitch, *Crisis in Kenya*, pp. 100–01; Odinga, *Not Yet Uhuru*, pp. 23, 27.

33. Odinga, *Not Yet Uhuru*, pp. 20–21. The British tended to appoint interpreters because of the ease of communication.

34. Cf. H. Fearn, *An African Economy*, p. 51.

35. See the summary discussion of the relevant laws in G. St. J. Orde-Browne, *The African Labourer*, pp. 147–53.

36. See GB *PP*, "Despatch."

37. See Milner to Governor Northey, 22 July 1920, in GB *PP*, "Despatch."

38. The relevant regulations were embodied in three Resident Native Ordinances passed in 1918, 1924 and 1925.

39. See the testimony of Chief Koinange in GB *PP*, Joint Parliamentary Committee on Closer Union in East Africa, "Minutes of Evidence," vol. 2, 1931, pp. 401–02 (House of Commons Paper no. 156, 1931). There is some evidence that the size of the land parcels granted to squatters for cultivation began to exceed the size of land shares within the reserves during the 1920s. See GB *CP* CO, G. St. J. Orde-Browne, "Labour Conditions in East Africa," Colonial Office Paper no. 193, 1946, pp. 82–83.

40. See S. H. Fazan, "Memorandum: Economic Survey of Kikuyu," in GB *CP* CO, Kenya Land Commission, "Evidence," Colonial Office Paper no. 91, vol. 1, 1934, p. 976.

41. See GB *CP* CO, G. W. B. Huntingford, "Nandi: Work and Culture," Colonial Office doc. 56987/1, mimeographed, 1950, pp. 73–76.

42. GB *CP* CO, Orde-Browne, "Labour Conditions," pp. 82–83.

43. See GB CPK, Department of Agriculture, "Annual Report, 1932"; and Salvadori, *La Colonisation*, p. 183.

44. GB CPK, Department of Lands, "Land and Land Conditions in the Colony and Protectorate of Kenya," 1926, p. 11.

45. Salvadori, *La Colonisation*, p. 184.

46. See L. P. Mair, *Native Policies in Africa* (London: Routledge, 1936), p. 90.

47. GB *CP* CO, Orde-Browne, "Labour Conditions," pp. 82–83.

48. GB *CP* CO, Huntingford, "Nandi: Work and Culture," pp. 73–76.

49. Fazan, "Memorandum," in GB *CP* CO, Kenya Land Commission, "Evidence," 1: 1011; see also Mair, *Native Policies*, p. 91; and N. Leys, *A Last Chance in Kenya*, p. 94.

50. "Proceedings of the Tukuyu Conference," *East Africa* 2, no. 64 (10 December 1925): 245. East Africa Pamphlet no. 98 (fol.).

51. Ross, *Kenya*, pp. 225–26.

52. GB *PP*, "Report of the East Africa Commission," Cmd. 2387, 1925, p. 41.

53. A. Holm, "Review of Agriculture in Kenya," in British East Africa Department of Agriculture Bulletin no. 9, pp. 4–5.

54. J. H. Oldham, "Kenya and its Problems," *Times* (London), 10 June 1926, in East Africa Pamphlet no. 108 (fol.), p. 17.

55. Cf. table 6.1. The mention there that 1925 and 1926 were years of insufficient supply is based solely on the evidence of European employers, who were at that time anxious about government competition for labor to construct the Uasin Gishu railway extension. Their evidence therefore was likely to be biased.

56. T. Sleith, *Report on Trade Conditions in British East Africa, Uganda and Zanzibar* (Cape Town: Union of South Africa Department of Mines and Industries, 1919) (italics added). Note that it is an observer familiar with South African conditions who makes such a remark.

57. See GB *PP*, "Tours in the Native Reserves and Native Development in Kenya," Cmd. 2573, 1926.

58. GB CPK, "Report of the Labour Bureau Commission," 1921, p. 4.

59. GB CPK, "Annual Medical Report for 1922," pp. 21, 63. Ibid., 1932, p. 33.

60. N. Leys, *Kenya*, p. 286.

61. GB CPK, "Annual Medical Report for 1932," p. 33.

62. Cf. GB *PP*, "Report of the East Africa Commission," Cmd. 2387, 1925, pp. 46, 50–61.

63. See A. Beck, *A History of the British Medical Administration of East Africa, 1900–1950*, pp. 26–27 and 198–208. The available evidence also suggests that individual European settlers rarely if ever expended their own funds to provide adequate housing, sanitary, or medical care facilities.

CHAPTER 7

1. L. C. A. Knowles, *The Economic Development of the British Overseas Empire*, vol. 1, passim.

2. Ibid., p. 42. Cf. also G. J. L. Burton, "Wheat Growing in Kenya Colony," in British East Africa Department of Agriculture Bulletin no. 2, pp. 2–3.

3. Knowles, *Economic Development*, pp. 42 ff.

4. The Federation of British Industries sponsored a major research project which culminated in the ten-volume series, *The Resources of the Empire*. Most volumes carried an introduction by H. R. H. the Prince of Wales. Comprehensive topical studies carried the following titles: Crops and Fruits; Meat, Fish, and Dairy; Timber and Timber Products, including Paper-Making Materials; Textile Fibers and Yarns; Fuel; Rubber, Tea, and Cacao, with Special Sections on Coffee, Spices,

and Tobacco; Leather, Hides, Skins, and Tanning Materials; Chemicals; Ferrous Metals; Non-Ferrous Metals and Other Minerals; Oils, Fats, Waxes, and Resins; and Communications.

5. Knowles, *Economic Development*, pp. 159-60, 204.

6. Ibid., p. 127.

7. Knowles, *Economic Development*, p. 138.

8. GB, *Parliamentary Debates*, 4th ser., vol. 30 (1895): columns 698-701.

9. By contrast, British officials in Uganda found and finally fixed on a third alternative: African peasant cash-crop agriculture, chiefly cotton. The geographic position of Uganda in the interior of the continent greatly reduced the economically damaging effects of the slave trade and its abolition. Furthermore, the relatively strictly structured and "stable" Buganda Kingdom offered the attractive possibility of organizing African peasant agricultural production managed at middle and lower levels by Africans already accustomed to workable hierarchical relationships. After some unsuccessful experiments with European settlers, the British opted for this possibility. Cf. C. C. Wrigley, "The Christian Revolution in Buganda," *Comparative Studies in Society and History* 2 (1959): 33-48.

10. European farmers also supported settler immigration, generally on the assumption that more Europeans, particularly Britons, lessened the chance that worldwide imperial interests might lead London to arrangements detrimental to white farmers in the protectorate.

11. See GB *PP*, "Report of the East Africa Commission," Cmd. 2387, 1925, pp. 80-94, 156. See also GB *CP* CO, "Report of the Commission Appointed to Enquire into and Report on the Financial Position and System of Taxation of Kenya," Colonial Office Paper no. 116, 1936, p. 133. (The report of this commission, chaired by Sir Allen Pim, will hereafter be referred to as GB *CP* CO, "Pim Report"). This report describes the period 1923 to 1929 in the following terms: "Up to this time practically nothing had been done by the Department [of Agriculture] for Native agriculture."

12. GB *CP* CO, "Pim Report," pp. 215-15, and app. 9, p. 260B.

13. W. S. Churchill, *My African Journey*, p. 65.

14. D. K. Fieldhouse, *The Colonial Empires*, p. 289.

15. Cf. remarks by J. Ainsworth in *Journal of the Manchester Geographical Society*, 1900, East Africa Pamphlet no. 9, p. 192.

16. Cf. *East Africa Quarterly* 1 (January-March 1904): 30-32.

17. See GB *PP*, "Agricultural Report on the District Between Voi and Kui in the East Africa Protectorate," Cd. 1953, 1904.

18. Cf. "Report of the Malindi Cotton Farm," *East Africa Quarterly* 2 (April-June 1905): 360-63.

19. J. E. Jones, "Native Cotton and Native Cultivation," *Agricultural Journal of British East Africa* 3, pt. 2 (July 1910): 146-50.

20. GB EA, Economic Commission, "Final Report: Part 1," 1919, p. 19.

21. *Proceedings of the Tukuyu Conference, 1925, East Africa* 2, no. 64 (10 December 1925), East Africa Pamphlet no. 98 (fol.), pp. 245-46.

22. GB *PP*, "Report of the East Africa Commission," Cmd. 2387, 1925, pp. 34, 36, 153.

23. Ibid., pp. 72–74.

24. S. H. Fazan, "Memorandum on the Kikuyu," in GB *CP* CO, Kenya Land Commission, "Evidence and Memoranda," vol. 1, 1934, p. 988 (italics added).

25. N. Leys, *Last Chance in Kenya*, p. 61.

26. Cf. J. R. Schott, "The European Community of Kenya" (Ph.D. diss., Harvard University, 1964). See esp. p. 166: "Prior to World War Two, the development of the African sector of the economy received virtually no assistance from the British Government."

27. Fazan, "Memorandum," p. 1012.

28. Leys, *Last Chance*, p. 95.

29. Cited in T. R. Batten, *Problems of African Development, Part 2*, 3d ed., rev. (London: Oxford University Press, 1960), p. 17.

30. A. Holm, "Memorandum," in GB *CP* CO, Kenya Land Commission, "Evidence," vol. 3, 1934, p. 3067.

31. H. Fearn, *An African Economy*, pp. 69, 72, 74, 209, 231–32, 234.

32. See M. Yoshida and D. G. R. Belshaw, "The Introduction of the Trade Licensing System for Primary Products in East Africa, 1900–1939," mimeographed, Conference Paper no. 336 (Kampala, Uganda: Makerere Institute for Social Research, 1965).

33. Cf. Fearn, *African Economy*, p. 232.

34. GB CPK, Department of Agriculture, "Annual Report for 1935," p. 95; see also Fearn, *African Economy*, pp. 76, 156; and Leys, *Last Chance*, p. 63.

35. See GB *CP* CO, "Pim Report," pp. 129–30.

36. Fearn, *African Economy*, pp. 76 ff.

37. The criterion of efficiency as used here can be considered as the minimal conception of achieving maximum output, given factor inputs and the level of technological knowledge available to persons in Kenya.

38. Cablegram by Lord Delamere, 1930, quoted in E. Huxley, *White Man's Country*, 2: 279.

39. See the excellent study on just this point by M. R. Dilley, *British Policy in Kenya Colony*, 2d ed., passim.

40. Cf. M. A. Buxton, *Kenya Days;* and W. R. Foran, *A Cuckoo in Kenya*.

41. S. H. Frankel, *Capital Investment in Africa*, p. 269.

42. Lord Hailey, *An African Survey*, p. 750.

43. Cf. Schott, "European Community," pp. 86 ff.; see also C. C. Wrigley, "Kenya: The Pattern of Economic Life, 1902–1945," in V. Harlow, E. M. Chilver, and A. Smith, eds., *History of East Africa*, 2: 209–64.

44. See the suggestive summary in R. Dumont, *False Start in Africa*, trans. P. N. Ott, 2d ed. rev. (New York: Praeger, 1969), pp. 37 ff.

45. Cf. D. L. Barnett and K. Njama, *Mau Mau From Within*.

Bibliography

DOCUMENTS

Statistical Series

GB. *Statistical Abstract for the United Kingdom.*
GB. *Statistical Abstract for the Several Colonies and Other Possessions of the United Kingdom.* (Title varies.)
GB *CP* CO. "Annual Blue Book." Colonial Office, CO 543.

The three items listed above were annual, official publications covering part or all of the period under review, 1870–1930.

Parliamentary Papers

A. REPORTS ON THE EAST AFRICA PROTECTORATE

GB *PP.* "Report by Sir A. Hardinge on the Condition and Progress of the East Africa Protectorate from Its Establishment to the 20th July 1897." C. 8683. 1897.
———. "Report by Sir A. Hardinge on the British East Africa Protectorate for the Year 1897–98." C. 9125. 1899.
———. "Report by H.M. Commissioner on the East Africa Protectorate." Cd. 769. 1901.
———. "Report on the East Africa Protectorate for the Year 1902–03." Cd. 1626. 1903.
———. "Report of the Commissioner of the East Africa Protectorate for the Year 1903–04." Cd. 2331. 1904.
———. "Reports Relating to the Administration of the East Africa Protectorate." Cd. 2740. 1905.

Among many reports, those listed above were the most useful. These early reports, issued while the Foreign Office controlled the Protectorate, were general compendia of whatever information colonial officials could gather. After 1905 the Colonial Office issued annual reports, of which the following two were of special importance.

GB *PP.* "East Africa Protectorate, Report for 1907–08." Colonial Report no. 592. Cd. 4448–1. 1908.
———. "Annual Report for the Colony and Protectorate of Kenya, 1919–20."

B. PAPERS ON SPECIAL TOPICS

GB *PP.* Sir G. Portal. "Reports Relating to Uganda." C. 7303. 1894.
———. Board of Trade. "Statement on Tea and Coffee." Trade Paper no. 351. 1900.

———. "Correspondence Relating to the Murder of Mr. Jenner, and the Ogaden Punitive Expedition." Cd. 591. 1901.

———. "Report on the Agricultural Prospects of the Plateaux of the Uganda Railway." Diplomatic and Consular Reports Miscellaneous Series no. 577. Cd. 1787–13. 1902.

———. "Report by Mr. A. Whyte on his Recent Travels Along the Sea-Coast Belt of the British East Africa Protectorate." Cd. 1534. 1903.

———. "Report on Slavery and Free Labour in the British East Africa Protectorate." Cd. 1631. 1903.

———. "Agricultural Report on the District Between Voi and Kui in the East Africa Protectorate." Cd. 1953. 1904. This document offers considerable information on the kinds of questions and expectations current among officials and private interests concerned with the economic future of the Protectorate.

———. "Correspondence Relating to the Resignation of Sir Charles Eliot and to the Concession to the East Africa Syndicate." Cd. 2099. 1904.

———. "Final Report of the Uganda Railway Committee." Cd. 2164. 1904.

———. "Reports from the Director of Agriculture on the Government Farms at Nairobi and Naivasha in the East Africa Protectorate for the year 1904, and on the Prospects of Settlers." Cd. 2410. 1905.

———. "Report on the Uganda Protectorate for 1904." Cd. 2250. 1905.

———. Board of Trade. "Memorandum on Coffee and Tea." 1905.

———. "Report on the Possibilities of Cotton-Growing in the East Africa Protectorate for 1904." Cd. 2406. 1906.

———. (Lords). "Papers Relating to British East Africa." House of Lords Paper no. 158. 1907.

———. "Report on the Survey Department, East Africa Protectorate." Colonial Report, Miscellaneous no. 44. Cd. 3794. 1907.

———. "Annual Report of the Veterinary Department for 1906–1907." Colonial Report, Miscellaneous no. 49. Cd. 3917. 1908.

———. "Correspondence Relating to Affairs in the East Africa Protectorate." Cd. 4122. 1908. This collection of documents provides detailed insights into the tensions between European settlers and British officials around the issue of implementation of the Protectorate's economic policies.

———. "Correspondence Relating to the Tenure of Land in the East Africa Protectorate." Cd. 4117. 1908. This collection of documents provides some early examples of the resolution of tensions between settlers and officials in favor of the former.

———. "Report of the Committee on Emigration from India to the Crown Colonies and Protectorates." Part I, The Report; Part II, Minutes of Evidence; Part III, Papers Laid before the Committee. Cd. 5192, 5193, and 5194. 1910.

———. "Memorandum on Government Action in Encouragement of Cotton-Growing in Crown Colonies." Cd. 5215. 1910.

———. "Correspondence Relating to the Masai." Cd. 5584. 1911.

———. "Despatch to the Governor of the East Africa Protectorate Re-

lating to Native Labour and Papers Connected Therewith." Cmd.
873. 1920.
———. "Compulsory Labour for Government Purposes." Cmd. 2464. 1925.
———. "Report of the East Africa Commission." Cmd. 2387. 1925. This
comprehensive survey of the general state of the area in 1925 provides as well examples of attitudes and expectations among Europeans developing the protectorate economy at that time.
———. Joint Parliamentary Committee on Closer Union in East Africa.
3 vols. House of Commons Paper no. 156, and House of Lords Paper
no. 184. 1931.
———. "Report of the Kenya Land Commission." Cmd. 4556. 1934.

Generally, parliamentary papers were prepared by the current government and hence reflected that government's selectivity in choosing
which facts to make public. However, these papers contain a vast
amount of invaluable information.

Cabinet Papers

A. FOREIGN OFFICE

In the Foreign Office Archives, located at the Public Record Office,
London, are the following items of special interest.

GB *CP*. Series FO 107. These documents contain all correspondence
between the Foreign Office and its chief agents in Zanzibar, who,
until 1898, also supervised affairs in the East Africa Protectorate.
———. Series FO 2. These documents contain the official correspondence
after 1898 until the transfer of responsibility for the protectorate to
the Colonial Office in April 1905.
———. Charles Eliot. "Report on the Native Tribes in East Africa, April
9, 1902." FO 2/570.
———. History Section of the Foreign Office, "Peace Handbook No. 96:
Kenya, Uganda and Zanzibar." 1920.

Foreign Office Confidential Prints is a series of documents containing
despatches or papers not always included in the regular Foreign
Office Archives.

B. COLONIAL OFFICE

In the Colonial Office Archives, also located at the Public Record
Office, London, are the following.

GB *CP*. Series CO 533. These documents contain the official correspondence after April 1905.
———. Series CO 519. These documents contain some interesting information on imperial intentions in East Africa. They comprise the cor-

respondence between the Foreign Office and the Colonial Office prior
to the protectorate's transfer from the former to the latter.
——. Series CO 534. These documents contain valuable material on in-
ternal problems in the protectorate.
——. Series CO 543. These are the Annual Blue Books of the East Africa
Protectorate, i.e. the annual compendia of all available statistics.
——. Series CO 544. These documents contain Sessional Papers and such
items as minutes of the Executive Council.

In general, CO 519, 534, 543, and 544 are subsets of the Series CO 533.

Colonial Office Confidential Prints is a series of documents comparable to the Foreign Office Confidential Prints.

The Colonial Office Published Papers listed below are all sources of
much valuable data on their topics. Each is a massive research study
by specialists who wrote expressly for the guidance of colonial policy
makers.

GB *CP* CO. Kenya Land Commission. *Evidence and Memoranda.* 3 vols.
Colonial Office Paper no. 91. 1934.
——. *Report of the Commission Appointed to Enquire into and Re-
port on the Financial Position and System of Taxation of Kenya.*
Colonial Office Paper no. 116. 1936.
——. G. St. J. Orde-Browne. *Labour Conditions in East Africa.* Co-
lonial Office Paper no. 193. 1946.

East Africa Protectorate Publications

GB EA. Department of Agriculture for British East Africa. "Annual Report[s]" for the following years: 1907–08 (1908), 1908–09 (1909), 1909–
10 (1910), 1910–11 (1911), 1911–12 (1912), 1912–13 (1914), 1914–15 (1915).
——. "Report of the Labour Inquiry Board." 1908.
——. "Annual Report of the Principal Medical Officer, 1908–1909." CO
544/1. 1909.
——. "Report of the Native Labour Commission." 1913.
——. Economic Commission, "Final Report, Part I," 1919. This document provides a glimpse into the official assessment of postwar economic intentions and expectations among the Europeans in Kenya.
——. "Report of the Land Settlement Commission." 1919.

Colony and Protectorate of Kenya Publications

GB CPK. "Report of the Labour Bureau Commission." 1921.
——. "Report on the Proceedings of the Coffee Conference." 1922.
——. "Annual Medical Report[s]" for the years 1922 (1923), 1927 (1927),
1932 (1933).
——. "Official Gazette." 1922.

——. "Kenya Law Reports," vol. 9, pt. 2. 1923.

——. Department of Native Affairs, "Annual Report[s]" for the years 1925 (1925), 1926 (1927), 1927 (1928).

——. Department of Lands, "Land and Land Conditions in the Colony and Protectorate of Kenya." 1926.

——. Department of Agriculture, "Annual Report[s]" for the years 1927 (1928), 1932 (1933), 1935 (1936).

Miscellaneous Documents

Report of the Sixth International Geographical Congress Held in London, 1895. London: J. Murray, 1896.

U.S., Congress, Senate, *Production and Consumption of Coffee,* 57th Cong., 2d sess., 1903, Doc. no. 35. The documents in this collection provide some uniquely detailed information on problems of the international coffee market with special reference to "corners" on coffee supplies.

T. Sleith. *Report on Trade Conditions in British East Africa, Uganda and Zanzibar.* Cape Town: Union of South Africa Department of Mines and Industries, 1919.

G. Walsh and H. R. Montgomery, *Report on Native Taxation.* 1936. This report was officially commissioned. It is the most comprehensive treatment of its topic available. It is not clear why the report did not appear as a formal government document.

R. B. Mitchell and P. Deane. *Abstract of British Historical Statistics.* Cambridge, 1962.

EAST AFRICA PAMPHLETS

Starting in 1893, the Colonial Office staff began to clip and file all the articles they could find that related to East Africa. These were later bound into sequential volumes and constituted a stock of background material for policy makers in the Colonial Office. They are found in the Colonial Office (now renamed the Commonwealth Office) Library in London.

Ainsworth, J. (no title) *Journal of the Manchester Geographical Society,* 1900. No. 9. Ainsworth, personally familiar with conditions in East Africa, outlines some of their geographical aspects.

British East Africa Department of Agriculture. *Settlers' Prospects.* Nairobi, 1905, No. 22.

Buckley, R. B. "Colonization and Irrigation in the East Africa Protectorate." *Geographical Journal,* April 1903. No. 16.

"The Financial Position of the East Africa Protectorate." Letter to the *East African Standard.* Nairobi, 27 January 1909. No. 29.

Hewitt, G. "A Profitable Postwar Settlement Scheme." London, 1918. No. 43.

"The Importance of Kenya's Sisal Industry." *African World,* supplement, London, 5 December 1925. No. 96. Folio.

Maxwell, G. V. "Memorandum on Native Progress." Nairobi, 1928. No. 13. This article contains important data on the conditions of African workers in the mid-1920s.

Oldham, J. H. "Kenya and Its Problems." *Times* (London), 10 June 1926. No. 108. Folio.

Parry, F. "The Capabilities of Eastern IBEA." *Imperial and Asiatic Quarterly Review,* July 1893. No. 1. An example of optimistic economic forecasting.

"Proceedings of the Tukuyu Conference." *East Africa* 2 (10 December 1925). No. 98. Folio. Useful information contained in these discussions among settlers concerned with problems of African labor supply.

"Report of the Labour Commission." Nairobi, 1927. No. 217. Folio.

"Report on the Pastoral and Agricultural Capabilities of the East Africa Protectorate." Johannesburg, 1904. No. 21.

Wigglesworth, Edwin and Company. "Notes on the Growing and Preparation of Flax for Fibre." London, 1918. No. 51.

BOOKS AND ARTICLES

Ainsworth, J. "The East Africa Protectorate and Development." *East Africa Quarterly* 4 (October–December 1906): 840–47. Most issues of this periodical contain useful information.

———. "East Africa and Agriculture." *East Africa Quarterly* 1 (January–March 1904): 14–16.

———. "Staple Products for East Africa." *East Africa Quarterly* 3 (April–June 1906): 685–89.

Ainsworth's articles are important not only for their factual content but also for their tone and general orientation. Ainsworth was the leading agricultural specialist in the Protectorate; his ideas on how to develop agriculture had a great influence on officials and settlers during the first twenty years of the protectorate's history.

Burton, G. J. L. "Wheat Growing in Kenya Colony." British East Africa Department of Agriculture Bulletin no. 2. Nairobi, 1925.

Burton, R. F. *The Lake Regions of Central Africa.* 2 vols. London: Longman, Green, Longman & Roberts, 1860.

Buxton, M. A. *Kenya Days.* London: E. Arnold, 1927. Diary of a settler's wife.

Churchill, W. S. *My African Journey.* London: Hodder and Stoughton, 1908. A direct account of Churchill's official mission to many of Britain's possessions in Africa.

Dawson, W. J. "The Importance of Plant Introduction with Special Reference to the Highlands." *Agricultural Journal of British East Africa* 4, pt. 2 (January 1912): 106–09.

Eliot, C. *The East Africa Protectorate*. London: E. Arnold, 1905. Chiefly an apologetic description of his term as governor.

Elliot, G. S. "Commercial Prospects of British Central and East Africa." *Journal of the Society of Arts* 44 (March 1896): 423–31.

Evans, G. W. "Report." *East Africa Quarterly* 1 (April–June 1904): 64.

Foot, C. E. "Transport and Trading Centers from Eastern Equatorial Africa." *Journal of the Society of Arts* 28 (March 1880): 362–67.

Foran, W. R. *A Cuckoo in Kenya*. London: Hutchinson, 1936. Memoirs which are useful in providing a picture of settler life, including settler attitudes toward their own proper roles in Kenya's economic development.

Fyffe, R. "Rubber in Uganda: Retrospective and Prospective." In J. Torrey and A. S. Manders, eds. *The Rubber Industry*. London: International Rubber and Allied Trades Exhibition, 1911.

Harris, J. H. "Back to Slavery." *Contemporary Review* 120 (July–December 1921): 190–97.

———. "Making the 'Lazy Nigger' Work." *Contemporary Review* 105 (June 1914): 819–25.

Hindlip, Lord. *British East Africa: Past, Present and Future*. London: Unwin, 1905. An aristocratic settler's perceptions.

Hobley, C. W. *Kenya: From Chartered Company to Crown Colony*. London: Cass, 1929. Personal accounts of important political and economic events by an official who spent much of his adult life in Kenya.

———. *The Ethnology of A-Kamba and Other East African Tribes*. Cambridge: Cass, 1910. Useful for its reflection of British officials' estimates of African capabilities and patterns of behavior.

———. "Native Problems in Eastern Africa: Part One." *Journal of the African Society* 22 (April 1923): 184–207.

Hollis, A. C. *The Nandi*. Oxford: Clarendon Press, 1909.

Holm, A. "Review of Agriculture in Kenya." British East Africa Department of Agriculture Bulletin no. 9. Nairobi, 1926. As chairman of the Department of Agriculture, Holm was in an excellent position to know and summarize agricultural conditions.

Hutchinson, E. *The Slave Trade of East Africa*. London: Sampson Low, Marston, Low and Searle, 1874. A very useful collection of material from official and unofficial sources by the lay secretary of the Church Missionary Society. The book presents descriptions of the contemporary state of the slave trade in East Africa.

Jackson, F. *Early Days in East Africa*. London: E. Arnold, 1930. A moderately useful record of one official's acts and thoughts in the early period of the Protectorate.

Jones, J. E. "Native Cotton and Native Cultivation." *Agricultural Journal of British East Africa* 3, pt. 2 (July 1910): 146–50.

Kenyatta, J. *Facing Mount Kenya: The Tribal Life of the Gikuyu*. London: Secker and Warburg, 1938. A thorough study going beyond the scope that its anthropological tone might suggest. For my purposes its value lies in the presentation of an indigenous *African* view of the tribal economy and the effect of British rule upon it.

Krapf, J. L. *Travels, Researches, and Missionary Labour in Eastern Africa.* London: Trübner, 1860. An early explorer's records.

Leggett, E. H. M. "The Economic Development of British East Africa and Uganda." *Journal of the Royal Society of Arts* 63 (February 1915): 213–26.

"Letter from an Old Resident." *Agricultural Journal of British East Africa* 1, pt. 4 (January 1909): 369.

Leys, N. *Kenya.* 2d ed. London: Hogarth Press, 1925. A discussion of current affairs by an on-the-spot observer, this book is remarkable for its critical position vis-à-vis the policies of settlers and officials. Some useful material, unavailable elsewhere, is drawn from this work.

Lindblom, G. *The Akamba in British East Africa.* 2d ed. Uppsala: Appelberg, 1920. An anthropological study.

Livingstone, D. *The Last Journals of David Livingstone in Central Africa.* Compiled by H. Waller. 2 vols. London: J. Murray, 1874.

Livingstone, D. and C. *Narrative of an Expedition to the Zambezi and its Tributaries.* London: J. Murray, 1865. The particular relevance of this famous work lies in its presentation of an early British understanding of the potential economic importance of a British empire in Africa.

Lugard, F. D. *The Rise of Our East African Empire.* 2 vols. London: Blackwood, 1893. This is by far the most complete statement of the British imperialist vision of East Africa. Lugard's position in the highest circles of British society accounts for much of the valuable factual material contained in these volumes.

McDermott, P. L. *British East Africa or IBEA.* 2d ed. London: Chapman and Hall, 1895. This is the official, and hence very apologetic, history of the chartered company which first established British rule in East Africa.

Meinertzhagen, R. *Kenya Diary, 1902–1906.* Edinburgh: Oliver and Boyd, 1957. The memoirs of a British colonel who was very active in many of the earliest punitive and pacification actions against the African tribes.

Odinga, O. *Not Yet Uhuru: An Autobiography.* New York: Hill and Wang, 1967. As with Kenyatta's work, this book's chief importance derives from the presentation of an African's memory of the impact of British rule on African life.

Orde-Browne, G. St. J. *The African Labourer.* London: Oxford, 1933. Essentially a statistical survey of current conditions.

Paish, G. "The Export of Capital and the Cost of Living." *The Statist,* supplement, 79 (February 1914): i-viii.

Perham, M. and Bull, M., eds. *The Diaries of Lord Lugard.* Vol. 1. London: Faber and Faber, 1959.

"Report of the Malindi Cotton Farm." *East Africa Quarterly* 2 (April–June 1905): 360–63.

Ross, W. M. *Kenya from Within*. London: Allen & Unwin, 1927. The most careful and best documented criticism of European policies in Kenya then available from the pen of any European. The book contains important analyses of economic aspects of European policies.

Routledge, W. S. and K. *With a Pre-historic People: the Akikuyu of British East Africa*. London: Arnold, 1910. An anthropological study.

Sandford, G. R. *An Administrative and Political History of the Masai Reserve*. London: Waterlow and Sons, 1919. An officially sponsored and supported work designed to present all that was known from government and other records on the topic. Very comprehensive.

Speke, J. H. *Journal of the Discovery of the Source of the Nile*. London: Blackwood, 1863. An explorer's diary.

Stanley, H. M. *Through the Dark Continent*. 2 vols. London: Low, Marston, Searle & Rivington, 1878. The famous explorer's diary and general reflections. The latter are interesting as evidence of early British interest in the economic potential of a possible British empire in Africa.

Tate, H. R. "Native Tenants on European Farms." *Agricultural Journal of British East Africa* 1 (January 1909): 359–63.

Taylor, F. W. "Canadian Loans in London." *United Empire: the Journal of the Royal Colonial Institute*, n.s. 3 (1915): 985–94.

Thomson, J. "East Africa As It Was and Is." *Contemporary Review* 55 (January 1889): 41–51.

———. *To the Central African Lakes and Back*. 2 vols. Boston: Houghton, Mifflin, 1881. An early explorer's records.

Wagner, J. *Deutsch-Ostafrika*. Berlin, 1886. An early German account of conditions and possibilities in East Africa.

Waller, Reverend H. "The Two Ends of the Slave Stick." *Contemporary Review* 55 (April 1889): 528–38.

Wilson, C. T., and Felkin, R. W. *Uganda and the Egyptian Sudan*. Vol. 1. London: S. Low, Marston, Searle and Rivington, 1882. Travelers' accounts interlaced with general reflections.

Wissmann, H. von. *My Second Journey through Equatorial Africa: From the Congo to the Zambesi, 1886 and 1887*. Translated by M. J. A. Bergmann. London: Chatto and Windus, 1891.

SECONDARY SOURCES

Aaronovitch, S. and K. *Crisis in Kenya*. London: Lawrence & Wishart, 1947. This Marxist analysis seeks to explain the "crisis in Kenya" as a consequence of the severe and economically wasteful "misuse" of Kenya's resources by British imperialism. Useful in part for its method of analysis.

Adler, J. H., and Kuznets, P. W., eds. *Capital Movements and Economic Development*. New York: Macmillan, 1967. The first group of essays in this volume provides a useful summarization of the state of our knowledge on this question.

Aldcroft, D. H., ed. *The Development of British Industry and Foreign Competition, 1875–1914.* London: Allen & Unwin, 1968. This collection of essays on different major British industries presents an excellent summary of what is known about the impact of foreign competition on British industry.

Baran, P. A. *The Political Economy of Growth.* New York: Monthly Review Press, 1957.

Barnett, D. L., and Njama, K. *Mau Mau from Within.* New York: Monthly Review Press, 1966.

Beck, A. *A History of the British Medical Administration of East Africa, 1900–1950.* Cambridge, Mass.: Harvard University Press, 1970.

Bennett, G. *Kenya: A Political History.* London: Oxford University Press, 1963.

Bennett, N. R. *Studies in East African History.* Boston: Boston University Press, 1963.

Bennett, N. R., and Brooks, G. E., Jr., eds. *New England Merchants in Africa: A History through Documents, 1802–1865.* Boston: Boston University Press, 1965.

Bodelsen, C. A. *Studies in Mid-Victorian Imperialism.* London: Gyldendal, 1924.

Brady, C. T., Jr. *Commerce and Conquest in East Africa.* Salem, Mass.: Essex Institute, 1950.

Brown, M. B. *After Imperialism.* London: Heinemann, 1963.

Cairncross, A. K. *Home and Foreign Investment, 1870–1913.* Cambridge: University Press, 1953. The most thorough and definitive work on this subject from the statistical standpoint.

Collister, P. *The Last Days of Slavery.* Dar es Salaam, East African Literature Bureau. Nairobi, 1961. A general history of the end of East African slavery, a rarely studied topic.

Coupland, R. *The Exploitation of East Africa, 1856–1890: The Slave Trade and the Scramble.* London: Faber and Faber, 1939. A massive, thorough and extremely valuable study of early European and other exploitation in East Africa.

Court, W. H. B. *British Economic History: Documents, 1870–1914.* Cambridge: University Press, 1965.

Davidson, B. *The African Slave Trade: Pre-Colonial History, 1450–1850.* Boston: Little, Brown, 1961.

Deane, P., and Cole, W. A. *British Economic Growth, 1688–1959.* Cambridge: University Press, 1962.

Dilley, M. R. *British Policy in Kenya Colony.* 1st ed., London: T. Nelson & Sons, 1937; 2d ed., London: Cass, 1966. This is, to date, the definitive political history of the early colonial period in Kenya. The treatment of economic problems is particularly valuable.

Dobb, M. *Political Economy and Capitalism.* London: G. Routledge & Sons, 1937.

Fearn, H. *An African Economy: A Study of the Economic Development of the Nyanza Province of Kenya, 1903–1953.* London: Oxford University Press, 1961. A useful, pioneer monograph on the course of economic change in one Kenya province. Of special interest is the analysis of changing European economic policies in the 1930s.

Federation of British Industries. *Resources of the Empire*. 10 vols. London: E. Benn, 1924.

Feinstein, C. H. "Income and Investment in the United Kingdom, 1896–1914." *Economic Journal* 71 (June 1961): 367–85.

Feis, H. *Europe, the World's Banker, 1870–1914*. New Haven: Yale University Press, 1930.

Fieldhouse, D. K. "Imperialism: An Historiographical Revision." *Economic History Review*, 2d ser., 14 (1961): 187–209. The basic statement of a neo-Hobsonian criticism of "economic imperialism" and of the general line of Leninist analysis.

———. *The Colonial Empires*. New York: Delacorte, 1967. A general history of the main European empires since the eighteenth century. There is also some treatment of the "United States Colonial Empire."

Foran, W. R. *The Kenya Police, 1887–1960*. London: R. Hale, 1962.

Frankel, S. H. *Capital Investment in Africa*. London: Oxford University Press, 1938. Still the most thorough, careful and thoughtful study on the subject.

Goldsmith, F. H. *John Ainsworth, Pioneer Kenya Administrator, 1864–1946*. London: Macmillan, 1955.

Graham, G. S. *Great Britain in the Indian Ocean: A Study of Maritime Enterprise, 1810–1850*. Oxford: Clarendon Press, 1967.

Gray, R., and Birmingham, D., eds. *Pre-Colonial African Trade*. London: Oxford University Press, 1970.

Hailey, Lord. *An African Survey*. London: Oxford University Press, 1938. Rev. ed., London: Oxford University Press, 1957.

Hall, A. D. *Agriculture after the War*. London: J. Murray, 1916.

Harlow, V.; Chilver, E. M.; and Smith, A., eds. *History of East Africa*. Vol. 2. Oxford: Clarendon Press, 1965.

Henderson, W. O. "Germany's Trade with Her Colonies, 1884–1914." *Economic History Review* 9 (November 1938): 1–16.

Hieke, G. E. *Zur Geschichte des deutschen Handels mit Ostafrika*. Part 1. Hamburg: Hans Christians, 1939.

Hilferding, R. *Das Finanzkapital*. Berlin: J. H. W. Dietz, 1947.

Hill, M. F. *Permanent Way: The Story of the Kenya and Uganda Railway*. 2d ed. Nairobi: East African Railways and Harbours, 1961. The official history of the railway.

———. *Planters' Progress: The Story of Coffee in Kenya*. Nairobi: Coffee Board of Kenya, 1956. The official history of the European coffee planters and plantations.

Hobson, C. K. *The Export of Capital*. London: Constable, 1914. The first systematic and still valuable study of British capital outflows during the nineteenth century.

Hobson, J. A. *Imperialism: A Study*. Rev. ed. London: J. Pott, 1905. The classic liberal study of and sharp critical attack upon the "new imperialism" of Great Britain after 1870.

Hoffman, R. J. S. *Great Britain and the German Trade Rivalry, 1875–*

1914. New York: Russell and Russell, 1964. The most comprehensive study of this topic available.

Hoffmann, W. G. *British Industry, 1700–1950.* Translated by W. O. Henderson and W. H. Chaloner. Oxford: Basil Blackwell, 1952.

Hollingsworth, L. W. *The Asians of East Africa.* London: Macmillan, 1960. A useful, although short, general history.

Holmberg, A. *African Tribes and European Agencies.* Gothenberg: Akademiförlaget, 1966. A general study from an anthropological viewpoint.

Huntingford, G. W. B. "Nandi: Work and Culture." Colonial Office Document DS 56987/1. 1950. Mimeographed.

———. *The Nandi of Kenya.* London: Routledge and Kegan Paul, 1953. General studies emphasizing anthropological perspectives.

Huxley, E. *White Man's Country: Lord Delamere and the Making of Kenya.* 2 vols. London: Macmillan, 1935. An adulatory biography useful for some factual material, but chiefly for its reflection of dominant European settler attitudes.

Imlah, A. H. *Economic Elements of the Pax Britannica.* Cambridge: Harvard University Press, 1958. A basic statistical study of British foreign economic relations during the nineteenth century.

Ingham, K. *A History of East Africa.* Rev. ed. New York: Praeger, 1965.

Jackson, M. V. *European Powers and South-east Africa.* London: Longmans, Green, 1942.

Jenks, L. H. "British Experience with Foreign Investments." *Journal of Economic History,* supplement, December 1944, pp. 68–79.

———. *The Migration of British Capital to 1875.* New York: A. A. Knopf, 1927. An excellent study, balancing statistical, political, and institutional aspects into a comprehensive economic history of the subject. Some provocative theories of foreign capital investment are developed.

Kiewiet, M. J. de (Hemphill). "History of the Imperial British East Africa Company, 1875–1895." Ph.D. dissertation, University of London, 1955.

Knowles, L. C. A. *The Economic Development of the British Overseas Empire.* Vol. 1. London: Routledge, 1924.

Kuczynski, R. R. *Demographic Survey of the British Colonial Empire.* Vol. 2. London: Oxford University Press, 1949.

Langer, W. L. "A Critique of Imperialism." *Foreign Affairs* 24 (1935): 94–110.

Lenin, V. I. *Imperialism, the Latest Stage of Capitalism.* Moscow: Foreign Languages Publishing House, 1959.

Levine, A. L. *Industrial Retardation in Britain, 1880–1914.* New York: Basic Books, 1967.

Leys, N. *A Last Chance in Kenya.* London: Hogarth Press, 1931.

———. *Kenya.* 2d ed. London: Hogarth Press, 1925. Both works are important for their documented, critical appraisals of the impact of administration officials and policy on the African population.

Lowe, C. J. *The Reluctant Imperialists: British Foreign Policy, 1878–1902.* 2 vols. London: Routledge and Kegan Paul, 1967.

Luxemburg, R. *The Accumulation of Capital.* Translated by A. Schwarzs-child. New York: Monthly Review Press, 1951.

Lyne, R. N. *An Apostle of Empire.* London: Allen & Unwin, 1936. The biography of the English commander of the sultan of Zanzibar's military force offers important insight into British policy in East Africa before the declaration of the Protectorates.

Mangat, J. S. "Aspects of 19th Century Indian Commerce in Zanzibar." *Journal of African and Asian Studies* 2 (Autumn 1968): 17–27.

————. *History of the Asians in East Africa, 1886–1945.* Oxford: Clarendon Press, 1969.

Marsh, Z., and Kingsnorth, G. W. *An Introduction to the History of East Africa.* 3d ed. Cambridge: University Press, 1965.

Meyer, J. R. "An Input-Output Approach to Evaluating the Influence of Exports on British Industrial Production in the Late Nineteenth Century." *Explorations in Entrepreneurial History* 8 (October 1955): 12–34.

Müller, F. F. *Deutschland-Zanzibar-Ostafrika: Geschichte einer deutscher Kolonialeroberung, 1884–1890.* Berlin: Rütten and Loening, 1959. An excellent Marxist treatment.

Mungeam, G. H. *British Rule in Kenya, 1895–1912.* Oxford: Clarendon Press, 1966. This careful, political study is particularly useful for its detailed treatment of new sources of information in the archives.

Ogot, B. A. and Kieran, J. A., eds. *Zamani: A Survey of East African History.* Nairobi: East African Publishing House, 1968.

O'Leary, P. J. and Lewis, W. A. "Secular Swings in Production and Trade, 1870–1913." *Manchester School* 23 (1955): 113–52.

Oliver, R. *The Missionary Factor in East Africa.* London: Longmans, Green, 1952. A study of the missionary pioneers in East Africa before formal rule was established.

Oliver, R., and Mathew, G., eds. *History of East Africa.* Vol. 1. Oxford: Clarendon Press, 1963. A sourcebook of long essays by specialists in their various regions and periods. A useful introduction to the subject.

Page, W. *Commerce and Industry.* 2 vols. London: Constable, 1919. Useful for its statistical compilations of Britain's and the empire's international economic relations.

Parker, M. "Political and Social Aspects of the Development of Municipal Government in Kenya with Special Reference to Nairobi." Colonial Office Document DH 65550/1. N.d. Mimeographed.

Platt, D. C. M. "Economic Factors in British Policy During the 'New Imperialism.'" *Past and Present* 39 (April 1968): 120–38. Much of this carefully reasoned article is devoted to a refutation of the argument in the Fieldhouse article cited above.

Remole, R. A. "White Settlers or The Foundation of Agricultural Settlement in Kenya." Ph.D. dissertation, Harvard University, 1959.

Robinson, R. E. and Gallagher, J., with Denny, A. *Africa and the Victorians.* New York: St. Martins Press, 1961. A major study which supports the proposition that British colonialism in Africa was a political phenomenon focused on safeguarding routes to India rather than deriving economic gain from Africa.

Rosberg, C. G., Jr. and Nottingham, J. *The Myth of 'Mau-Mau': Nationalism in Kenya*. New York: Praeger, 1966.

Russell, C. E. B., ed. *General Rigby, Zanzibar and the Slave Trade*. London: George Allen and Unwin, 1935.

Salvadori, Max. *La Colonisation Europeene au Kenya*. Paris: Larose, 1938. A short but useful general account.

Saul, S. B. *Studies in British Overseas Trade, 1870–1914*. Liverpool: Liverpool University Press, 1960.

Savage, D. C., and Munro, J. F. "Carrier Corps Recruitment in the British East Africa Protectorate, 1914–1918." *Journal of African History* 7 (1966): 313–42.

Schlote, W. *British Overseas Trade from 1700 to the 1930's*. Translated by W. O. Henderson and W. H. Chaloner. Oxford: Blackwell, 1952. This is the classic statistical survey of the subject.

Schooling, J. H. *The British Trade Book*. 4th ed. London: Murray, 1911. This statistical volume contains some interesting tables, compiled as part of the author's effort to alarm British businessmen about the inroads of Britain's competitors.

Schott, J. R. "The European Community of Kenya." 2 vols. Ph.D. dissertation, Harvard University, 1964.

Semmel, B. *Imperialism and Social Reform, 1895–1914*. Cambridge: Harvard University Press, 1960.

Sorrenson, M. P. K. *Origins of European Settlement in Kenya*. Nairobi: Oxford University Press, 1968.

Stahl, K. M. *History of the Chagga People*. The Hague: Mouton, 1964.

Stamp, J. *The National Capital*. London: King, 1937.

Sweezy, P. M. *The Theory of Capitalist Development*. New York: Monthly Review Press, 1956.

Turton, E. R. "Kirk and the Egyptian Invasion of East Africa in 1875: A Reassessment." *Journal of African History* 11, no. 3 (1970): 355–70.

Ukers, W. H. *All About Coffee*. 2d ed. New York: Tea and Coffee Trade Journal, 1935.

Wagner, G. *The Bantu of North Kavirondo*. 2 vols. London: Oxford University Press, 1949 and 1956. A useful anthropological study.

Weisbord, R. G. *African Zion*. Philadelphia: Jewish Publication Society of America, 1968.

Wrigley, C. C. "The Christian Revolution in Buganda." *Comparative Studies in Society and History* 2 (1959): 33–48.

Yoshida M., and Belshaw, D. G. R. "The Introduction of the Trade Licensing System for Primary Products in East Africa, 1900–1939." Mimeographed. Conference Paper no. 336. Kampala, Uganda: Makerere Institute for Social Research, 1965.

Index

African Carrier Corps, 108–09, 111, 112, 172n62
Africans in Kenya: tribal distinctions, xiv; socioeconomic effects of slave trade on, 44–45, 159n56; allocated, 61, 63–66, 85; early social structure of, 89–90; socioeconomic effects of Britain's labor force policies on, 90–131; net income statistics, 138; reserve population statistics, 142; curtailed as merchants, 143. *See also* Kenya agriculture; Kenya labor force
Ainsworth, John, 92, 161n24; on white settlers, 54; agricultural studies of, 72, 184; on sisal production, 84
Akamba tribe, 100
Amory, Colonial Secretary: approves African forced labor, 123
Anglican Church: political influence of, 34
Anglo-Indian Review: on sisal fiber prices, 83
Arab Empire: East African holdings of, 30; growth of Britain's economic and political control of, 32–46. *See also* East Africa; Sultan of Zanzibar
Arabs: Kenya population statistics, 107
Arab-Swahili aristocracy. *See* East Africa
Arms and munitions: empire's import statistics, 15
Arnold, B. G., 165n18
Asians, xv
Australia, 1; wheat export statistics, 8; sugar export statistics, 9; wool export statistics, 10; ore export statistics, 10–11; Britain's

investments in, 28; cotton export statistics, 81
Austria-Hungary: coffee consumption statistics, 77

Bantu tribe, 30; Eliot on, 48
Barth, Jacob: land tenure ruling of, 65
Beans: Kenya's planting statistics, 72
Belgium: steel export statistics, 24; Britain's investments in, 26; East African interests of, 32, 33
Berlin Conference of *1884–85*, 35
Books: empire's import statistics, 15, 16
Brazil: as source of rubber, 21–22; as source of coffee, 74–76; coffee export statistics, 75
Brick industry: Britain's labor force allocation in, 5
Britain: increases empire, 1; affected by protectionism and competition, 3, 17, 20, 26–27, 29; labor force allocation in, 5, 12, 14; core industries of economy in, 5; import trade, 5–12; export trade, 12–17; re-export trade, 17–24, 153n24; trade control policies of, 23–24; foreign and colonial investments of, 24–29, 155n44; protests Northey Circulars, 122. *See also* Colonialism
Britain, export statistics of: textiles, 12, 20; foods, 13; livestock, 13; ships, 13; unclassified raw materials, 13; manufactures, 13, 14; iron and steel, 13, 20, 24; foreign trade, 20, 24, 27; machinery, 24; locomotives, 27
Britain, import statistics of: ores and metals, 6; unclassified raw

198   INDEX

Jenks, L. H.: on Britain's railway investments, 26
Jute: import value to Britain of,
6; Britain's import statistics, 10,
11; sources of, 10, 12

Kamba tribe, 109, 139
Kavirondo, 115, 142
Kenya (East African Protectorate):
Uganda compared to, 47–48; administrative budget statistics, 49;
private enterprises' interests in,
52–55, 66, 135; administrative
subdivisions in, 64; urban crowding in, 66–67, 164n58; population statistics, 107; becomes colony, 110, 173n2; new currency
system in, 112, 117; evaluation of
Britain's economic development
policies in, 132–48; net national
income statistics, 138
Kenya agriculture: Uganda Railway related to, 56–57, 85, 87;
rainfall pattern, 58; farm settlement pattern, 59; cultivated acreage, 60; Britain's economy related to, 68–88, 134–48; planting
statistics, 72, 73; wheat, 72–73,
84, 128; coffee, 72–74 passim,
78, 97, 128–29, 136, 141, 164n12,
173n11; maize, 72–74 passim, 84,
128, 136, 137; sisal, 73, 84, 94,
97, 128, 136, 137, 164n54; cotton,
81–82, 144, 167n39 and n43; rubber, 83, 167n48; flax, 84–85,
162n34; tax exemptions for, 87,
101, 118; labor force supply related to, 93–110; squatting related to, 104; wartime mobilization for, 111–12; postwar labor
statistics, 113, 114, 116, 128–29;
reserves' overcrowding related to
native production, 126, 141, 143;
sugar and tea, 128, 137; coconuts, 128; labor saving devices introduced, 129; experimental
work, 129–30, 136, 138; native
production restricted, 138, 139–

43, 177n11; revised policies for
native production, 142–44; Land
Regulations of 1897 specifics,
165n16
Kenya and Uganda Railway. See
Uganda Railway
Kenya Colonists Association, 87
Kenya commissions and committees: Land, 56, 98–99, 111, 122,
142, 143, 171n40; Native Labour,
100, 114–16, 119, 131–32, 172n50,
173n6 and n7; East Africa, 129,
140–41
Kenya departments: Agriculture,
78, 84, 87–88, 138–39, 142, 177n11;
Forestry, Survey, Trade, and
Veterinary, 87; Native Affairs,
101, 116, 173n6; Public Works,
138–39
Kenya Highlands: grants and settlements in, 52, 55–57, 146; squatting in, 104; Indians ask settlement rights in, 170n18
Kenya labor force: role of Indians
in, 51, 55, 90–91, 107; settlers'
role in establishing, 82, 93–110;
for railway, 90–91, 107, 169n7;
economy related to reorganization
of, 90–110; experiments in developing, 92–93; effects of World
War I on, 93, 108–10, 111–13, 130,
172n62; postwar establishment of,
93–131; taxation related to, 96,
98, 99–101, 103, 116–18, 121, 123,
170n24; inadequacy of, 96–97;
reserves as source of, 98–99, 103–
04, 110, 114; recruitment for, 102–
03; headman control of (forced
labor), 103, 104, 122, 124–25;
squatting related to, 104, 116,
125–27, 173n11, 175n39; pass system related to, 105, 109, 112,
119–21, 123; physical deteriora-
tion in, 106, 109, 114, 130–31,
172n56, n59, and n63; proliferation
tion of policies for, 107–08; conscription for, 109–10; postwar
policies for increasing, 111–31;